I0023852

The New World Order Paradigm
versus
The New System of International Order

The End of Pax Americana
and the Beginning of the Era of United Eurasia

Alexander Plashchinsky

2017

1ˢᵗ Edition

GlobalSouth
P R E S S

Copyright © 2017 by
Alexander Plashchinsky

Published in the United States by GlobalSouth Press Inc TM.
All rights reserved. Published in the United States of America

No part of this book may be reproduced or utilized in any form or by any
means, electronic or mechanical, including photocopying, recording, or
by any information storage and retrieval system, without written
permission from the publisher, except in the case of brief quotations
embodied in critical articles and reviews. For information,
address GlobalSouth Press Inc., 199 E. Montgomery Suite 100,
Rockville-MD. 20850. GlobalSouth Press books are available at exclusive
discounts for bulk purchases in the U.S. by corporations, institutions,
and other organizations.

For more information, please contact
info@globalsouthpress.com or go to
http://www.globalsouthpress.com/

The New World Order Paradigm versus
The New System of International Order
By Plashchinsky, Alexander

—1st ed. — 2017

Includes bibliographical references and index

ISBN: 978-1-943350-71-1

1. POLITICAL SCIENCE / International Relations / General

2. POLITICAL SCIENCE / Globalization

3. POLITICAL SCIENCE / World / Russian & Former Soviet Union

GlobalSouth
P R E S S

Editorial Board

Bulent Acma, Ph.D.
Anadolu University, Eskişehir, Turkey.

Flavio Saraiva, Ph.D.
Universidade de Brasília, Brasilia, Brazil.

Helmunt Schlenter, Ph.D.
Institute for Global Dialogue, Pretoria, South Africa.

Tullo Vigevani, Ph.D.
Sao Paulo State University, Sao Paulo, Brazil.

Monica Arruda Almeida, Ph.D.
Georgetown University, Washington, D.C., United States of America.

Yong J. Wang, Ph.D.
Ohio University, Columbus, United States of America.

Chih-yu Shih, Ph.D.
National Taiwan University (ROC), Taipei, Taiwan.

Irene Klumbies, Ph.D.
Jacobs University Bremen, Bremen, Germany.

Sai Felicia Krishna-Hensel, Ph.D.
Center Business and Econ. Develop., Auburn University, Montgomery, United States of America.

José Álvaro Moisés, Ph.D.
Universidade de São Paulo (USP), São Paulo, Brazil.

Martina Kaller, Ph.D.
Standford University, California, United States of America

Contents

Introduction

*"World-conquest is believed in most firmly by those
who know it to be impossible."*

George Orwell

At present the mankind faces one of the turning points in history - the end of Pax Americana and the beginning of a new era of world development - the era of united Eurasia. The new turning point and global power shift occurred as a result of clashing between two fundamental historical trends and geopolitical processes. The first trend has been implementation of the new world order paradigm. It implies establishing "liberal" system of global governance and, thus, gaining control over international development. The second trend has been re-launching the Eurasian integration process after the collapse of the Soviet Union. Each of these trends projects an opposed scenario for the future of mankind, namely, the expansion of global chaos that eventually might bring about "clash of civilizations" or, alternatively, creation of balanced, equitable and peaceful world order.

The new world order paradigm has wide theoretical and conceptual spectrum. It originated yet in Ancient Egypt. Since then it comprised certain system of beliefs, knowledge and policy doctrines advocating the idea of "novus ordo seclorum". This idea has been officially interpreted as being "a new order of the ages" or a new American era. Yet its ethos appeared as gaining world hegemony. In the late 18th century the U.S. Founders added that idea as a cornerstone to U.S. development. In pursuit of Pax Americana, the paradigm was incorporated into U.S. foreign policy strategy. Thus the "grand strategy" has been established as being a tool to constructing the new world order. The interconnection between the "grand strategy" and the new world order paradigm is a prerequisite to understanding common factors within world political and historical process both in the past and at present [201].

The problem of war and peace has been an important part of the paradigm. Many prominent thinkers and philosophers articulated that problem in their writings, specifically, in terms of uniting the whole mankind under a single authority. They believed that the world government might foster world's peaceful development. However, implementing the paradigm has been a constant warfare, which incorporates World War I, World War II, the Cold War, the War on Terror, and the ongoing Cyber War. The process of establishing the new world order reflects the so-called "big picture". It expands conventional insight into many historical events, demonstrates cause and effect connection between them, and explains how the United States became the only global superpower at the end of the 20th century.

The "big picture" can be viewed through the prism of the following stages of American development: the stage of isolationism (since proclamation of the Monroe Doctrine in 1823 until the beginning of World War I), the stage of globalism (since carrying out the Truman Doctrine in 1947 until the end of the Cold War), the stage of hegemony (since adoption of the Clinton Doctrine in the early 1990-s until the inception of the Obama Doctrine) and, finally, the current stage of declining Pax Americana.

The "Anglo-American establishment" [222] has been the driving force promoting the paradigm. It was carried by various social and political movements including the world revolution movement, the world peace movement (i.e. "world peace" congresses, then "peace educators" movement), the world government movement, etc. The Roundtable Group (The Group), Council on Foreign Relations, Carnegie Endowment for International Peace, the Club of Rome, the Trilateral Commission, the Bilderberg Group as well as many other influential forums and organizations of transnational elites have been projecting the "liberal" scenario of world's development. Accordingly, The Inquiry, The War and Peace Studies, The WOMP, the 1980s Project, and other think tanks incorporated the paradigm into global political agenda through the activities of international organizations, particularly, the League of Nations and the United Nations.

In the wake of the collapse of the Soviet Union the term "new world order" has been widely used by experts and politicians, including U.S. Presidents, declaring that the new world order was emerging. In the early 1990s the term became a "catch phrase". It was widely applied by scholars and experts to describing new trends arising in the international system. In academic works the "new world order" was associated, mainly, with globalization processes, economic interdependence, technological breakthrough as well as global issues facing the mankind.

Until now, however, the paradigm has not been conceptualized in political science to a full extent, especially, in terms of formation and development of U.S. foreign policy strategy. Instead, various conspiracy theories emerged marginalizing that phenomenon. Many of them have been ridiculing the "new world order", thus, serving as a "smoke screen" for the promotion of the paradigm.

Since the very term "world government" has become a political liability in the second half of the 20th century, the global governance doctrine was introduced in the mid 1990-s. The doctrine encompassed the following concepts: "global village", "cosmopolitan democracy", "democracy enlargement", "shared sovereignty" as well as many others. These liberal concepts have identified the process of transforming the international system, re-ordering its hierarchy and consolidating sub-national mechanisms of global control. Yet, in contemporary political theory arguments advocating the world government re-emerged again.

Most of the modern concepts of global governance suggest ceding traditional rights of sovereignty to supranational institutions and redistributing state power between civil society, non-state actors, social movements, NGO-s, inter-governmental institutions, etc. They also suggest establishing "global governance networks" or "a networked world order", building "global regulatory regimes" upon international institutions to solving the global issues. At the same time, the main strategic objective of establishing the world supranational authority remains unchanged.

The U.S. messianic vision of world`s future, which has been based on self-perceived Manifest Destiny, contradicts other civilizational paradigms, including the Russian Orthodox doctrine having Christian values in its core, as well as the Chinese dream based on traditional Chinese values, or Indian dream, which constitutes another ancient philosophy, etc. The idea of global hegemony is incompatible with the very principle of peaceful coexistence. Therefore, the promotion of the new world order paradigm from a position of strength, but under the pretext of expanding liberal values and democracy around the globe has a high conflict potential.

The "liberal" matrix of world order conceals the roots of international conflict. It might approach the mankind towards possible eruption of a "long-predicted World War III" [11; p. 330]. Indeed, the U.S. military engagement into the Middle East has radicalized the entire region. Such policy might eventually generate the so-called *third force* directed against the Eurasian power centers, namely, Russia, China, India, Iran as well as others impeding the establishment of the U.S. global control.

In this connection, the Islamic State movement (IS) has been infiltrating worldwide, for instance, into Pakistan`s radical movements, Russia`s Northern Caucasus, the EU countries, etc. Since the majority of world`s Muslim population inhabits South-East Asia, therefore, the global chaos might seek to spreading from the Middle East through the New Silk Road, thus, covering the Greater Middle East and the Greater Central Asia regions.

Considering newly emerged global security threats, there is a need to implementing a modified matrix of international order to uniting Eurasia and deterring the expansion of the global chaos. With this purpose, modern types of think tanks are to be established to elaborating joint Eurasian strategy. Implementation of such strategy, exclusively, might create geopolitical, economic, and philosophical synergy between the key power centers in Eurasia mentioned above. This synergy is important to ensuring world`s peaceful development and forging ahead the era of united Eurasia. The United Eurasia, so far, seems to be the true end of history.

Chapter 1
Theoretical Development
of New World Order Paradigm

World War I

To establish theoretical and conceptual framework of the new world order paradigm, at first, the origin of the term "new world order" must be determined within scientific works as well as milestones of its evolution. Theoretical spectrum of the paradigm consists of specialized scholarly literature, program speeches of U.S. political leaders, foreign policy documents, and archival sources. Conceptual spectrum of the paradigm encompasses policy concepts and doctrines, including the concept of "universal peace", the concept of "new world", the world revolution doctrine, the world government doctrine, the new world order doctrine, the global governance doctrine as well as American Dream, American Century (Pax Americana), New American Century, New American Moment, etc. Therefore, it is necessary to systemize academic works towards what might be the theoretical and conceptual development of the new world order paradigm in the 20th century, specifically, through the milestones of World War I, World War II, the Cold War, and beyond.

The idea of building a "new world" has been influential both in European political affairs and academic thought before World War I broke out. This idea was inspired by the Revolution in France of 1789. Initially, the international revolutionary and labour movement, the International, was used as a tool fostering the "new world". The first International was incepted in 1847 in London by Marx and Engels. According to its leaders, a different world order must have been built on the remnants of the European empires. The world revolution movement had been propagated as a means towards that end.

In 1917, Bolsheviks` coup in Russia was undertaken. In a wider context of establishing the new world order the coup d`etat in Russia pursued the objective of subverting the monarchy in Russia. Similarly, to the European revolutions of the second half of 19th century, the revolution in Russia was aimed at challenging the Westphalian order having national sovereignty doctrine in its core. Notably, the appeal towards building a "new world" was incorporated into the national anthem of the Soviet Russia in 1918, namely, The International. The original text of The International had been written in France yet in 1875. The idea of the world revolution was further promoted by Trozky and his followers in the framework of the activities of The Communist International, abbreviated as Comintern and known as the Third International (1919–1943).

The "new world" concept was advocated by many intellectuals. In 1915, Hugh Black, an American theologian, published a book entitled "The New World". In a chapter "The Changing Order" Black pointed out that, "The world is always passing through transition… No doubt there are times of sharp crisis… But usually change is gradual. Even when it looks sudden, as in a French Revolution, it really had been prepared for long, and the sudden crisis is the climax of a slow process… It has taken more than two centuries for the truth to filter through." [21, p. 28]. In this publication, Black observed "The Principles of Reconstruction" of the international system as well as "The Forces of Unrest". He elaborated these issues mainly from a theological and religious point of view.

In 1916, Frederick Lynch wrote a book entitled "Challenge: The Church and the New World Order" [159], in which the term "new world order" was used, perhaps, for the first time in the literature of that time. Before that, yet in 1911 Lynch propagated the idea of world's unification into a single federation of states abided by a set of international treaties. In his book entitled "The Peace Problem: The Task of the Twentieth Century" he pointed out, that "no one who has closely observed the movements gathering greatest headway at the beginning of this century can fail to see that the century is to witness a somewhat similar to unifying process among the nations to that which the nineteenth century witnessed among the states" [160, p.12]. He suggested, that "the twentieth century will witness… a federation which shall insure justice, right understanding, and happiness for all" [160, p. 13].

Considering the prospects of world's unification Lynch focused on the importance of the two Hague (Peace) Conferences held in 1899 and 1907 accordingly. He argued that these two conferences marked "the beginning of the Federation of the World" [160, p. 27-28]. The role of the Second Hague (Peace) Conference has been especially important. According to Lynch, the conference "made some very definite and momentous steps towards world unity. It passed fourteen conventions, every one of which cemented the ties of the nations in more or less degree and brought federation nearer" [160, p. 19]. Thus, Lynch identified "the task of the twentieth century, namely the federation of the nations" [160, p. 27-28].

The idea of building a "new world" in the form of the "federation of the nations" must be considered in the following historical context. Yet in 1898 the Emperor of Russia issued a Peace Manifesto proposing to all governments an international conference on the means of ensuring peace. The Russian initiative resulted in organizing the First Hague (Peace) Conference of 1899. The conference established the Permanent Court of Arbitration (PCA) to facilitate arbitration and other forms of dispute resolution.

The United States, from its side, suggested creating a Permanent Court of International Justice at the Third Hague (Peace) Conference in 1914. The U.S. Secretary of State Philander Knox publicly announced that the conference would find the court already constituted. Although the conference did not take place due to the eruption of World War I, the Permanent Court of International Justice was set up by the League of Nations in 1920. The CFR admitted, that the Hague Conventions influenced the formation of the League of Nations [102].

Lynch urged that, "the Third Hague Conference cannot think of dissolving its sessions without having constituted a Permanent Supreme Court of the World" [160, p. 114]. He considered founding such an international institution as being "the first thing the century should see... The second immediate task is... to insist that all the nations present at the Third Hague Conference sign a general treaty of obligatory arbitration binding them ... to refer to the Permanent Court of Arbitral Justice... The third thing that should be consummated either before the Third Conference or simultaneous with it, is a League of Peace" [160, p. 113-115].

So far, the idea of establishing the League of Peace and the Permanent Court of International Justice, in case of gaining U.S. preeminent position in these organizations, might be considered as being the first attempt by the Anglo-American establishment to create a prototype of the world government. Notably, this idea was promoted by Lynch yet in 1911, that is three years before the beginning of World War I and seven years prior the League of Nations was established in 1919. According to Lynch, there were two ways of conceiving the League of Peace, such as establishing an international police force, which would be large enough to "simply enforce the decrees of the Permanent Court when it shall be in operation; the other as a combination, if we do not get the Permanent Court soon, [consisting] of the three or four great powers with their then irresistible armaments, to insist that all the rest of the world keep the peace" [160, p. 115-116].

More than two decades after Lynch published his work the same idea of establishing a World Federation or a World State possessing the international police force, the world parliament and legally binding authority (i.e. the International Court) was further developed by the World Federalist Movement, that is, the World Government Movement. The movement was brought into being in the late 1930-s - before World War II erupted. It reached its apogee in the aftermath of World War II serving as a tool of establishing the world government, though, under the pretext of promoting international peace.

The roots of the world government movement and the promotion of the idea of world's unification under the aegis of a single world authority can be identified within political agenda of the United States and its allies yet in the middle of the 19th century. These ideas had been promoted in the framework of the international peace congresses that might be identified as *the world peace movement*. The latter had been the predecessor of *the world government movement*.

In this regard, Lynch mentioned several international peace congresses as well as other official and unofficial meetings and gatherings that took place around the world on different issues. These meetings were "drawing more and more delegates and exercising greater influence" [160, p. 51-53]. Lynch also stated that "they were held in the last century, but they become one of the most promising features of this century... A list of organizations that hold international congresses has been made and they number over two hundred" [160, p. 45-46].

The world peace movement constituted the international peace conferences so far. It lasted for almost exactly one century, from 1843 until

World War II. During this period, more than 75 international conferences took place. Among the first international peace conferences Lynch indicated the one held in London in 1843 (on the initiative of the American Peace Society), then in Brussels in 1848 (the first after the French Revolution of February 1848). The most significant meeting, according to Lynch, took place in Paris in 1849. It was presided by Victor Hugo who introduced the concept of the United States of Europe and suggested consolidation of its transatlantic ties with the United States of America [160, p. 51-53]. Following the first international peace congress at London in 1843, an annual series of congresses called International Congress of the Friends of Peace or "International Peace Congress" were organized from 1848 until 1853. In total, seven meetings of the International Peace Congress took place.

Starting from 1867 and until 1889 the International League of Peace and Liberty organized four international peace congresses. The first congress took place in Geneva. Since then 33 congresses were held before 1939. This trend was identified by historians as *the Universal Peace Congress.*

Besides, the trend for world unification was further promoted by the Inter-Parliamentary Union (IPU). It was founded in 1889. Its initial objective was the arbitration of conflicts. Initially, its forums were intended for individual parliamentarians. Since then IPU has transformed into an international organization of the parliaments of sovereign states. At present, the national parliaments of 163 countries are members of the IPU, and 10 regional parliamentary assemblies are associate members [119]. At its early stage, however, IPU contributed significantly to the development of the world government movement. Since then it has been conducting congresses on a regular basis.

So far, since the middle of the 19th century the world peace movement fostered the idea of international peace and, thus, promoted the concept of creating "world federation". Referring to the congresses and meetings of the movement Lynch acknowledged that, "This is all a sign that the movement has become so universal and sure of success that the multitude gathers to it. It is the sure movement of our day" [160, p. 83].

Because of the activities of the world peace movement, *the concept of "world federation"* was incorporated into international political agenda. This was reflected in establishing the League of Nations. The successor of the world peace movement, that is, the world government movement, contributed significantly to the creation of the United Nations system as well as the Bretton Woods institutions. Thus, both movements played a key role in the process of world's unification (globalization) and establishing sub-national institutions aimed at managing that process. Yet, the two currents have been the integral parts of the same global mainstream, which had been aimed at establishing the world government.

On the eve of U.S. entering World War I the *concept of universal peace* was incorporated into the new world order paradigm. The U.S. President Woodrow Wilson referred to the idea of ensuring universal peace based on liberal principles. In 1918, the League for Permanent Peace in Boston (Massachusetts) published Wilson's Fourteen Points program. The League issued a leaflet titled "President Wilson's Fourteen Points, The Basis of the New World Order" [213, p. 4].

Publication of the Fourteen Points in the United States might be considered as being the first official declaration of the new world order agenda by the U.S. government in the early 20th Century. The leaflet, so far, reflected adoption of Wilson's universalism doctrine and the concept of world reconstruction in terms of realization of the U.S. foreign policy strategy. This fact also testifies, that in the wake of World War I the idea of re-ordering the world was promoted not only in Bolsheviks' Russia, but also in the United States and Britain.

Yet, different slogans and ideologies were used for achieving the same objective, namely, the idea of the world revolution promoted by Trozky's camp in Bolshevik's Russia, from one side, and universalism and liberal democracy advocated in the United States, from the other side. The promotion of such an agenda was aimed, mainly, at eroding the concept of state sovereignty to create sub-national system of global governance.

In 1919, the American Baptist Publication Society published a book by Samuel Butten entitled "The New World Order". In a preface dated January 1, 1919, which was less than two months after the Armistice in World War I was achieved, Butten claimed his book as being "the outline of a great subject". He urged, that "A few aspects only of the great social task are noted, with constant recognition, however, that these must be viewed together in their relation to the one enterprise" [41, preface].

Butten emphasized the role of World War I in transforming the international system as follows: "The world war represents the passing of the old order and the end of an epoch. A new day is begun, a page of new achievements is upturned. The old order passes from view; the new world is rising upon our vision" [41, preface]. Butten further acknowledged, that "The world war... represents the close of an age and the opening of a new epoch; it began as a world war, it has developed into a world revolution" [41, p. 3].

Thus, Butten identified the role of World War I in carrying out the world revolution doctrine and, more specifically, within the process of transformation of the world order. World War I might be considered, so far, as being the first attempt at implementing the new world order paradigm. This attempt was institutionalized in the form of the League of Nations. It was a prototype of the world government.

In identifying the principles and foundations of the new world order Butten stressed: "In this period of reconstruction it is imperative that men should know... what are the true principles that should be built in as the very foundations of the house that is to be. What kind of world order do we want? What are the principles and ideals that should guide us in our planning? What are the immediate things in our efforts, and what are the ultimate ends? What are the forces and factors on which we may count for aid and inspiration? These are questions of first importance in this hour" [41, preface]. He suggested that, "The only alternative is World Federation... There must be a League of free nations, a federation of the world... There must be a world parliament made up of representatives of the nations... There must be an international court to interpret international law and decide all questions that arise between nations and states... There must be also an international police force large and strong enough to enforce international law against any offending member" [41, p. 123-124]. Thus, advocating establishing global institutions or, in other words, executive branches of the world government, namely, a world parliament, an international court, an international police force Butten further developed the idea of creating the World Federation, which had been put forward in Frederick Lynch`s publication of 1911 mentioned above.

Among other publications of that period, Frederick Hicks` book entitled "The New World Order, International Organization,

International Law, International Cooperation" must be noted [106]. This author argued that with the defeat of Germany a world balance of powers had been established. The League of Nations was founded to maintain that balance. Hicks emphasized that a Society of Nations existed for centuries. The League of Nations was an effort to improve this society. At the same time, he maintained that the ancient idea of state sovereignty can be limited only by time and practice. Thus, in our view, the concept of state sovereignty was again considered as being an impediment in the context of the promotion of the sub-national system of global governance.

In scholarly publications, the term "world government" was coined already in the first volume of Foreign Affairs magazine dated December 15, 1922. The article entitled "From Empire to Commonwealth" was written by Philip Kerr, Secretary to British Prime Minister Lloyd-George from 1917 to 1922 and editor of the "Round Table" magazine [133]. According to Carrol Quigley, Philip Kerr (Lord Lothian) was an important figure in the "Anglo-American Establishment" and leader of the so-called "The Roundtable Group" from 1925 to 1940 [222]. Therefore, the article by Philip Kerr appeared an important milestone in terms of the theoretical evolution of the new world order paradigm. Hence, the latter was endorsed by the Council on Foreign Relations.

Kerr put forward a question: "What of the future?" In answering this question, he argued that, "It is no longer a question of maintaining law and order and promoting orderly self-government over sections of the earth's surface, but over the earth as a whole. Obviously, there is going to be no peace or prosperity for mankind if it remains divided into fifty or sixty independent states... yet with no real machinery for adjusting their relations... Equally obviously there is going to be no steady progress in civilization... until international system is created which... will hold in check, under a mandatory or other regime, those deleterious forces of civilization... The real problem today is that of the world government" [133, p. 97-98].

Kerr considered that, "If peace and freedom and prosperity are to be made universal over the earth, the United States and other powers must take their share of the burden and cooperate in some such scheme as the League of Nations. The alternatives before us, indeed, are obvious – on the one side *chaos ending in another world war*, on the other side the work and self-sacrifice necessary to substitute law for force throughout the world. What part is the United States going to play? Is she going to take a hand in the greatest enterprise for human betterment that has ever been presented to people?" [133, p. 97-98]. So far, already in the aftermath of World War I the Anglo-Saxon elites considered the mechanisms of establishing sub-national governance based on a universal law, as if it was aiming at "human betterment". Important enough, the possibility of "chaos ending in another world war" was stated already in 1922.

It is also worthy to note, that a copy of Foreign Affairs' first issue contains penciled annotations by Lenin and Radek. In 1992, this copy of the magazine was exhibited during a visit of the then former head of the Soviet Union Gorbachev to the CFR`s premises in Harold Pratt House in New York. During the visit Gorbachev remarked that he, too, had made some notes on the margins of his own copy of the CFR's journal which was translated for him [60]. The CFR observed on that regard, that "Gorbachev has yet to contribute his own annotated copy of Foreign Affairs to the Council archives" [60].

Despite the first attempt at implementing the idea of subnational governance in the framework of the League of Nations failed, the new world order paradigm was further developed in academic works. During the interwar period (between World War I and World War II) several conceptual publications appeared suggesting possible scenarios for re-ordering the world. The key concept of world reconstruction was still establishing a federation of states. For example, in the essays "New World Order", which were arranged and edited by F.S. Marvin in 1932, this author pointed out that, "Something of a world-wide order has been set up, by the general consent of mankind, and is in active work, of which it is impossible to say that any parallel existed before" [171; 277].

Between 1934 and 1937 British intellectual Lionel Curtis further elaborated the idea of organization of all human society into one commonwealth. Curtis was one of the founders of The Round Table Group, which created The Royal Institute of International Affairs in Britain and the Council on Foreign Relations in the United States. His book titled "Civitas Dei: The Commonwealth of God" was published in London in 1938 [63]. He advocated establishing the World Federal Government. In 1939, this publication appeared in the United States under the title "World Order: (Civitas Dei)" [64].

Curtis' earlier work was entitled "The Commonwealth of Nations". It was published in 1916. It advocated similar concepts of world unification, but its main theses were developed yet in 1911. As Carroll Quigley mentioned referring to Curtis, "Lionel Curtis is one of the most notable members of the Milner Group, or, as a member of the Group expressed it to me, he is the *fons et origo*. It may sound extravagant as a statement, but a powerful defense could be made of the claim that what Curtis thinks should be done to the British Empire is what happens a generation later. I shall give here only two recent examples of this. In 1911 Curtis decided that the name of His Majesty's Dominions must be changed from "British Empire" to "Commonwealth of Nations" [222, p. 63], which came into being more than three decades later in 1949.

Despite Curtis used the term "commonwealth" regarding British Empire, the prospects were to establish the World-State. It was planned to be built around Britain, the United States and British depending territories engaging them into a single bloc. With this purpose, perhaps, Curtis put forward the question of how to adapt peoples' thinking to a one-world concept, abandoning tribal and nationalist sentiment.

Foreign Affairs' review of Curtis' "World Order: (Civitas Dei)" noted, that "The growth of the idea of Commonwealth is traced from the beginning of recorded time until now, and the conclusion is reached that man can realize his best possibilities only through unremitting service to the common good in a democratic State. The argument is made in terms of thought that are in some respects deeply personal. The conclusions have significance in view of the fact that Mr. Curtis, as a practical politician during the past thirty years, working on South African, Indian and Irish affairs, has had a direct influence on the transformation of Empire into Commonwealth" [327].

In his later book entitled "World Revolution in the Cause of Peace" Lionel Curtis demonstrated a clear globalist' vision of the "big picture" of history. He acknowledged, that the historical events linked together represent a trend towards "world revolution" culminating in a world government: "We shall end the World Revolution, as they ended the American Revolution, only when our leaders have prepared an international constitution and have laid it before us ordinary people to accept or to reject" [65, p. 106]. Notably, similar concepts were later developed by H.G. Wells, who applied the idea of ensuring "world peace" in terms of the promotion of the world revolution doctrine.

In 1940, Carnegie Endowment's for International Peace issued a document titled "The New World Order: Select List of References on Regional and World Federation; together with some Special Plans for World Order after the War" [286]. The publication included the list of scientific works that appeared from 1938 to 1940 elaborating "designs for a world order" such as "federation of free states", a "world state", "unarmed world federation", etc. For example, John Foster Dulles urged "America to lead the transition to a new order of less independent, semi-sovereign states bound together by a league of federal union". Landone Brown advocated "a super state which shall have power to act only as a world police to enforce permanent peace on earth". Wilson Duncan examined "how federalism might be adopted on a world-wide scale". Lothar von Wurmb promoted the idea of "the world federal state" [286, p. 10-17].

The list of references included many other publications of the type, suggesting various models for the post-World War II international order. Interesting enough, the address by Pontific Pius XII, which was delivered on December 24, 1939 outlining "five points considered essential for the setting-up of a new world order", was also included in the list. Besides, the so-called "source of inspiration" of globalists, that is, Immanuel Kant's "Perpetual Peace", was introduced with the following comment: "Advocates a federation of free states" [286, p. 10].

Many of the notorious intellectuals of that time contributed to theoretical and conceptual evolution of the new world order paradigm. They promoted *the concept of a world federation* or a world state which, in their view, must have been built by means of establishing a federal world government along with its executive branches, such as international police force, world parliament, and international court. For instance, E.J. Housden urged "strong international army governed by a new league of nations". L. Einaudi insisted to "unify Europe and European dependencies on the pattern of the Napoleonic empire or, better, the Roman empire: one ruler, one law, one religion or, alternatively, unify Europe and dependencies on a federal plan on the pattern of the United States of America" [286].

Other authors suggested establishing a world federation using the concepts of "the United States of Europe", "a federal world" or "federation of free people". They insisted on "the collapse of sovereignty". From this assumption, they deduced *the concept of world government* [286, p. 10]. Eventually, the proposed ideas inspired the world government movement. The movement emerged as a successor to the world peace movement. It incorporated the ideas of the world peace congresses held from 1843 until 1939.

World War II

On the eve of World War II *the world government movement* has become an influential international force promoting the new world order paradigm. British writer, futurist and historian Herbert Wells made an important contribution in that regard. He was one of the founding members of the Round Table Group along with Lionel Curtis and Philip Kerr [222]. Upon publication of Well's books entitled "Open Conspiracy: Blue Prints for a World Revolution" and "The New World Order" the term "new world order" became a widely discussed topic [316; 315].

Yet in 1902 Wells wrote: "The Open Conspiracy will appear first, I believe, as a conscious organization of intelligent and quite possibly in some cases, wealthy men, as a movement having distinct social and political aims, confessedly ignoring most of the existing apparatus of political control, or using it only as an incidental implement in the stages, a mere movement of a number of people in a certain direction who will presently discover with a sort of surprise the common object toward which they are all moving... In all sorts of ways, they will be influencing and controlling the apparatus of the ostensible government" [314, p. 285].

In "Open Conspiracy" Wells further developed the idea of rebuilding the international system. He emphasized, that "reorganizing the affairs of the world on quite a big scale, which was "Utopian," and so forth, in 1926 and 1927, and still "bold" in 1928, has now spread about the world until nearly everybody has it.... Hundreds of thousands of people everywhere are now thinking upon the lines foreshadowed by my Open Conspiracy, not because they had ever heard of the book or phrase, but because that was the way thought was going.... to make over the New World amidst the confusions of the Old" [315, p. 7-8].

Wells advocated the idea of "Open Conspiracy" in pacifist terms using the ideology of the world peace movement. He propagated refusal of military service, world economic control, population control as would be basic pillars for the new world order. Wells urged, "From the outset, the Open Conspiracy will set its face against militarism. There is a plain present need for the organization now, before war comes again, of an open and explicit refusal to serve in any war... The time for a conscientious objection to war service is manifestly before and not after the onset of war... And a refusal to participate with one's country in warfare is a preposterously incomplete gesture unless it is rounded off by the deliberate advocacy of a world pax, a world economic control, and a restrained population, such as the idea of the Open Conspiracy embodies" [315, p. 51].

In "The New World Order" Wells suggested to working out "a clear conception of the world order" [316, p. 14]. In doing so, he updated the world revolution doctrine and introduced the concept of "the new Revolution". The main purpose of this intellectual effort was "to examine the way in which we are to face up to this impending World Revolution" [316, p. 69]. The idea of "Open Conspiracy" was proposed as being the means towards that end. This idea differed from the concept of "closed conspiracy" or secret conspiracy which, as some scholars argue, had inspired the Revolution in France.

Referring to World War II Wells urged that, "There will be no possible way of ending it until the new Revolution defines itself" [316, p. 73]. It is important to emphasize, that Hitler's "new order" doctrine also invoked the idea of a revolution. Hitler declared: "With the notion of race, National Socialism will use its own revolution for the establishing of a new world order." [143, p. 138].

In elaborating the concept of "the new Revolution" Wells considered the role of revolutions that had taken place in Europe. He identified the two types of revolutions. The first type of revolution, according to him, was the "Catholic type of Revolution" which represented only a specimen of "one single type of Revolution". The second type of revolution was identified as follows: "revolution conspiracy... in which many people set about organizing the forces of discomfort and resentment and loosening the grip of the government's forces, to bring about a fundamental change of system. The ideal of this type is the Bolshevik Revolution in Russia..." [316, p. 69-71]. Comparing the mentioned two types of revolutions Wells concluded: "Neither is lucid enough and deliberate enough to achieve a permanent change in the form and texture of human affairs" [316, p. 72].

Therefore, Wells urged that a different type of revolution, the new revolution, is needed, "which aims essentially at a change in directive ideas. In its completeness, it is an untried method" [316, p. 72]. The process of carrying out the new revolution brings about "a choice between so carrying on and so organizing the process of change in our affairs as to produce a new world order or suffering an entire and perhaps unrepairable social collapse" [316, p. 14; 72].

It appears, so far, that the development of the new world order paradigm reflected transformation of the existing social order as well as peoples` mentality. The means was the ideas powerful enough to inspire Wells's new type of revolution aimed at reconstructing human society and its social order. Such a new revolution might be identified today as being the revolution in people`s minds and human values. At present, it has been driven primarily by globalization processes, its secular trends as well as certain "liberal" movements eroding the system of traditional values.

Wells urged that, "The reorganization of the world has at first to be mainly *the work of a "movement"* or a Party or a religion or cult, whatever we choose to call it. We may call it New Liberalism or the New Radicalism or what not… but if a sufficient number of minds irrespective of race, origin or economic and social habituations, can be brought… then their effective collaboration in a conscious, explicit and open effort to reconstruct human society will ensue" [316, p. 73]. This movement clearly demonstrated itself as being *the world government movement*. Gaining its apogee in the wake of World War II, it was inspiring the new type of revolution that Wells had articulated. Thus, in a wide historical context of the "big picture", World War II seems to be *the second attempt* at creating the new world order.

Wells viewed the new world order as a "collective achievement" and a "social product". He argued that "no man, no group of men, will ever be singled out as its [new world order`s] father or founder… but Man, that being who is in some measure in every one of us" [316, p. 105]. He also referred to "the overruling conception of a secular movement towards a single world order" [316, p. 101]. Eventually, this secular principle has become one of the strategic constants of the U.S. foreign policy strategy. In 2000, Condoleezza Rice observed: "Powerful secular trends are moving the world... American policies must help further these favorable trends by maintaining a disciplined and consistent foreign policy" [229].

In both "The Open Conspiracy" and "The New World Order" Herbert Wells advocated "a World Pax", where the mankind would be "united and free and creative" [316, p. 106]. With this purpose, he proposed to adopt a "Declaration of the Rights of Man" or "Declaration of Human rights", which "must become the common fundamental law of all communities and collectivities assembled under the World Pax" [316, p. 90; 120]. The Universal Declaration of Human Rights (UDHR) was adopted in 1948. Notably, this happened eight years after Wells drafted a Declaration in his book [316, p. 91-94].

The idea of the "World Pax" foreshadowed *the concept of Pax Americana*. It was incorporated into the new world order paradigm, so far, underpinning its implementation during the second half of the 20th century. The concept of Pax Americana included the ideas of "The American Dream", "The American Destiny" and "The American Century".

The term "American Dream" was coined by James Adams, an American writer and historian. Yet in 1931 he believed that the American way of life was "a dream of social order." Initially, the title of his book was planned to be "The American Dream". However, considering the period of the Great Depression it was eventually released as "The Epic of America" [2]. This work was reprinted again in 1941, making "the American Dream" and "the American Way of Life" commonly used phrases.

The concept of the "American Destiny" emerged in 1939 following the publication of an article entitled "The American Destiny" [149]. It was published in Life magazine by Walter Lippmann, a famous journalist, an adviser to the U.S. President Woodrow Wilson and a member of the Council of Foreign Relations, who assisted in the drafting of Wilson`s Fourteen Points speech and, also, coined the term "The Cold War". Besides, Lippman along with CFR`s members George Kennan, Paul Nitze, Dean Acheson, and others took part in elaboration of the Marshall Plan and NSC-68 in the aftermath of World War II.

"The American Destiny" demonstrated striving of the U.S. political establishment towards global hegemony. The article emphasized the role of World War I and World War II in the context of such evolution. Referring to World War I Lippmann claimed: "The American people were right… that because of the War they had become the strongest creditor power, and this gave them a vital interest and a clear obligation to take a leading part in the reconstruction of the money and the credit and the commerce of the world" [149, p. 72]. The article further maintained that the U.S. mission after World War II was to become a world leader. Its key theses were based on the so-called American exceptionalism and belief in Manifest Destiny.

Lippman considered the interwar period in terms of missed opportunities for the United States: "Twenty years ago the Congress refused to proceed with the challenging work of organizing the world for peace. The refusal has not settled the issue… Ten years ago we refused to go on with the task of reconstructing the shattered economy of the world. The refusal has not made easier, in fact it has aggravated, the difficulty of restructuring our own domestic economy" [149, p. 73]. Thus, the problem of Great Depression in the United States was connected with the issue of re-structuring the world economy. It was mainly the Great Depression on the one hand and the process of establishing the new world order on the other hand that required the U.S. participation in World War II.

World War II represented an opportunity for the United States to reshaping international economy, according to American interests, in the wake of the war. From this perspective, perhaps, Lippman concluded that, "when a nation refuses to do the great things which it has to do, it is… the general refusal to accept the American destiny in the post-War world" [149, p. 73]. Therefore, Lippman criticized American isolationism, which used to be a foreign policy concept laid out yet in the Monroe Doctrine: "we still cling to the mentality of a little nation on the frontiers of the civilized world, though we have the opportunity, the power, and the responsibilities of a very great nation at the center of the civilized world" [149, p. 73].

"The American Destiny" advocated the U.S. engagement into world affairs in global dimension. Such an approach would later become known as a *concept of globalism* or American global engagement. It was embodied within the Truman Doctrine and every consecutive doctrine of the U.S. presidential administrations since then.

Lippman emphasized the strategic opportunity for extending American power overseas. He stated that, "In the lifetime of the generation to which we belong there has occurred one of the greatest events in the history of mankind. The controlling power in western civilization has crossed the Atlantic. America, which was once a colony on the frontiers of Europe, is now, and will in the next generations become even more certainly, the geographic and the economic and the political center of the Occident. All the world knows this and acknowledges it. The American people have known it under Wilson, under Coolidge, under Roosevelt, in their great undertakings after the World War. They were following the American destiny. And... they will have to go on with it. There is no way to refuse this destiny. What Rome was to the ancient world, what Great Britain has been to the modern world, America is to be to the world of tomorrow... when the destiny of a nation is revealed to it, there is no choice but to accept that destiny and to make ready to be equal to it" [149, p. 73]. So far, "The American Destiny" might be considered as an important milestone in terms of conceptual underpinning of the new world order paradigm. It adopted the U.S. globalism as a foreign policy concept.

The concept of Pax Americana was adopted in 1941. An influential media magnate, the founder of Time, Life, and Fortune magazines, Henry Luce, proposed theoretical framework of that concept in Life magazine's editorial entitled "The American Century" [154]. As Walter Lippmann and many other representatives of American elites did, Luce considered the entrance of the United States into World War II as an opportunity to transforming the international system and asserting U.S. leadership role in world affairs. He stressed that, "its participation is deeply needed for the shaping of the future of America and of the world" [154]. According to Luce, the U.S. participation in World War II was "a question of choice and calculation" [154].

The article read: "The 20th Century is the American Century... it is America's first century as a dominant power in the world... And ours is also a revolutionary century... as a corollary in politics and the structure of society" [154]. Luce insisted on taking American "complete opportunity of leadership" and suggested to promote "the vision of America as the dynamic leader of world trade" and "guarantor of the freedom of the seas". These ideas fully corresponded to Wilson`s universalism doctrine and its conceptual basis – The Fourteen Points program.

"The American Century" advocated the U.S. global engagement into world affairs. It criticized isolationism as a policy concept. Luce criticized the first Presidential terms of Franklin Roosevelt. He considered Roosevelt as "a complete isolationist" and urged "Franklin Roosevelt`s great opportunity to justify his first two terms and to go down in history as the greatest rather than the last of American Presidents" [154]. He stated, that "Without our help he cannot be our greatest President. With our help, he can and will be. Under him and with his leadership we can make isolationism as dead an issue as slavery, and we can make a truly American internationalism... In 1919, we had a golden opportunity, an opportunity unprecedented in all history, to assume the leadership of the world - a golden opportunity handed to us on the proverbial silver platter. We did not understand that opportunity. Wilson mishandled it. We rejected it. The opportunity persisted. We bungled it in the 1920`s and in the confusions of the 1930`s we killed it. To lead the world would never have been an easy task. To revive the hope of that lost opportunity makes the task now infinitely harder than it would have been before. Nevertheless, with the help of all of us, Roosevelt must succeed where Wilson failed... Once we cease to distract ourselves with lifeless arguments about isolationism, we shall be amazed to discover that there is already an immense American internationalism" [154].

Luce concluded that, "finally there is the belief - shared let us remember by most men living - that the 20th Century must be to a significant degree an American Century. This knowledge calls us to action now" [154]. Notably, in the beginning of the 20th century the concept of "New American Century" emerged within the neo-conservative part segment of the U.S. political establishment [225].

"The American Century" pursued globalists` agenda of establishing the world state. Luce considered, however, that the world government was hardly achievable in the 20th century: "in postulating the indivisibility of the contemporary world, one does not necessarily imagine that anything like a world state - a parliament of men - must be brought about in this century. Nor need we assume that war can be abolished. All that it is necessary to feel... is that terrific forces of magnetic attraction and repulsion will operate as between every large group of human beings on this planet. Large sections of the human family may be effectively organized into opposition to each other" [154].

Thus, the article advocated the implementation of the so-called "divide and rule" principle. It had been traditionally applied by the Anglo-Saxon civilization with a purpose of splitting Eurasia and expanding its liberal paradigm of world order. Luce confirmed, that "of course there would always be a better than even chance that, like the great Queen Elizabeth, we could play one tyrant off against another" [154].

As follows from the above, the concepts of "The American Dream", "The American Destiny", "The American Century" and "The New American Century" contributed to theoretical evolution of the new world order paradigm. Proclamation of the 20th century as the American century symbolized the end of isolationism and the beginning of Pax Americana, that is, the era of globalism. Interesting enough, Rockefeller Brothers Fund's Special Studies Project defined Pax Americana "as an imperial ambition to call nations into being, to set them against one another in a balance of power, to divide and break up any too massive concert" [233, p. 25]. Thus, the "divide and rule" geopolitical principle was applied with regard to major Eurasian powers.

In the context of the above it must be noted, that during World War I Washington aimed, primarily, at weakening geopolitical power capacity, mostly, of Russia and Germany. According to the U.S. Department of State, the United States was interested in "keeping Russia in the war" [178]. During World War II the White House used the same geopolitical approach with regard to Russia and Germany. The U.S. President Harry Truman suggested: "If we see that Germany is winning we ought to help Russia and if Russia is winning we ought to help Germany, and that way let them kill as many as possible..." [6].

The White House considered the concept of Pax Americana as the most perceptive postwar vision corresponding to the process of implementation of the new world order paradigm. Therefore, the editorial has been reprinted several times, including in the New York Times, The Washington Post, the Reader's Digest etc. Besides, Time Inc. distributed the article in high schools, colleges and universities around the United States. It also appeared in the U.S. Congress [154-157].

The *pro* and *contra* arguments regarding the idea of "The American Century" have been more a matter of tones and nuances rather than disagreements in principles on the conduct of the United States' foreign policy. However, among a few critics of that idea was Oswald G. Villard, a former editor of The Nation magazine. He asserted that, "'The American Century' was a "dangerous mixture of imperialism and aggression, roughly the counterpart to Mein Kampf in announcing a pursuit of "world domination", making the U.S. as ominous a threat to humanity as the Third Reich, or Soviet Russia, or Japan" [71, p. 42-43; 333].

Graeme Howard's book "America and a New World Order" (1940) also argued, that neither isolationism, nor interventionism (globalism) could be a practical policy option for the United States. Instead, the book urged a pattern of the world which would be based on a policy of "cooperative regionalism" and in effect mean pursuing the tradition of the Monroe Doctrine by letting European Powers divide the Eastern Hemisphere while the U.S. would take over the Western Hemisphere [111].

Cold War

In the aftermath of World War II the euphoria of omnipotence had an overwhelming impact on the U.S. government. To a greater extent it can be explained due to American atomic monopoly. The U.S. Secretary of State Dean Acheson (1949-1953) entitled his memoirs "Present at the Creation." This book demonstrated determination of the United States' political establishment to create Pax Americana immediately after the war. However, the beginning of the Cold War and the invention of the atomic weaponry by the USSR made the liberal paradigm of new world order evolving, mainly, within U.S. think tanks' projects. Therefore, during the Cold War the paradigm evolved as an elitist agenda which was kept beyond the debates of the existing schools of thought.

During the Cold War *the orthodox, revisionists and post-revisionists* schools of thought focused on the conflict between the two superpowers - the United States and the Soviet Union. Academic efforts of scientists both in the U.S.A. and in the USSR sought to identify "the guilty side", that is, the initiator of the Cold War and, from this perspective, explaining its causes. For example, the traditional, or orthodox, school blamed the Soviet Union as if it was an aggressor.

The orthodox supported foreign policy approaches put forward by the Truman administration. It urged containing the "Soviet threat". That is why, this school of thought has been also known as "official historians".

The revisionists' school opposed the "traditionalists" (i.e. the orthodox). It provided additional arguments regarding the Cold War. This current emerged, mainly, due to American military failure in Vietnam. The revisionists considered economic causes of the U.S. geopolitical expansion after World War II. They viewed the "open door" policy as a requirement of promoting Pax Americana and the U.S. development as an imperialist power.

Finally, starting from the 1970-s *post-revisionists'* school of thought emerged. It challenged the "revisionists" by accepting some of their findings but rejecting many of their key claims. Post-revisionism applied geopolitical principles of foreign policy analysis.

The majority of "orthodox", revisionists and post-revisionists scholars kept the factor of threat to U.S. national interests as their North Star. It is this factor that linked together the Cold War, the War on Terror and the ongoing Cyber War. Besides, World War I and World War II followed the same strategic line of carrying out world's transformation. From this perspective, each of the named warfares served as a stage in terms of establishing the new world order. The Cold War, in its turn, appeared as being an episode in the framework of the "big picture" and realization of the U.S. "grand strategy".

In 1948, Sir Harold Butler, a CFR member serving as Director of the International Labor Office, and then as a Minister in charge of information at the British Embassy in Washington, published an article in Foreign Affairs entitled "A New World Takes Shape". He urged that the countries of Western Europe were "on the threshold of a very difficult enterprise" [40]. Butler put forward the following question: "How far are they prepared to sacrifice a part of their sovereignty without which there can be no effective economic or political union?" [40]. In seeking to answering this question Butler concluded that, *"Out of the prevailing confusion* [i.e. chaos] a new world is taking shape. When it finally settles into its mold, its structure will be so different from anything that has gone before that a comfortable Victorian risen from the dead would detect in it little resemblance to the world which he knew. At present, however, everything is still fluid; hardly any fixed points have yet emerged.

But there are signs of incipient consolidation here and there, which may point the way toward the new order" [40]. The latter, in Butler's view, would be "held together by a common faith" [40].

In 1949, The Social Science Foundation of the University of Denver issued a collection of essays entitled "Foundations for World Order" [325]. These essays represented a collective work performed by seven intellectuals from the United States and Europe, who have been both renowned scholars and active participants in the public affairs. The purpose of the publication was to identify, for each author in a specific area, the foundations on which a new world order could be established. The authors of the essays were E. L. Woodward, J. Robert Oppenheimer, E. H. Carr, William E. Rappard, Francis Bowes Sayre, Edward Mead Earle, Robert M. Hutchins [328]. Each author dealt with an issue of building a new world order from political, scientific, moral, economic, constitutional, and power perspectives.

E. L. Woodward considered several historical pre-conditions of world order. In "The Historical and Political Foundations" chapter of the book, he argued that despite the first failure at world organization (League of Nations) the U.S. have made a second attempt through the United Nations. The earlier publication by Woodward in 1947 viewed "The Historical and Political Foundations for World Order" [326].

J. Robert Oppenheimer focused on the contributions of science and technology in "The Scientific Foundations of the New World Order." He stated, that "the notion of order, the notion of law, implies reason – implies the ability of men by discussion and thought to come to agreement where there had been no agreement before." E. H. Carr interpreted of the hazards of moral value-judgments referring to international politics in "The Moral Foundations". Particularly, he pointed out an assumption "that one's own conception of the good is identical with the good itself, and can and should be imposed on others." William E. Rappard analyzed "The Economic Foundations" and concluded that in solving the question of world's unification "the political would dominate the economic" [325; p. 87]. He believed that political ideas and psychological forces would create greater motivation than the economic forces. Francis Bowes Sayre discussed the application of the United Nations' Charter to the problem of "Dependent Peoples." Edward Meade Earle offered an analysis of the nature of power politics in "National Power." He insisted that in building the new world order the United States must "confront Soviet power with our own power." Earle viewed two alternatives regarding the international system, namely, "the hegemony of a single power in Europe and Asia" or the "restoration of some sort of balance of powers" [325].

Robert M. Hutchins, who has been chairman of the Chicago Committee to frame a world constitution, has made his views on "The Constitutional Foundations". He vigorously advocated for the world government. He affirmed that, "World Government is necessary, and therefore possible… tinkering with the United Nations will not help us… an entirely different constitutional foundation is required" [325]. In claiming the world government, Hutchins appealed to the issue of peace and justice. He considered, that the "price of peace is justice", but the way to promote the international community must be exclusively through the world government. According to him, there was no alternative: world federation or world destruction.

Finally, the named authors agreed on the fact that new foundations for world order were needed, yet they could not be offered by the United Nations in the framework of "institutional approach" [325]. All of them concluded that independent states must be brought into some other form of organization that can prevent or at least delay the next devastating war. Thus, *the issue of war and peace* remained central in terms of the promotion of the new world order paradigm.

Further theoretical elaboration of the paradigm can be traced in many of Foreign Affairs' magazine publications, including articles and book reviews. Robert Gale Woolbert reviewed two books on the subject. The first book entitled "The Foundations of a More Stable World Order" was written by Walter H. C. Laves. It comprised six lectures delivered at the Harris Institute of the University of Chicago in 1940 [279]. The second book titled "World Order: Its Intellectual and Cultural Foundations" was written in 1946 by F. Ernest Johnson. It included eighteen lectures delivered "by men of diverse faith under the auspices of the Jewish Theological Seminary of America" [124].

Since then theoretical elaboration of the foundations for the new world order has been steadily increasing in Foreign Affairs. In 1999, for example, the magazine published a review of the book by Francis Anthony Boyle entitled "Foundations of World Order: The Legalist Approach to International Relations, 1898-1922" [26]. This book examined the period of constructing the new world order from the Spanish American War to the establishment of the League of Nations and the Permanent Court of International Justice (1922-1946).

In the late 1950-s the Rockefeller Brothers Fund launched a Special Studies Project. It gathered together a group of influential individuals including Henry Kissinger, John Gardner, Dean Rusk, Charles Percy, Henry Luce, Nelson Rockefeller, Laurance S. Rockefeller (president of the Fund) and roughly a hundred other. Leading academic and government authorities in the United States were engaged in the project activities. The Project was inspired by Nelson A. Rockefeller, who served as president of the Rockefeller Brothers Fund from 1956 until 1960. Its objectives were to "define the major problems and opportunities facing the U.S. and clarify national purposes and objectives, and to develop principles which could serve as the basis of future national policy" [232].

Henry Kissinger was selected to serve as the director for the project. The papers and discussion sessions resulted in the final reports by each panel, which were published as "Prospect for America: The Rockefeller Panel Reports" (1961) [232]. These reports included "The challenge to America: its economic and social aspects"; "Foreign economic policy for the twentieth century"; "International security, the military aspect"; "The mid-century challenge to U.S. foreign policy"; "The pursuit of excellence; education and the future of America" [234]. Portions of the project papers are still restricted.

The project considered "The Mid-Century Challenge to U.S. Foreign Policy" report as "an attempt to assess the major problems of foreign policy over the next decade, as they appear to one group of citizens" [233, p. V]. Section IV of the report entitled "Elements of a New World" urged to consider the future world order. It argued that, "In a world changing rapidly it is important to discern the next phase as well as to grasp the fundamentals of the present one" [233, p. 48-51]. It also insisted on "the decline of the nation-state." The report urged: "The nation-state as it was conceived in the sixteenth century and as it has existed throughout the modern age is now transforming itself... the nation-state, as traditionally conceived, is no longer the sole possible unit of political power" [233, p. 51].

The Special Studies Project identified *driving forces* of the new world order as well as its major *dimensions*. It acknowledged that the Cold War was an episode in terms of the "world drama", that is, the "big picture" in our view. The U.S. foreign policy was considered as being *an instrument* aimed at confronting threats to American interests around the globe. The project urged "a foreign policy which seeks to shape events" [233, p. V].

Thus, Section VIII of the report entitled "On Entering a New Phase" read: "Events and upheavals which shake the surface may have already occurred; but men suddenly become aware of forces at work on a deeper level..." [233, p. 72]. It further stated that, "The United States has been jolting along from crisis to crisis, viewing foreign policy, as a rather unpleasant device for warding off threats all over the world... The fateful rivalry of the cold war may persist for a long time; nevertheless, this is an incident in a far greater world drama. We cannot escape - and indeed should welcome - the task which history has imposed on us. This is the task of helping to shape a new world order in all its *dimensions - spiritual, economic, political, social.* There is the challenge. There also is a hope and the practical possibility" [233, p. 74]. The named dimensions of the new world order have been shaped as a result of realization of the U.S. foreign policy strategy.

The Rockefeller`s project challenged the concept of national sovereignty. It envisaged the new world order as a subnational phenomenon: "the United States has an objective which needs to be defined in additional terms, broader than the old concept of "national interest" [233, p. 12]. The U.S. elites agreed upon time-consuming and lengthy period of its implementation: "Only slowly, however, are we grasping the implications of a world in which forces hardly yet measurable and peoples still in political infancy form essential elements of *the total structure*" [233, p. 58]. The project put forward *the concept of population control* as if to provide higher living standards [233, pp. V; 41; 58].

Moreover, messianic beliefs and American exceptionalism were considered essential to bringing about the global transformation: "The United States at its best has always seen its national life as an experiment in human liberty. It established its independence and made its Constitution in an age of large and liberal hopes... A sense of being watched - in an almost Biblical sense of being judged - has remained with the United States... On a deeper level, Americans have cared what history thought of them, what the ultimate judgment would be upon their work. They have known that the hopes of the world were, in some measure, bound up with their success" [233, p. 13].

The new world order paradigm was clearly confirmed at the U.S. presidential level during the Nixon administration. On December 7, 1971 Richard Nixon applied liberal slogans of "peace, justice and progress" to identify that phenomenon. He declared, that "in the presence of new events and new circumstances, in the presence of a reality which is ever changing and above which we must rise to build a new world order in the spheres of political, diplomatic, economic, financial, and monetary activity. We must approach this new world without preconceived ideas and without inflexible positions. And what seems imperative to us is that this new world order must also bring about an entirely new phase of peace, justice, and progress for all the members of the family of nations" [195; 215]. In October 1975, Nixon`s National Security Advisor Henry Kissinger expanded such a policy approach at the UN level. Kissinger appealed to the UN General Assembly suggesting to "fashion together a new world order" [180, p. 155].

Following the above mentioned political declarations by Richard Nixon and Henry Kissinger, the Center of International Studies, Woodrow Wilson School of Public and International Studies at Princeton University, published a book by Cyril Edwin Black entitled "A New World Order?" [20]. This book included papers which had been originally presented on November 14-15, 1974 at the first of a series of Princeton University Conferences. Thus, the academic thought and intellectuals were shaping *theoretical models for the future*.

In 1974, Foreign Affairs` published an article entitled "The Hard Road to World Order" [89]. The U.S. Ambassador Richard N. Gardner, the author of the article, argued that *"three ambitious strategies"* had been implemented by previous generation in pursuit of the new world order, namely, "world federalism", "world peace through world law", and the UN "charter review". As our research has demonstrated so far, these strategies were carried by the world government movement, the world peace movement (congresses) as well as the "peace educators" movement.

The U.S. Ambassador put forward the following question: "If instant world government, Charter review, and a greatly strengthened International Court do not provide the answers, what hope for progress is there?" [89]. Gardner maintained that the answer to that question must come down not to building up international institutions of universal membership, but rather "inventing or adapting institutions of limited jurisdiction and selected membership to deal with specific problems on a case-by-case basis..." [89]. He urged, that "the "house of world order" will have to be built from the bottom up... around national sovereignty, eroding it piece by piece" [89].

Gardner concluded that, "even as nations resist appeals for "world government" and "the surrender of sovereignty", technological, economic and political interests are forcing them to establish more and more far-reaching arrangements to manage their mutual interdependence... Thus, while we will not see "world government" in the old-fashioned sense of a single all-embracing global authority, key elements of planetary planning and planetary management will come about on those very specific problems where the facts of interdependence force nations, in their enlightened self-interest, to abandon unilateral decision-making in favor of multilateral processes" [89].

Almost two decades after Richard Gardner`s publication, the U.S. government adopted *multilateralism* as a foreign policy doctrine aimed at larger engagement of international organizations into the process of establishing the new world order. The United States intended to apply multilateral mechanisms and institutions to deal with global issues and various crises. In doing so, however, Washington insisted on exclusive American leadership role while relying on preemptive actions and shared responsibility.

On August 26, 1992 the U.S. Senator David Boren, a CFR member, confirmed such an intention in The New York Times article entitled "The World Needs an Army on Call". He acknowledged that, "For the United States to act, the burden must be shared... In the aftermath of World War II, President Truman wanted to empower the United Nations to create a new world order... That promise was never realized because of the cold war and the Soviet Union`s use of its veto power on the Security Council... Richard Gardner, a professor of international law at Columbia University, proposes that 40 to 50 member nations contribute to a rapid-deployment force of 100,000 volunteers that could train under common leadership and with standardized equipment. Intelligence could also be shared to allow the United Nations to anticipate problems and take preemptive action... It is time for us to create such a force, and the

United States should take the lead in proposing it... Still, the existence of such a force, uniformly trained and ready to act, would go a long way toward making the "new world order" more than just a slogan... We must seize this moment. History will hold us accountable if we do not" [25].

It might be assumed, so far, that the Cold War stage coincided with the third attempt undertaken by the global elites to establish the new world order. Yet in 1977 The Atlantic Monthly published an article entitled "The Trilateral Connection". In this publication, former Washington Post columnist Jeremiah Novak stated: "For the third time in this century, a group of American scholars, businessmen, and government officials is planning *to fashion a New World Order*" [196].

Beyond the Cold War

After the end of the Cold War the process of transformation of the international system entered a new stage. It might be identified as being the stage of U.S. hegemonism, which lasted until the global rising of China and creating the BRICS. Before that, the unipolar moment opened wide strategic opportunities for the United States to further implementing its "liberal" model of global governance. At the same time, changing geopolitical conditions required further theoretical elaboration and legitimization of the paradigm.

Starting from the early 1990-s many experts and statesmen, including U.S. Presidents, declared that a new world order was emerging. The term "new world order" became a widely debated topic in scholarly works and political agenda, especially, after the speech given by U.S. President George H. W. Bush entitled "Toward New World Order" on September 11, 1990. Since then "the new world order" became a catch phrase and a commonly used term.

However, it was associated, mainly, with the process of transformation of the post-World War II international order. The U.S. preeminent position in world affairs as well as fundamental changes in the international system that followed the collapse of the Soviet Union were identified as the new world order. Many authors viewed the latter in terms of Wilsonian universalism and liberal rhetoric. For example, Bruce Russett and James S. Sutterlin urged that, "The new world order envisioned by

Presidents Bush and Gorbachev would be founded on the rule of law and on the principle of collective security" [241].

Since then hundreds of academic works emerged applying the term "new world order" from different perspectives. It was widely referred to globalization processes as well as various models of global governance developed by international institutions and forums (G20, BRICS, EU, World Economic Forum, etc.). Many authors referred the term, primarily, to modern trends in world's economic and technological development, international security and law issues, arms proliferation, military engagement, crises management, etc. [340]. Interesting enough, Daniel W. Drezner, Associate Professor of International Politics at the Fletcher School of Law and Diplomacy at Tufts University, argues about "The New New World Order". He considers that the way for a multipolar era in world politics has been "a challenge to the U.S.-dominated global institutions that have been in place since the 1940s" [74].

The ideas of the grand strategists, such as Henry Kissinger and Zbigniew Brzezinski, must be especially emphasized in the same context of identifying the new world order paradigm after the Cold War. Both Kissinger and Brzezinski have applied the term "new world order" in their works [136; 137; 36]. Notably, Kissinger's most recent book "World Order" (2014) has been different in comparison with most of the existing approaches towards the subject [137]. Its distinctive feature appears not the concept of "world order" itself, but rather the idea of viewing the phenomenon in a wide historical context.

Kissinger demonstrates the contemporary "world order" as a descendant of the Westphalian system that emerged in Europe in response to the religious violence of the Thirty Years War (1618-48). In this historical context, he examines "the varieties of world order" and refers to European Order, Islamic World Order, Asian Order and, finally, illustrates the U.S. concept of order and its implications in terms of the nuclear age and cyber technology. Despite declining Pax Americana Kissinger asserts that constructing a new international system can only be possible under the U.S. leadership. However, the driving forces projecting the new world order paradigm through world's history or, in other words, those *forces at work on a deeper level*", which were mentioned by the Special Studies Project under Kissinger's directorship in 1959, remain within the uncharted territory of the U.S. foreign policy strategy.

Although many critical issues were raised in the framework of scholarly debates, existing approaches towards the new world order paradigm have been fragmentary. They have been focused mostly on the Cold War period and its aftermath while leaving earlier stages of the promotion of the system of global governance, including World War I and World War II, its deep historical roots as well as interconnection with the U.S. foreign policy strategy largely unexplored. This oversimplified the paradigm and brought about doubtful interpretations.

Considering a variety of approaches towards identifying the new world order paradigm as well as significant amount of literature on the subject, it is important to systemize the most influential schools of thought and currents that have influenced on its theoretical and conceptual evolution at the modern stage. In 1997, American intellectual John C. Hulsman summarized a paradigm *for* the new world order. He identified its key features in the framework of schools` of thought analysis and debates on U.S. foreign policy issues after the Cold War. Hulsman focused on *the democratists, the neo-realists, the institutionalists currents*, which advocated for the U.S.-led world order and suggested various foreign policy tools to further promote American leadership. Besides, Hulsman demonstrated foreign policy preferences of many political figures in the United States as well as their affiliation, yet implicit, with the named currents of thought.

According to Hulsman, the key ideas of the democratists have been the shared values and promotion of democracy worldwide. The neo-realists adhered to the concept of national interests and relied upon the U.S. military power and unilateral actions, if necessary, to attain strategic goals. The institutionalists` approach has been based on the concept of shared interests. They appealed mainly to the economic power and the role of multilateral institutions to promote the U.S. leadership. The institutionalists have challenged the concept of nation-state and advocated sub-national level of governance [112].

The democratists, republican theorists and critical theorists have been considering the international order in the context of *the concept of global governance*. They deal with that subject in terms of the issue of war and peace and, therefore, consider the interstate war as being the key security threat. From this perspective, the named currents advocate various theoretical models and patterns for global governance [330].

Since the very term "world government", as it was mentioned before, has become a political liability, that is why, the concept of global governance was introduced into world`s political agenda. In 1992, Strobe Talbott[1], the current president of the Brookings Institution[2] and former Deputy Secretary of State (1994 – 2001), confirmed: "The advocacy of any kind of world government became highly suspect. By 1950 "one-worlder" was a term of derision" [270]. In 1995, the first periodical magazine entitled "Global Governance" was issued in Boston, the USA.

In 1997, Anne-Marie Slaughter, Professor of International, Foreign, and Comparative Law at Harvard Law School, asserted that Bush`s idea of new world order was a 'chimera'. In the article entitled "The Real New World Order" she pointed out: "Many thought that the new world order proclaimed by George Bush was the promise of 1945 fulfilled, a world in which international institutions, led by the United Nations, guaranteed international peace and security with the active support of the world`s major powers. That world order is a chimera. Even as a liberal internationalist ideal, it is infeasible at best and dangerous at worst. It requires a centralized rule-making authority, a hierarchy of institutions, and universal membership. Equally to the point, efforts to create such an order have failed. The United Nations cannot function effectively independent of the major powers that compose it, nor will those nations cede their power and sovereignty to an international institution. Efforts to expand supranational authority, whether by the U.N. secretary-general`s office, the European Commission, or the World Trade Organization (WTO), have consistently produced a backlash among member states" [256].

Instead, "the end of the nation-state" concept was considered in the article as the leading alternative to liberal internationalism. This concept implied the increasing role of "supra-state, sub-state, and, above all,

---

1 Strobe Talbott is also a member of the Trilateral Committee, the Council on Foreign Relations (CFR), Carnegie Endowment for International Peace board of directors member, and, as some sources argue, the then member of the Skull & Bones secret society at Yale University.

2 Brookings Institution is one of the most influential think tanks promoting world government (or "global governance," the euphemism the internationalists prefer to use today). Interesting enough, the ex-chairman of the Federal Reserve Ben Bernanke is a distinguished Fellow in Residence at the Brookings Institution

nonstate actors." These new players have multiple allegiances and global reach: "The result is not world government, but global governance" [256].

According to Stanford Encyclopedia, "Today, proposals for a world government with coercive powers and centralized authority structures compete with proposals for noncoercive, decentralized structures of "global governance." Critical assessments of this evolution from "world government" to "global governance" have accompanied a revival of arguments for world government in intellectual debates in international relations theory as well as political theory about global order and justice" [330]. In the framework of contemporary political science and, especially, international relations theory such arguments were put forward, for example, by realists, neo-realists, liberal theorists, etc.

Realists (Hans Morgenthau, Edward H. Carr, Reinhold Niebuhr, John Herz, Frederick Schuman etc.) consider that wars between states are unavoidable since the anarchy is an unalterable social fact. As concerns the issue of governance, they support a global reformist agenda, prompted by the globalization processes, technological change etc. According to Reinhold Niebuhr, the global political change towards a world government in the form of a global federal system would depend on deeper social integration in global dimension and cohesion comparing to the mid-twentieth century [246, p. 72-76]. As far as the "global political unity" (i.e. the world government in other words) currently lacks the required social and cultural basis, Niebuhr concludes that, "the achievement of world government would be undesirable, since in such conditions, a world government would require authoritarian devices to rule, raising the specter of a global tyrannical power" [330].

Neorealists (Robert J. Art, Richard K. Betts, Joseph Grieco, Robert Jervis, Christopher Layne, John Mearsheimer, Stephen Walt etc.) represent one of the most influential currents in contemporary political science. This current emerged in the late 1970s as a modification of classical realism. As realists do, proponents of neorealism explain the causes of interstate war in the context of anarchy as if it is the very nature of the international system. They argue, however, that the anarchy exists due to the absence of a world supreme authority. From this point of view, the neorealists appear to be the most active proponents of the world government and creation of a world state.

Liberal theorists basically reject a unified global political regime. They consider such a regime as a might be global despotism or a fragile empire torn by civil upheavals of people striving towards freedom and political autonomy. Liberalism, in general, assumes that nonstate actors, such as political parties, social groups, movements and individuals at the national level, and NGOs at the international level, also play a key role in international system, which they consider as being less anarchical than realists assert. Therefore, most of liberal thinkers reject the concept of world government or a world state covering the entire globe [14, p. 182; 125, p. 229; 272; 202, p. 285; 244, p. 77-78]. They advocate global governance instead urging "the legitimacy and desirability of establishing international or transnational institutions to regulate cooperation between peoples and even to discharge certain common inter-societal duties" [330].

Besides, liberalism implies restrictions on the powers of state sovereignty. It undermines the nation state doctrine suggesting vertical dispersion of sovereignty, "upwards towards supranational bodies, and downwards toward particular communities within states" [272, p. 101]. For example, Thomas Pogge considers that realizing "a peaceful and ecologically sound future will … require supranational institutions and organizations that limit the sovereignty rights of states more severely than is the current practice" [202, p. 213]. According to David Held, the liberal ideal of autonomy (derived from Kant) requires long-term institutional developments leading to the creation of a global parliament, an international criminal court, the demilitarization of states, and a guaranteed annual income for each global citizen [104, p. 279-280].

Globalists (internationalists), constructivist theorists, libertarians, and conspiracy theorists are among other influential currents that shape theoretical and conceptual spectrum of the new world order paradigm. According to globalists, the process of globalization might lead the mankind towards "one world" or, possibly, a "world state" united under a single authority as if it would approach the new era of peace, well-being and prosperity. The globalists' current appears today as being the main advocate of the world government. It influenced significantly on the formation of the global political agenda as well as the activities of international organizations and think tanks.

Globalists` ethos is to bring about the "new order of the ages" into being. This is their key ideal which had originated yet in Ancient Egypt. Since the early history of the American republic it was incorporated into the U.S. foreign policy strategy. Therefore, historically, there have been two distinct approaches to the conduct of the United States foreign policy – isolationism and internationalism (globalism).

Despite "globalism" on the one hand and "isolationism" on the other hand have been, seemingly, two conflicting approaches to the conduct of United States foreign policy, the historical players in each of these two camps, while clashing over different foreign policy options and pushing multiple soft power or hard power concepts agree on fundamental principles of the American foreign policy. The key principle has been the defense of U.S. national interests. Eventually, globalsits and isolationists, realists and idealists, unilateralists and multilateralists, "hawks" and "doves" have always come together to confront threats to U.S. national interests. Simultaneously, they have been suggesting different means in attaining the same strategic objectives. As Robert Kagan put it, "Even most American multilateralists are unilateralists at the core" [127].

Globalists consider the concept of national sovereignty as the main impediment to the promotion of sub-national model of governance. Yet in 1931 a famous historian Arnold J. Toynbee stated at the Fourth Annual Conference of Institutions for the Scientific Study of International Relations, which was initiated by the League of Nations: "We are at present working discreetly with all our might to wrest this mysterious force called sovereignty out of the clutches of the local nation states of the world. All the time we are denying with our lips what we are doing with our hands, because to impugn the sovereignty of the local nation states of the world is still a heresy for which a statesman or publicist can perhaps not quite be burned at the stake but certainly be ostracized or discredited" [295].

As it was mentioned, since the first half of the 18th century the Anglo-American establishment has been the main driving force in the promotion of the new world order paradigm. The paradigm has been carried by various social, political, scientific and cultural movements, including world peace congresses (*the world peace movement*), *the world revolution movement, the world federalists' movement,* etc. On the eve of World War II, merging of these movements into *the world government movement* occurred. Its apogee was marked by publication of the Preliminary Draft of a World Constitution by the University of Chicago Committee to Frame a World Constitution in 1947 [211].

The Soviet Union opposed globalists` idea of establishing the world government in the wake of World War II. Therefore, during the Cold War the world government movement transformed into *the "peace education" movement*. The agenda of globalists was evolving mostly within U.S. think tanks` and organizations of international elites such as the Bilderberg group, the Trilateral Commission, the Club of Rome etc. The CFR has been very influential in that regard. Its key think tanks, such as The Inquiry, The War and Peace Studies, The WOMP, the 1980-s Project as well as several others have been *projecting the paradigm*.

After dissolution of the USSR globalists` influence on formulating world`s political agenda increased. Since then one of the main arguments of transnational elites, in terms of implementing the paradigm, has been the idea of natural evolution of mankind from its early tribal organization towards sophisticated cities and states which, in their turn, developed into nation-states and, finally, globalization process emerged approaching a world state. Describing the "big picture" of history globalists assume that the world government would inevitably appear as an apogee of the evolution of mankind bringing about the "new order of the ages". However, it must be noted, that globalists have always omitted in their analysis the very fact that all historical attempts to impose a single authority eventually led to tyranny and, therefore, failed.

In a 1992 essay for Time magazine, entitled "The Birth of the Global Nation," Strobe Talbott supported the idea of a global government over nation-states. Being an influential representative of the U.S. political establishment, Bill Clinton's Russia advisor and former Deputy Secretary of State, Talbott demonstrated *globalists` perception of the "big picture"*, spanning from the Stone Age until the present. Specifically, though, he viewed the development of the mankind in terms of devolution of power from national states towards supranational institutions, commonwealths, common markets and, thus, urging that the global governance would eventually come into being.

Giving a special emphasis on eroding nation-states doctrine, the vision that seems to be materialized today, Talbott approached the logic of history (i.e. historical mechanism of cause and effect connections between the events) since prehistoric times through the periods of the empires and further to the formation of the modern nation states and, finally, towards universal organizations such as the League of Nations and the United Nations.

According to Strobe Talbott, the optimist's reason for believing that unity or, in other words, the world government will eventually prevail over disunity appears as follows: "nationhood as we know it will be obsolete; all states will recognize a single, global authority. A phrase briefly fashionable in the mid-20th century – "citizen of the world" – will have assumed real meaning by the end of the 21st century." In this connection, he claims: "All countries are basically social arrangements, accommodations to changing circumstances. No matter how permanent and even sacred they may seem at any one time, in fact they are all artificial and temporary" [270].

Therefore, in Talbott's mind, "The best mechanism for democracy, whether at the level of the multinational state or that of the planet as a whole, is not an all-powerful Leviathan or centralized super state, but a federation, a union of separate states that allocate certain powers to a central government while retaining many others for themselves... Federalism has already proved the most successful of all political experiments, and organizations like the World Federalist Association have for decades advocated it as the basis for global government. Federalism is largely an American invention. For all its troubles, including its own serious bout of secessionism 130 years ago and the persistence of various forms of tribalism today, the U.S. is still the best example of a multinational federal state. If that model does indeed work globally, it would be the logical extension of the Founding Fathers' wisdom, therefore a special source of pride for a world government's American constituents. As for humanity as a whole, if federally united, we won't really be so very far from those much earlier ancestors, the ones huddled around that primeval fire beside the river; it's just that by then the entire world will be our valley" [270].

Considering the issue of war and peace, Talbott further argued that the conquest was the main driving force of the process of political expansion and consolidation: "The big absorbed the small, the strong the weak. National might made international right. Such a world was in a more or less constant state of war." In this context he, as most of the globalists do, appeals to the ideas of "the best minds" and philosophers who had wondered of "a way to run a planet": Dante in the 14th century, Erasmus in the 16th, Grotius in the 17th advocated international law as a means over use of force in settling differences between the states [270].

Strobe Talbott concluded that, "perhaps national sovereignty wasn't such a great idea after all." He also appealed to the ideas that had been given rise by the Enlightenment in the 18th century and represented by Rousseau in France, Hume in Scotland, Kant in Germany, Paine and Jefferson in the United States. They propagated basic liberties, rights and freedoms, including that of choosing their leaders.

The key Talbott's sentiment in the above context, so far, has been as follows: "Once there was a universal ideology to govern the conduct of nation toward their own people, it was more reasonable to imagine a compact governing nations' behavior toward one another. In 1795 Kant advocated a "peaceful league of democracies." But it has taken the events in our own wondrous and terrible century to clinch the case for world government" [270]. From the perspectives on institutionalizing the world government, Talbott identified the IMF and GATT (WTO) "as the protoministries of trade, finance and development for a united world" [270].

It must be especially emphasized, that regarding the above mentioned "case for world government" Talbott identified *the role of wars* in the promotion of the new world order paradigm: "Each world war inspired the creation of an international organization, The League of Nations in the 1920's and the United Nations in the '40s…" He continued that, "The cold war also saw the European Community pioneer the kind of regional cohesion that may pave the way for globalism" [270].

According to U.S. President Barack Obama, the modern world has been "at a crossroads between war and peace" [190]. In view of this fact, it might be assumed that World War III, in case it erupts, might bring about the "order out of chaos" in the face of the world government. The latter is the key globalists' concern.

In 2008, Strobe Talbott further projected the new world order paradigm, theoretically, in his book entitled "The Great Experiment: The Story of Ancient Empires, Modern States, and the Quest for a Global Nation". It appears that "Great Experiment" goes back to the most ancient times. Thus, Talbott expanded the "big picture" from the Garden of Eden into the present, yet, with a globalists' eye into the future. Talbott urged, so far, that the whole mankind is being guided towards "an international system that is far more cohesive" and "far more effective than the one we have today" [271].

Considering Talbott's perception of the "big picture", it might be assumed that theoretical projection of the new world order paradigm by international (global) elites, their think tanks as well as political leaders sharing the idea of global governance gives the way towards institutionalization of the world government. The latter can be also identified as "the premises of international order," if using the phrase coined by Henry Kissinger.[3]

The "big picture", in which the world government appears as the ultimate end, emerges in the context of Strobe Talbott' book as he analyses the logic of history and power phenomena since consolidation of tribes into nations - starting with Israel - and the absorption of those nations into the past empires of Hammurabi in Babylon (1792-1750 BC), the Pharaohs (31 dynasties over the 3000 years of Ancient Egyptian history), Alexander the Great (ruled from 336 BC to 323 BC and conquered the Persian Empire), the Caesars in the Roman Empire (36 Roman Emperors from 27 BC to 393 AD), Charles the Great (ruled much of medieval Western Europe from 768 to 814), Genghis Khan in the Mongol Empire (became emperor of "all who lived in felt tents" in 1206 until his death in 1227), the Ottoman dynasty in the Ottoman Empire (made up of the members of the House of Osman and ruled from 1299 to 1922) and, finally, the Hapsburgs dynasty in the Austro-Hungarian Empire (1867-1918).

The missing parts in such a historical puzzle are the only two Orthodox empires in the history of mankind, that is the Byzantine Empire ("Great Romea") and the Russian Empire ("Katehon"). Hence, Western attempts at absorbing the former during the Four Crusades and the latter during World War I, World War II, the Cold War, and beyond to the ongoing War on Terror (using the IS movement as being an instrument to clashing Christianity with Islam) and further to Cyber War.

The issue of war and peace in Talbott's book can be traced through wars of territory and religion, to modern alliances and the global

---

3   This phrase was coined by Henry Kissinger in his book "World Order"

institutions of the twentieth century, that is through the breakthroughs and breakdowns of peace along the way of history: the Pax Romana, the Treaty of Westphalia, the Concert of Europe, the failure of the League of Nations, the creation of the United Nations and, finally, the effort to building the "new world order" after the Cold War. Thus, in our view, Talbott demonstrated the stages of the promotion of the new world order paradigm (the world government). However, some other parts of the historical puzzle, especially, those connected with Pax Britannica and Pax Americana, have been omitted from such an analysis of the "big picture."

Important enough, Talbott identifies the U.S. role in world's history as being "the master builder" of the international system. Although the collapse of the USSR gave the way to chaos in the Balkans in the 1990s, the emergence of a "terror threat", and the expansion of the global chaos, Talbott viewed America's "unipolar moment" as being the latest, but not the last, stage in the "Great Experiment" [271].

Constructivist theory has been important in fostering globalists' idea of the world government. It is based on the belief that reality is a socially constructed phenomenon. This theory emerged in the mid-1990s as a challenge to the dominant realist and liberal schools of thought. Constructivist theory argues that human beings generate knowledge and meaning from an interaction between their factual experiences and their ideas. It also focuses on the meanings that are assigned to material objects, rather than the mere existence of these objects themselves.

Nicholas Greenwood Onuf has been the first theorist who introduced the term "constructivism" in International Relations theory in 1989. He urged that not only individuals, but also states are living in a "world of our making." In such a reality, many entities such as "social facts", for example, are made by human action [193].

Since 1992 the constructivist theory was popularized by University of Chicago's researcher Alexander Wendt as well as other theorists who directly challenged neorealism. The core of Alexander Wendt's concept consists of his efforts to develop a theory of the international system as a "social construction" [13]. Important enough, this theory had a wide-ranging impact on learning theories and teaching methods in education and is a fundamental concept of many education reform movements. Thus, the constructivist theory might influence on shaping the *informational dimension* of the new world order.

From this perspective on constructing social and international reality, Wendt contributed to identifying the "big picture" of events in their causal connection. He considered the development of mankind as a sequence alignment from an anarchic system of states to (as if) inevitability of establishing a world state. In a publication entitled "Why a World State is Inevitable: Teleology and the Logic of Anarchy" he argues that, "the struggle for recognition between states will have the same outcome as that between individuals, collective identity formation and eventually a state" [317].

As well as other supporters of the idea of the world government maintain Wendt invoked philosophers of the past. He claimed that the world state would emerge out of the ruins of the eroded national sovereignty. According to Wendt, in the struggle of nation-states there can be no other outcome than the formation of a global authority to settle all the disputes [317].

So far, Wendt advocated the world government as if it was necessary and inevitable institution due to the current merging of nation-states and emerging of a global monopoly - a world state. In his view, the latter would imply the legitimate use of violence. He urged, that "Long dismissed as unscientific, teleological explanation has been undergoing something of a revival... to explain the tendency of systems to develop toward stable end-states. On that methodological basis, this article argues that a global monopoly on the legitimate use of organized violence - a world state - is inevitable. At the micro-level world state formation is driven by the struggle of individuals and groups for recognition of their subjectivity. At the macro-level, this struggle is channeled toward a world state by the logic of anarchy, which generates a tendency for military technology and war to become increasingly destructive. The process moves through five stages, each responding to the instabilities of the one before - a system of states, a society of states, world society, collective security, and the world state. Human agency matters all along the way, but is increasingly constrained and enabled by the requirements of universal recognition" [317].

Wendt followed the tradition of the Chicago`s Committee to Frame a World Constitution of 1945 arguing, that "Rather than go down with the ship of national sovereignty, states should try to "get the best deal" they can in the emerging global constitution." He proposed to absorb the intention by the states towards self-determination to bring about the world state: "Nationalist struggles for recognition are by no means over, and more new states- "more anarchy"- may yet be created. But while further fragmentation is in one sense a step back, it is also a precondition for moving forward, since it is only when difference is recognized that a larger identity can be stable... Far from suppressing nationalism, a world state will only be possible if it embraces it" [317].

Important enough, Wendt's article inspired further discussion, both pro and contra, on the issues concerning global governance and the world government. Thus, he further promoted theoretical and conceptual legitimization of the new world order paradigm both in academic realm and in the field of public policy. For example, the following publications are worth mentioning: "Wendt's Violation of the Constructivist Project: Agency and Why a World State is Not Inevitable" (2005) by Vaughn P. Shannon; "Agency, Teleology and the World State: A Reply to Shannon" (2005) by Alexander Wendt; "Review article: World government: Renewed debate, persistent challenges" (2010) by Luis Cabrera; "Obstacles to a world state in the shadow of the world market" (2012) by Bob Jessop; "Accelerating democratic global state formation" (2012) by Christopher Chase-Dunn; "Federal world government: The road to peace and justice?" (2012) by Ronald Tinnevelt; "Introduction: World state futures" (2012) by Mathias Albert, and etc. [317].

The libertarians shape a considerable part of the theoretical spectrum of the new world order paradigm. They support the concept of a society based on the ideas of freedom, liberty, and voluntary association with less government regulation. As globalists do, the libertarians also challenge the concept of national sovereignty. Moreover, they put forward a question whether a state system should exist at all and, if so, to what extent. This issue of state sovereignty divides libertarians into two camps: the minarchists and the anarchists. While minarchists propose to limit the state power to mainly preventing external aggression, anarchists advocate complete elimination of the nation state.

Thomas Woods, an American historian and political analyst, has been advocating a typical libertarian point of view with regard to the new world order. Woods has been considered as "one of the most influential minds in the subjects of history, economics and contemporary politics...

endorsed by several influential political and economic figures including Ron Paul" [145].

Thomas Woods' comments on a document entitled "Towards Reforming the International Financial and Monetary Systems in the Context of Global Public Authority" [205] released by Vatican on October 24, 2011 by the Pontifical Council for Justice and Peace, calling for a "global public authority" and a "central world bank" to rule over financial institutions, are important to considering. Woods suggested that, "From this point, we plunge straight away into a full endorsement of a world central bank, a world political authority, taxes on financial trading, and heavy regulations" [324]. He also suggested that the document by Vatican could have been written by any number of secular think-tanks in the United States [323]. Referring to conspiracy theorists' point of view that as if a "cabal of evil people" have been ruling the world, Woods stressed at his lecture, though quite ironically, that "this would explain a lot".[4]

William T. Still, who sought the Libertarian Party[5] presidential nomination in 2012, emphasized that, "an ancient plan has been hidden for centuries deep within secret societies. This scheme is designed to bring all of mankind under a single world government – A New World Order. This plan is of such antiquity that its result is even mentioned in the Bible – the rule of Antichrist mentioned in the Revelation of Saint John the Divine… Their "government of nations" is a deception, hiding an iron clad, world dictatorship. This is where their New World Order is taking us, and unless we realize from whence the danger comes, our ability to oppose it will be unfocused and therefore ineffective" [266, p. 7-8]. The end of the proponents of the new world order, so far, is "the destruction of Christianity" [266, p. 119].

Conspiracy theorists stand at the end of theoretical spectrum of the new world order paradigm. Although they have largely marginalized the phenomenon, they raise critical issues which contribute to its understanding. Conspiracy theorists have been dealing with new world order's issues in terms of secret societies, sub-national elites and global institutions. They analyze symbolism, knowledge and rituals which had

---

4   Personal observation by the author of this book who attended the lecture delivered by Thomas Woods at the University of Florida in October 2012.

5   "Minimum Government, Maximum Freedom" – the slogan of the Libertarian Party

originated yet in Ancient Egypt, but still exist in the American society (e.g. symbols of the Great Seal, the U.S. dollar bill, etc.). Some researchers even believe that the pattern of governance introduced to ruling the Ancient Egypt has been applied by world's elites as a model for the promotion of the current system of global governance.

Besides, conspiracy theorists argue that the most influential families, politicians and transnational elites form a worldwide network aimed at realizing a long-lasting and thoroughly planned project for the future of the whole mankind. In support of such arguments they focus on historical milestones of evolution of secret societies, including their documents. For example, the activities of the Order of Illuminati of 1776 as well as other esoteric and occult groups such as freemasonry, etc. have been in the focus of their analysis.

A lot in conspiracy theories' emphasis has been given on the activities of the international elitist organizations such as the Round Table group (The Group), the Bilderberg Group[6], the Trilateral Commission as well as many others which altogether might be considered as being a powerful political and economic sub-system managing the process of implementation of the new world order paradigm. According to Carol Quigley, the "Anglo-American Establishment" is an important international player whose role in the history of mankind has been underestimated [222; 223].

David Rockefeller, a famous American banker and former chairman and chief executive of Chase Manhattan Corporation, pointed out in his memoirs: "Some even believe we (the Rockefeller family) are part of a secret cabal working against the best interests of the United States, characterizing my family and me as "internationalists" and of conspiring with others around the world to build a more integrated global political and economic structure - one world, if you will. If that's the charge, I stand guilty, and I am proud of it" [235; p. 405].

In a book touching upon the activities of "Skull and Bones" secret society, which had been founded at Yale University in 1823, Alexandra Robbins, the Yale alumna, argues that secret societies are being associated in public eyes with "someone or something in control" [231; p. 205].

---

6 The activities of the Bilderberg Group have been explored by a Journalist Daniel Estulin.

While explaining the methods of functioning of secret societies, especially, the reason why they used to disclose a certain amount of hidden knowledge and rituals to wide public, Robbins refers to a member of "Skull and Bones" stating, that "It`s essential to have a certain amount of confusion and uncertainty about just what goes on because it actually projects what goes inside. It`s an effective smokescreen to project that privacy" [231; p. 200]. Besides, Robbins considered a point of view that, "In its quest to create a New World Order that restricts individual freedoms and places ultimate power solely in the hands of a small cult of wealthy, prominent families, Skull and Bones has already succeeded in infiltrating nearly every major research, policy, financial, media, and government institution in the country. Skull and Bones, in fact, has been running the United States for years" [231; p. 4].

Among members of the "Skull and Bones" were, allegedly, William Howard Taft, the 27th President of the United States (1909-1913); famous American diplomat William Averill Harriman; Henry Luce; George Herbert Walker Bush, the 41st President of the United States (1989-1993), John F. Kerry, George W. Bush, the 43rd President of the United States (2001-2009) as well as many other influential figures in U.S. political establishment. In his memoirs, George W. Bush confirmed: "During my senior year at Yale, I was a member of Skull and Bones; a secret society so secret, I can't say anything more." [39; p. 47].

Conspiracy theories consider numerous speeches and declarations made by influential political figures, including U.S. Presidents, regarding the new world order phenomenon. Although they have been often misinterpreted, such declarations and observations, indeed, represent valuable empirical basis and, therefore, must be taken into consideration. Yet in 1913, for example, the U.S. President W. Wilson emphasized in his memoirs: "Since I entered politics, I have chiefly had men`s views confided to me privately. Some of the biggest men in the United States, in the field of commerce and manufacture, are afraid of somebody, are afraid of something. They know that there is a power somewhere so organized, so subtle, so watchful, so interlocked, so complete, so pervasive, that they had better not speak above their breath when they speak in condemnation of it" [320; p. 134].

Wilson further urged that, "We have restricted credit, we have restricted opportunity, we have controlled development, and we have come to be one of the worst ruled, one of the most completely controlled and dominated Governments in the civilized world no longer a Government by free opinion, no longer a Government by conviction and the vote of the majority, but a Government by the opinion and duress of a small group of dominant men" [320; p. 210].

In addition to such an observation by the American President, the U.S. Congressman Wright Patman, former chairman of the House Banking Committee, suggested the existence of "two governments" in the United States. In a newsletter dated 6 June 1968 Patman argued that, "In the United States today we have in effect two governments .... We have the duly constituted government.... Then we have an independent, uncontrolled and uncoordinated government in the Federal Reserve System, operating the money powers which are reserved to Congress by the Constitution" [269; p. 174].

In 1920, Winston Churchill claimed the existence of a "world-wide conspiracy for the overthrow of civilization and for the reconstitution of society". The British Prime Minister declared, that "From the days of Spartacus-Weishaupt [The Order of Illuminati] to those of Karl Marx, and down to Trotsky (Russia), Bela Kun (Hungary), Rosa Luxembourg (Germany), and Emma Goldman (United States), this world-wide conspiracy for the overthrow of civilization and for the reconstitution of society based on arrested development, of envious malevolence, and impossible equality, has been steadily growing. It played, as a modern writer, Mrs. Webster, has so ably shown, a recognizable part in the tragedy of the French Revolution. It has been the mainspring of every subversive movement during the Nineteenth Century; and now at last this band of extraordinary personalities from the underworld of the great cities of Europe and America have gripped the Russian people by the hair of their heads and have become practically the undisputed masters of that enormous empire" [49].

Among other notorious speeches, which the conspiracy theorists have been referring to in their attempt at explaining the new world order phenomenon, is the Address by John F. Kennedy - "The President and The Press" - delivered before the American Newspaper Publishers Association in New York on April 27, 1961. Kennedy stated that, "Today no war has been declared - and however fierce the struggle may be, it may never be declared in the traditional fashion... For we are opposed around the world by a monolithic and ruthless conspiracy that relies primarily on covert means for expanding its sphere of influence – on infiltration instead of invasion, on subversion instead of elections, on intimidation instead of free choice, on guerrillas by night instead of armies by day. It is a system which has conscripted vast human and material resources into the building of a tightly knit, highly efficient machine that combines military, diplomatic, intelligence, economic, scientific and political operations. Its preparations are concealed, not published. Its mistakes are buried, not headlined. Its dissenters are silenced, not praised. No expenditure is questioned, no rumor is printed, no secret is revealed" [132].

In our view, conspiracy theories contribute to theoretical and social legitimization of the new world order paradigm and, therefore, perform a distinct role in terms of its promotion. On the one hand, conspiracy theories raise public attention to the paradigm. They urge that political and historical events are not random, but rather interconnected ones. Even chaos, from their point of view, has causality. On the other hand, the very fact of existence of some types of the conspiracy theories allows to ridicule critical approaches regarding the new world order phenomenon.

In fact, conspiracy theories manipulate public opinion and serve as a "smokescreen" in terms of implementation of the global agenda. As Julian Assange noted in an interview, "Any time people with power plan in secret, they are conducting a conspiracy. So, there are conspiracies everywhere. There are also crazed conspiracy theories. It's important not to confuse these two. Generally, when there's enough facts about a conspiracy we simply call this news." Commenting on the annual meetings of the Bilderberg conference Assange noted, "That [the conference] is vaguely conspiratorial, in a networking sense. We have published their meeting notes" [311].

Finally, the theoretical and conceptual spectrum of the new world order paradigm has a *theological dimension*. This issue has been beyond theoretical framework of our research. However, some aspects of that dimension are to be considered as they contribute to perceiving the "big picture". In 1940, "A Memorial to be Addressed to the House of Bishops and the House of Clerical and Lay Deputies of the Protestant Episcopal Church" stated that, "The term Internationalism has been popularized in recent years to cover an interlocking financial, political, and economic world force to establishing a World Government. Today Internationalism is heralded from pulpit and platform as a `League of Nations` or a `Federated Union` to which the United States must surrender a definite part of its National Sovereignty. *The World Government plan* is being advocated under such alluring names as the `New International Order`, `The New World Order`, `World Union Now`, `World Commonwealth of Nations`, `World Community`, etc. All the terms have the same objective; however, the line of approach may be religious or political according to the taste or training of the individual" [16; p. 158].

The Vatican has touched upon the new world order phenomenon in addressing *the issue of war and peace*. For example, on March 26, 1967 Pope Paul VI referred to the idea of establishing a single world authority and undertaking joint efforts to constructing the new world order. He stated: "As We told the United Nations General Assembly in New York: «Your vocation is to bring not just some peoples but all peoples together as brothers... Who can fail to see the need and importance of thus gradually coming to the establishment of a world authority capable of taking effective action on the juridical and political planes? »... Delegates to international organizations, public officials, gentlemen of the press, teachers and educators - all of you must realize that you have your part to play in the construction of a new world order" [209].

On January 1, 2004 during the World Day of Peace John Paul II referred to the drama of World War II: "That war, with the horrors and the appalling violations of human dignity which it occasioned, led to a profound renewal of the international legal order..." [207]. Further in his message the Pontiff appealed to the need of "A new international order". While acknowledging the role of the UN in "preparing the cultural and institutional soil for the building of peace", John Paul II emphasized the need for reforming the UN system: "the ideals of the United Nations have become widely diffused, particularly through the practical gestures of solidarity and peace made by the many individuals also involved in Non-Governmental Organizations and in Movements for human rights. This represents a significant incentive for a reform which would enable the United Nations Organization to function effectively..." [207]. John Paul II also emphasized: "People are becoming more and more aware of the need for a new international order that will make the most of the experience of the United Nations Organization and the results it has achieved in recent years: an order that can provide satisfactory solutions to the problems of our day..." [208].

Following the above statements, the Guardian published an article entitled "Pope calls for a new world order" [110]. The article interpreted Pontiff's words, specifically, in terms of replacing the post-war international system: "Pope John Paul II launched one of the most important diplomatic initiatives of his long papacy yesterday when he called for a new international order to replace the one that emerged from the second world war. Though he did not offer a detailed plan, his words appeared to show he wanted the UN replaced... The Pope called last month for the reform of world institutions and deplored any failure to respect international law. But in a sermon during a mass at St Peter's in Rome yesterday, he went much further, referring to the UN as if it were already a part of the past" [110]. Considering the above statements by the Vatican, the article put an emphasis on the reform of the present system of international organizations that emerged in the wake of World War II, including the UN, the IMF and the World Bank.

The Vatican considered re-ordering the international system in the framework of globalization processes. In 2009, the Pontiff Benedict XVI suggested "a greater degree of international ordering" to manage globalization processes. He pointed out, that "Globalization is a multifaceted and complex phenomenon which must be grasped in the diversity and unity of all its different dimensions, including the theological dimension... In order, not to produce a dangerous universal power of a tyrannical nature, *the governance of globalization must be marked by subsidiarity*, articulated into several layers and involving various levels that can work together. Globalization certainly requires authority, insofar as it poses the problem of a global common good that needs to be pursued. This authority, however, must be organized in a subsidiary and stratified way, if it is not to infringe upon freedom and if it is to yield effective results in practice.... The process of globalization could replace ideologies with technology" [204]. The Pontiff concluded that, "The integral development of peoples and international cooperation require the establishment of a greater degree of international ordering, marked by subsidiarity, for the management of globalization. They also require the construction of a social order that at last conforms... to the interconnection between moral and social spheres, and to the link between politics and the economic and civil spheres" [204].

The Pontiff Benedict XVI also referred to the role of media in the context of globalization processes as follows: "Given the media's fundamental importance in engineering changes in attitude towards reality and the human person, we must reflect carefully on their influence... above all when they are geared towards a vision of the person and the common good that reflects truly universal values... In fact, human freedom is intrinsically linked with these higher values. The media can make an important contribution towards the growth in communion of the human family and the *ethos* of society when they are used to promote universal participation in the common search for what is just" [204].

In 2011, the Vatican released the document "Toward Reforming the International Financial and Monetary Systems in the Context of a Global Public Authority" [205], which has been mentioned above. The publication of this document coincided with world's financial and economic crisis which had erupted yet in 2008. The document read: "The economic and financial crisis which the world is going through summons everyone, as individuals and peoples, to examine in depth the principles and the cultural and moral values that underlie social coexistence. What is more, the crisis engages private actors and competent public authorities on the national, regional and international level in serious reflection on causes and on solutions of a political, economic and technical nature" [205].

It must be especially emphasized, that the Vatican's Pontifical Council for Justice and Peace considered the crisis as an "opportunity" to establishing "A supranational Authority" urging that, "The crisis thus becomes an opportunity... to shape a new vision for the future" [205]. It further suggested to "reforming the international financial and monetary systems in the context of global public authority" [205].

The following excerpts of the document are especially important in terms of exploring the process of establishing the new world order paradigm: "This is a complex and delicate process. A *supranational Authority* in this arena should have a realistic structure and be set up gradually. It should be favourable to the existence of efficient and effective monetary and financial systems.... It is a matter of an Authority with a global reach that cannot be imposed by force, coercion or violence, but should be the outcome of a free and shared agreement and a reflection of the permanent and historic needs of the world... It [the new world order] ought to arise from a process of progressive maturation of consciences and advances in freedoms as well as awareness of growing responsibilities... Consent should engage an ever-greater number of countries... through a sincere dialogue that values the minority opinions rather than marginalizing them. So, the world Authority should consistently involve all peoples in a collaboration in which they are called to contribute, bringing to it the heritage of their virtues and their civilizations" [205].

The document stressed that, "The establishment of a *world political Authority* should be preceded by a preliminary phase of consultation from which a *legitimated* institution will emerge that is able to be an effective guide and, at the same time, can allow each country to express and pursue its own particular good. The exercise of this Authority at the service of the good of each and every one will necessarily be *super partes* or impartial: that is, above any partial vision or good, with a view to achieving the common good. Its decisions should not be the result of the more developed countries' superior power over weaker countries. Instead, they should be made in the interest of all, not only to the advantage of some groups, whether they are formed by private lobbies or national governments" [205].

Moreover, as the document further reads, "*A supranational Institution*, the expression of a "community of nations", will not last long, however, if the countries' differences from the standpoint of cultures, material and immaterial resources and historic and geographic conditions, are not recognized and fully respected. The lack of a convinced consensus, nourished by an unceasing moral communion on the part of the world community, would also reduce the effectiveness of such an Authority. What is valid on the national level is also valid on the global level. A person is not made to serve authority unconditionally. Rather, it is the task of authority to be at the service of the person, consistent with the pre-eminent value of human dignity. Likewise, governments should not serve the world Authority unconditionally. Instead, it is the world Authority that should put itself at the service of the various member countries, according to the principle of subsidiarity. Among the ways it should do this is by creating the socio-economic, political and legal conditions essential for the existence of markets that are efficient and efficacious precisely because they are not over-protected by paternalistic national policies and not weakened by systematic deficits in public finances and of the gross national products – indeed, such policies and deficits actually hamper the markets themselves in acting on the world stage as open and competitive institutions" [205].

The above-mentioned document by Vatican further advocated the U.N. reform to address the issues of governance, including the so-called "shared government." It argued that "a long road still needs to be travelled before arriving at the creation of a public *Authority with universal jurisdiction*. It would seem logical for the reform process to proceed with the United Nations as its reference because of the worldwide scope of the UN's responsibilities, its ability to bring together the nations of the world, and the diversity of its tasks and those of its specialized Agencies" [205]. The document suggested reforming the international financial and monetary systems established in the aftermaths of World War II, namely, the Bretton Woods system, arguing to create "a system of *government* for the economy and international finance" [205].

In concluding, the document acknowledged that, "Of course, this transformation will be made at the cost of a gradual, balanced transfer of a part of each nation's powers to *a world Authority* and to regional Authorities, but this is necessary at a time when the dynamism of human society and the economy and the progress of technology are transcending borders, which are in fact already very eroded in a globalized world. The birth of a new society and the building of new institutions with a universal vocation and competence are a prerogative and a duty for everyone, without distinction. *What is at stake* is the common good of humanity and the future itself" [205].

In the context of addressing *the war and peace issue*, another important statement by Vatican followed on the 100th Anniversary of the outbreak of World War I. On 13 September 2014 Pontiff Francis declared that, "Even today, after the second failure of another world war, perhaps one can speak of a third war, one fought piecemeal, with crimes, massacres, destruction.... Today, too, the victims are many.... It is so because in today's world, behind the scenes, there are interests, geopolitical strategies, lust for money and power, and there is the manufacture and sale of arms, which seem to be so important! And these plotters of terrorism, these schemers of conflicts, just like arms dealers... It is the task of the wise to recognize errors… the merchants of war have perhaps made a great deal of money, but their corrupted hearts have lost the capacity to cry" [206]. Indeed, since the second attempt at creating the new world order had failed [23], one might assume that the third period of world's transformation would require a new global conflict. At the 69th U.N. General Assembly U.S. President Barack Obama noted that, "We come together at a crossroads between war and peace" [190].

Global media shape the informational dimension of the new world order. Yet in 1991, at a Bilderberger Conference held in Baden-Baden (Germany) David Rockefeller acknowledged: "We are grateful to The Washington Post, The New York Times, Time magazine, and other great publications whose directors have attended our meetings and respected their promise of discretion for almost forty years. It would have been impossible for us to develop our plan for the world if we had been subject to the bright lights of publicity during those years. But the world is now more sophisticated and prepared to march towards a world government. The super-national sovereignty of an intellectual elite and world bankers is surely preferable to the national auto-determination practiced in past centuries" [322, p. 27].

In 2008, Financial Times published an editorial entitled "And now for a world government". The article suggested that, "For the first time since homo sapiens began to doodle on cave walls, there is an argument, an opportunity and a means to make serious steps towards a world government" [224] It also stated that, "a change in the political atmosphere suggests that "global governance" could come much sooner… The financial crisis and climate change are pushing national governments towards global solutions… A "world government" would involve much more than co-operation between nations. It would be an entity with state-like characteristics, backed by a body of laws. The European Union has already set up a continental government for 27 countries, which could be a model. The EU has a supreme court, a currency, thousands of pages of law, a large civil service and the ability to deploy military force… The world's most pressing political problems may indeed be international in nature, but the average citizen's political identity remains stubbornly local. Until somebody cracks this problem, that plan for world government may have to stay locked away in a safe at the UN" [224]. More specifically, the role of the global media in the promotion of the new world order paradigm can be viewed through the prism of *the informational and ideological component* of the U.S. foreign policy strategy (See Chapter 2).

In 2012, a publication entitled "Effective World Government Will Be Needed to Stave Off Climate Catastrophe" appeared within environmental scientists' realm [267]. Indeed, certain globalists' currents of thought have been urging unification of the mankind under the aegis of the single world authority as if to avert the perils of climate change, nuclear catastrophe as well as to counter the international terror threat and many other global issues facing the world today. The article advocated the idea of creating the world government under a pretext of countering environmental issues, particularly, the climate change.

In the context of coping with the climate change, the author of the above publication calls for resorting to "social engineering" rather than finding solely "technical solutions" to the existing environmental problems. To prove such an argument the article considers a report by environmental scientists which was produced in 2012 summarizing 10 years of research that had been undertaken to assessing "the capability of international institutions to deal with climate and other environmental issues". The report suggests "to reform world politics and government" and, among other proposals, insists on better handling the "emerging issues related to water, climate, energy and food security." While pursuing such benign purposes of protecting the Earth system from "rapid and irreversible change" the report urges that, "This requires fundamental reorientation and restructuring of national and international institutions toward more effective Earth system governance and planetary stewardship" [267].

The publication further insists that "far more is needed." It assumes that, "If we are ever to cope with climate change in any fundamental way, radical solutions on the social side are where we must focus..." In this regard, the article calls for establishing "a new set of institutions" with "heavy-handed, transnational enforcement powers." Thus, it suggests finding "answers to social problems that are usually dismissed by policymakers as academic naiveté" [267].

So far, there is an argument that the world government, if established, would be an answer to global issues the mankind faces today as well as to the problems it might encounter in the future. This widens the facets of the new world order paradigm from solely geopolitical and geoeconomic issues towards the global issues. At the same time, it is the idea of establishing the world government that appears central in such a discourse, yet, being proposed from different perspectives.

In this regard, the following questions are being put forward: "Would any institution be capable of instilling a permanent crisis mentality lasting decade, if not centuries? How do we create *new institutions with enforcement powers* way beyond the current mandate of the U.N.? Could we ensure against a malevolent dictator who might abuse the power of such organizations?" [267].

As follows from the above analysis, it might be concluded that the new world order paradigm has been evolving in the framework of various social and political movements and currents of thought, such as the world revolution movement, the world government movement, the world peace movement, etc. These social and political phenomena consolidated transnational elites (intellectuals, political figures, etc.) who have been striving towards establishing global control (i.e. the world government) and, therefore, urge world's unification on a "liberal" basis. Altogether they might be considered as being a single global mainstream aimed at constructing the new world order, simultaneously, on national and international levels.

So far, the new world order paradigm has theoretical and practical perspectives. From a theoretical perspective, *the new world order paradigm is a doctrine*. The political philosophy of this doctrine has been underpinned by the ideology of liberalism. The doctrine has been visible in Manifest Destiny, Pax Americana and many other concepts and strategic documents of U.S. foreign policy.

From a practical perspective, *the new world order paradigm is a matrix* applied to establish the system of global governance in the form of the world government. The latter is being established in the process of formation and development of the U.S. "grand strategy". It has been used by the U.S. as a tool to pass through key stages of its evolution, thus, enforcing the global control over the international development. Each of the stages reflects the "big picture".

Chapter 2
Conceptual Development of the Paradigm

World Revolution Doctrine

Most of the notorious revolutionaries, such as Rousseau in France, Lenin and, especially, Trozky in Russia advocated the idea of carrying out world revolution to bring about a "new world". In the first half of the 19th century the *world revolution movement* emerged in Europe. This movement intended to subvert sovereign European monarchies and empires. It was powered by means of erupting European Revolutions of 1848, the so-called Spring of Nations, and, especially, during the revolution in France in 1789. The world revolution movement reached its apogee during the "regime change" in Russia in 1917, which led to the collapse of the Russian Empire. Since then, the movement has become an influential mainstream aimed at transforming the world. It can be figuratively compared to a geopolitical Gulfstream influencing the world political climate.

During the 20th century the attempts at redistributing world power and resources have been undertaken, mainly, in the aftermaths of World War I, World War II, the Cold War, the War on Terror, and the ongoing Cyber War. The first stage of establishing the new world order paradigm followed World War I. With its nearly 39 million in casualties the war appeared to be one of the most tragic periods not only in the world's history, but also in the history of Russia.

In the aftermath of World War I, Bolsheviks overthrew the monarchy in Russia. The Civil War (1917-1923) and the so-called "red terror" followed along with first concentration camps being established in the country. Despite fruitful economic cooperation between Russia and Germany long before the war, the idea of *Drang nach Osten* had been actively generated among German militarists' circles since the end of the

19th century. Because of the war, European empires and sovereign monarchies were crashed. Russian Empire, its historical legacy and territories were partially divided.

The United States has been actively masterminding such plans. Washington also participated in the military intervention in Russia in 1918. According to Kerry Bolton, "New York and Washington have historically been the capitals of world revolution, with the globalist elites pumping money into revolutionary movements whilst Stalin was busily eliminating international bolshevism as a Trotskyite menace, and reversing many aspects of the Bolshevik social experiments at home" [23].

In such historical circumstances, the *world revolution doctrine* has been used as a key to implement the new world order paradigm. It was promoted by the Bolsheviks party in Russia, which, as it was mentioned, organized coup d`etat and subverted the country`s monarchy in 1917. As many historical sources and documents testify, the revolution in Russia was masterminded by external forces, which rendered financial support and, thus, participated in carrying out the world revolution doctrine. Therefore, the revolution in Russia can be viewed as a first regime change effort that had been undertaken in the 20th century. Trotsky and his adherents intended, in his words, to "throwing Russia into the fire of world revolution" [251]. In other words, while attempting to control Russia they aimed at gaining world hegemony.

On 10 June 1932 U.S. Congressman Louis T. McFadden gave a speech in the House of Representatives blaming the U.S. Federal Reserve for its possible connection with organizing the revolution in Russia in 1917. He urged that, "These bankers took money out of this Country to finance Japan in a war against Russia. They created a reign of terror in Russia with our money to help that war along. They instigated the separate peace between Germany and Russia, and thus drove a wedge between the allies in World War. They financed Trotsky`s passage from New York to Russia so that he might assist in the destruction of the Russian Empire. They fomented and instigated the Russian Revolution, and placed a large fund of American dollars at Trotsky`s disposal in one of their branch banks in Sweden so that through him Russian homes might be thoroughly broken up and Russian children flung far and wide from their natural protectors. They have since begun breaking up of American homes and the dispersal of American children" [173].

McFadden determined the U.S. Federal Reserve system as being "one of the most corrupt institutions the world has ever known" [173].

After the end of World War I, the United States emerged with a powerful economy and, for the first time in its history, became the creditor of the European states. Although the American might was yet insufficient enough to become a global power, the United States managed to institutionalize the concept of sub-national governance in the form of the League of Nations. The doctrine of universalism, which was proclaimed by U.S. President W. Wilson along with American "open door" policy clearly demonstrated the U.S. geopolitical shift from isolationism, which used to be a foreign policy doctrine (i.e. the Monroe Doctrine) towards more active role in world affairs under the pretext of promoting "liberal" model of world order and universal "common" values. Thus, the stage of American isolationism lasted until the adoption of the Wilson Doctrine. Then the concept of universalism was extended beyond to the Truman Doctrine which symbolized the era of U.S. globalism.

In the aftermath of World War I, the U.S. foreign policy strategy focused on restoration of German power center in Europe and, simultaneously, promoting economic diplomacy to transform the American economic might into its geopolitical influence. The U.S. rendered economic assistance to Germany in the framework of the Dawes Plan of 1924 and the Young Plan of 1929 (the prototypes for the Marshall Plan of 1948). Thus the U.S. increased its influence in Europe and, simultaneously, strengthened the German center of power.

Because of the American economic diplomacy, by the early 1920-s Germany restored its economic capabilities and potential for military development. The U.S. loans were provided by a consortium of American investment banks, led by the Morgan Guaranty Trust Company, under supervision by the U.S. State Department. Besides, in 1922, following the meeting in Berlin between American banker Paul Warburg and Hitler, the National Socialist German Workers` Party received financial support amounted to 10 million of U.S. dollars.

According to John Loftus and Mark Aarons, the Nazis could have remained a small political party in a weak and unarmed state of Germany which lacked financial resources provided that powerful investments of foreign capital had been arranged from overseas to support Hitler`s rising to power. This became possible because of the alliance between the

American oil concerns and the companies belonging to Saudi Arabia. By the 1930s, the first Saudi king Ibn Saud and famous British diplomat and adventurers Jack Philby had organized financial support of the Nazi rising to political power in Germany. The above-named authors also claim, that U.S. banking and investment firm of G. H. Walker and Company "was one of Hitler`s most powerful financial supporters in the United States. The relationship went all the way back to 1924, when Fritz Thyssen, the German industrialist, was financing Hitler`s infant Nazi party... there were American contributors as well" [152, p. 357-361].

Hitler`s rise to power was financed by a combination of major German, British, and American banks and industrial companies. This fact has been well documented, for instance, in the book by Fritz Thyssen entitled "I Paid Hitler" (1941) [293]. Allen Dulles (the then corporate lawyer for Sullivan & Cromwell and the future head of U.S. intelligence) as well as Averill Harriman (another important figure in the U.S. establishment and head of W. A. Harriman & Company) were linked with Thyssen. Since 1924 they invested in Germany through the Union Banking Corporation.

Before that, the U.S. industrial monopolies and concerns which possessed, perhaps, the best technologies of that time, had been active especially in those industrial areas of Kaiser`s Germany that eventually influenced on the growth of its military machine. Because of such policy, before World War II began Nazi Germany launched the production of new types of weaponry, including tanks and airplanes. Moreover, the U.S. industrial concerns continued oil supplies for the needs of the Nazi military machine until the second front, or the Western front of the European theatre of World War II was open in 1943. The apogee of the Western policies that were leading towards the clash between the Third Reich and the USSR was the so-called appeasement of Hitler and the decisions taken in Munich in September 1938.

Although trozkism failed in Russia, the idea of world revolution has been evolving further within the U.S. neo-conservative current. Leo Strauss, one of founding fathers of neo-conservatism, inherited trozkism as an ideological basis. In the wake of the collapse of the Soviet Union, the world revolution doctrine re-emerged in the framework of globalization processes.

In 1993, report by the Club of Rome entitled *The First Global Revolution* focused on global changes that marked the end of the 20th century. It considered, that "the magnitude of these changes amount to a major revolution on a worldwide scale" [278, p. 2]. The report put forward the following question, "But why do we regard the contemporary threats and changes as the first global revolution?" [278, p. 3]. In seeking to answer this question the think tank asserts that "the present brutal changes are taking place everywhere simultaneously from causes which are likewise ubiquitous, thus causing the `Sturm and Drang` of a universal revolution. The worldwide significance of this revolution becomes vastly greater if one considers that its management could endanger the whole human race" [278, p. 3]. Thus, the idea of the world revolution has evolved into *global revolution doctrine.*

The Club of Rome identified origins of the global revolution as "being shaped by an unprecedented mixture of geostrategic upheavals caused by social, economic, technological, cultural and ethical factors. Combinations of these factors lead to unpredictable situations. In this transitional period, humanity is therefore facing a double challenge – having to grope its way towards an understanding of the new world with its many hidden facets and… to learn how to manage the new world… Our aim must be essentially normative – to visualize the sort of world we would like to live in, to evaluate the material, human and moral resources available, to make our vision realistic and sustainable, and then to mobilize the human energy and political will to forge the new global society" [278, p. 3].

Besides, the Club of Rome produced at least 18 reports on the subject of global governance [243, p. 33]. The Club`s mission has been identified as follows: "to act as a global catalyst for change" [275]. Bringing together leading personalities from politics, business and science, the Club of Rome raised considerable public attention already in 1972 when it released a report entitled «Limits to Growth» (distributed in 12 million copies in more than 30 translations). It advocated the so-called "golden billion" doctrine.

The report entitled "Regionalized and Adaptive Model of the Global World System" was issued in 1973. It suggested the concept of dividing the world into ten political and economic regions restructured into a "horizontal system" which would include interdependent "world regions". The ten regions would then unite the entire world under a single government, which would be confronting global issues (e.g. depletion of natural resources, overpopulation, climate change etc.).

At present, the promotion of the world revolution doctrine has been posited as being a form of *global social movement* which fosters "an idea for a new, global activist social movement for progressive social change" [291]. The movement aims at establishing "the state of the world" under the pretext of addressing global issues in following areas - peace, human rights, the environment, world poverty and development [291]. At the same time, the world (global) revolution doctrine might be identified in the context of what Brzezinski has determined as being "global political awakening" of mankind. This phenomenon expands globally: "For the first time in human history almost all of humanity is politically activated, politically conscious and politically interactive... That awakening is socially massive and politically radicalizing..." [170; 341]. It exploits religious extremism, ethnic intolerance, poverty, inequality etc.

Brzezinski further argues that it goes beyond "sovereign borders and pose a challenge both to existing states as well as to the existing global hierarchy, on top of which America still perches..." [170]. He asserts that, "The youth of the Third World are particularly restless and resentful. The demographic revolution they embody is thus a political time-bomb, as well... these millions of students are revolutionaries-in-waiting, already semi-mobilized in large congregations, connected by the Internet and pre-positioned for a replay on a larger scale of what transpired years earlier in Mexico City or in Tiananmen Square. Their physical energy and emotional frustration is just waiting to be triggered by a cause, or a faith, or a hatred..." [170; 341]. Such radicalization might eventually empower the global revolution by means of connecting regional centers of violence.

On April 23, 2010, Brzezinski, being a Co-Chairman of the Advisory Board, Centre for Strategic and International Studies (CSIS) of Washington, gave a speech "America`s Geopolitical Dilemmas" at the Council on Foreign Relations` branch in Montreal. He confirmed "a total new reality" which is the politically awakened mankind. During the discourse Brzezinski advocated replacing the United Nations system with a new system of global governance which would be based on a "one world organization", that is, de-facto, the world government. He urged that, "There should be such an organization" [341].

Further in 2012, in the book "Strategic Vision: America and the Crisis of Global Power" Brzezinski advocated America`s new role in the world due to changing global balance of power caused by "the dynamic shift in the world`s center of gravity from the West to the East..." [35]. He asserted, therefore, that "the changing distribution of global power and the new phenomenon of massive political awakening intensify, each in its own way, the volatility of contemporary international relations. As China`s influence grows and as other emerging powers – Russia or India or Brazil for example – compete with each other for resources, security, and economic advantage, the potential for miscalculation and conflict increases. Accordingly, the United States must seek to shape a broader geopolitical foundation for constructive cooperation in the global arena, while accommodating the rising aspirations of an increasingly restless global population..." [35].

At the modern stage, so far, a new global trend arises having a world-wide impact. Some researchers identify this trend as being "the start of a global revolution" [170]. Indeed, the events of the "Arab spring" and "colour revolutions" that took place on the post-soviet space and around the world can be viewed regarding the so-called "managed chaos" doctrine. This doctrine incorporates the "regime change" concept. It explains to a considerable extent social uprisings and unrest worldwide and poses a threat to peaceful world development.

World Government Doctrine

According to Stanford Encyclopedia of Philosophy, "'World government' refers to the idea of all humankind united under one common political authority. Arguably, it has not existed so far in human history, yet proposals for a unified global political authority have existed since ancient times - in the ambition of kings, popes and emperors, and the dreams of poets and philosophers" [330]. Indeed, Socrates, Plato, and Aristotle in ancient Greece suggested their models of social order. From the medieval times and onwards Dante Alighieri, Thomas Hobbes, Jean-Jacques Rousseau, Immanuel Kant and many other famous thinkers touched upon the ideal of a universal community of humankind. To achieve this objective, they introduced different concepts, including establishing a "world empire" ruled by a universal monarch (Dante);

lawful interstate order (Hobbes); Commonwealth of Europe in the face of "Federation" or "League of Europe" (Rousseau); "perpetual peace", "federation of peoples" or "international state" (Kant)[7], etc.

Following the failure of the first attempt at implementing the new world order paradigm in the form of the world revolution doctrine, *the world government movement* emerged in the United States and in Europe. Starting as a U.S. Campaign for World Government in Chicago in 1937, it was divided between two offices - with the international campaign headquartered in New York and the U.S. national campaign located in Chicago. The Campaign's early platform was outlined in 1937 in a brochure written by its organizers "Chaos, War or a New World Order?" [43]. In 1939 the movement was identified in *Peace News* magazine (London) as "the American campaign for world government" [286]. British Parliamentary Group for World Government was founded in 1945. Both currents - American and European - merged into the world government movement.

After the end of World War II, the U.S. overwhelming military, financial and economic might shaped a strategic opportunity for Washington to bring about the new world order into being. In the conditions of the U.S. atomic monopoly, Bertrand Russell wrote about the perspectives on American hegemony in case a world war would erupt: "In the near future, a world war, however terrible, would probably end in American victory without the destruction of civilization in the Western hemisphere, and American victory would no doubt *lead to a world government under the hegemony of the United States* - a result which, for my part, I should welcome with enthusiasm" [240].

As Bertrand Russell further urged, "It is entirely clear that there is only one way in which great wars can be permanently prevented, and that is the establishment of an international government with a monopoly of serious armed force. When I speak of an international government, I mean one that really governs, not an amiable façade like the League of Nations, or a pretentious sham like the United Nations under its present constitution. An international government, if it is to be able to preserve peace, must have the only atomic bombs, the only plant for producing them, the only air force, the only battleships, and, generally, whatever

---

7   As many experts claim, Kant's work used to be a source of inspiration for globalists.

is necessary to make it irresistible. Its atomic staff, its air squadrons, the crews of its battleships, and its infantry regiments must each severally be composed of men of many different nations; there must be no possibility of the development of national feeling in any unit larger than a company. Every member of the international armed force should be carefully trained in loyalty to the international government" [240].

Therefore, the promotion of the *world government doctrine* in the wake of World War II became possible, primarily, due to the American atomic monopoly. The United States applied the idea of "internationalization" of the atomic power as a method to imposing the world government. The Baruch Plan envisaged gaining American control over the atomic power and, thus, remaining the only superpower after the war possessing the atomic bomb. However, due to the strong position of the Soviet Diplomacy in the UN on that regard, and creation of the "atomic shield" by the USSR in 1949 - the idea of establishing the world government in the aftermath of the war became a "paper dragon".

The world government movement was supported, on the one hand, by the U.S. Atomic Scientists, who invented the atomic bomb and, on the other hand, by U.S. intellectuals and hard-liners within American political establishment who considered that a "world state" could be the only option for the post-war international system. Among the most active supporters of the world government doctrine, advocating "a peace based on the rule of law," was Albert Einstein. Einstein had been supporting the idea of the world government since as early as October 1914. Long before the atomic bomb demonstrated its destructive potential Einstein believed in a "League of Europeans" and supported Wilson`s doctrine of universalism. Besides, in 1932 he argued in favour of "unconditional surrender by every nation, in a certain measure, of its liberty of action – its sovereignty" [11, p. 301-302]. It is worthy to note, that Saul Mendlovitz, who was engaged in developing the globalists` agenda in the framework of the World Order Models Project (the WOMP) in 1968, invoked an atomic scientist from Germany (Carl von Weiszäcker) in the activities of the project. Weiszäcker was considered to being "an outspoken critic of nuclear weapons, and a leader in Germany`s anti-nuclear movement" [76].

The origins and evolution of the world government movement are well documented. The movement has been substantially explored by Professor Joseph P. Baratta in a book titled "The Politics of World Federation: From world federalism to global governance" [11]. Ronald J. Glossop[8] stated that, "Baratta knows the movement from within as well as through intensive study". Indeed, Baratta has been engaged in the activities of the movement as the head of the UN office of the World Federalists in 1985-1988.

Baratta described his work as "a critical, documented history of the practical, political efforts to establish a constitutionally limited, democratically representative, federal world government to effectively abolish war" [108]. He maintains that, "Historically, during the coming, waging, and aftermath of World War II, a number of people in and out of government in America and in the eventually 51 allied countries in the wartime "United Nations" urged that the failed League of Nations not be simply revived, even with U.S. membership, but be transformed into the beginnings of a representative world government" [108].

According to the definition given by Baratta, there have been two currents in the "World Federalist Movement" in the United States: the maximalists and the minimalists. *The first current*, the maximalists, originated from the University of Chicago. They argued for the global federal government to be established immediately after the end of World War II. With this purpose, the Committee to Frame a World Constitution was established at the University of Chicago in 1945. The Chicago Committee elaborated a Preliminary Draft of a World Constitution by 1948. The maximalists adhered to traditional hard-liners` approach about implementing the new world order paradigm.

The second current of the world government movement, the minimalists, was promoted by U.S. legislators Grenville Clark, Glan Taylor and Louis Sohn. In contrast to maximalists` approach, they suggested "soft power" methods to ensuring the transition towards world government, and initiated the so-called "peace education" process. This current has been identified as "peace educators". During the Cold War, the minimalists remained the mainstream within the world government movement.

On 12 August 1945 Robert M. Hutchins, the University of Chicago Chancellor, emphasized the need for world government at Chicago

---

8   Professor Emeritus of Philosophy and Peace Studies at Southern Illinois University at Edwardsville.

Round Table radio discussion. As a follow up of the discussion Richard P. McKeon, dean of the Division of the Humanities at Chicago University, and G. A. Borgese, professor in the University, asked Hutchins "for financial and moral support for an institute to formulate a world constitution" [101]. On September 16th, 1945, the Chancellor supported the initiative and, thus, the Committee came into effect. Its first document was worked out by November 1945. In total, from June 1947 through June 1951 the Committee published 150 documents, including The Preliminary Draft of a World Constitution, and a journal, Common Cause. According to a historian George T. Peck, these documents were since then determined as "World Federalist Papers" [198, p. x-32]. These documents were used as the basis for the discussions held during the thirteen meetings of the Chicago Committee. Hutchins believed that "any future consideration of the shape of world government would have to take the Committee's draft into account" [116, p. 35-36].

The objective of the Committee was "to embody the idea of world government" [11, p. 316]. Therefore, it established close relations with "other organizations advocating some form of world government" [100]. In 1947, the Committee became a member of the world government movement. Then it was identified as World Movement for World Federal Government (WMWFG) [101]. Among its members at the time of the publication of the Draft were: Robert M. Hutchins, G. A. Borgese, Mortimer J. Adler, Stringfellow Barr, Albert Guérard, Harold A. Innis, Erich Kahler, Wilber G. Katz, Charles H. McIlwain, Robert Redfield, and Rexford G. Tugwell. Despite the members of the Committee had distinct approaches on how the world government might be achieved, they shared common belief that the "competing anarchy" of nation states must be transformed into a "universal world state".

According to Erich Kahler, who was a supporter of the then popular "citizens of the world" concept, "The Committee was performing the "ideological preparation" for such a revolution ... analogous to what Locke and Montesquieu had done for the English and French Revolutions, Rousseau for the French, and Marx and Engels for the Russian" [128, p. 6-7]. Borgese put it even more bluntly: "world government is necessary; therefore, it is possible" [11, p. 315]. Richard McKeon believed that "an open proposal of a world federal state would itself become a force in history" [11, p. 321]. He proposed to create an "Institute for World

Government" [11, p. 320]. Illustratively enough, Baratta summarized such arguments in a section of his book named "the age of nations must end" [11, p. 321].

The Draft of the World Constitution declared that, "nation-state is by definition and nature the enemy and antagonist of the World State" [211]. The Draft called for "The jurisdiction of the World Government". It appealed to establishing the "Federal Republic of the World". Its key idea was that the "primary Government" of such a world state shall be vested in "the Federal Convention, the President, the Council and the Special Bodies, the Grand Tribunal, the Supreme Court, and the Tribune of the People, the Chamber of Guardians" [211]. The Chamber of Guardians, for example, was planned for "The control and use of the armed forces of the Federal Republic of the World... under the chairmanship of the President, in his capacity of Protector of the Peace" [211]. To enforce law globally the World Constitution provided for creation of a "World Council" in addition to the Chamber of Guardians. The Draft also suggested a world police force. In Preamble, the document called upon all nations to surrender their arms to the world government.

In a review of the Chicago's Draft, Professor Ely Culbertson stated: "Backed up by the prestige of the University of Chicago, a Committee of Eleven to Frame a World Constitution labored for two years to produce The Preliminary Draft of a World Constitution" [61]. He stressed that, "The Constitution is designed for what its architects call, grandiloquently enough, the Federal Republic of the World. This Republic shall be, they proclaim, "indivisible and one." The bizarre and extraordinarily naive structure of this Federal World Republic, as it emerges from the mist of noble generalities and quasi-poetic allusions, is neither divisible by any common-sense denominator nor at one with reality. I have read, during my life, many scores of proposed constitutions of the world. I confess I have never read anything so childish and at the same time ferocious; so grimly utopian and yet so ominous as this Federal Constitution for the World State" [61].

Culbertson further acknowledged that, "The ideal of World Federation is the oldest in the universe. The best way to destroy this ideal in the American conscience is by proposing fantastic or totalitarian plans for World Federation. In its Foreword, the Committee somewhat rashly proclaims that their Constitution "is meant, no less humbly than confidently, as a proposal to history." As a proposal to history, their Constitution has a certain value. It is the value of pointing to a blind alley" [61].

Important enough, yet in 1948 the Chicago Committee advocated redistribution of world`s resources which might be identified today as being globalists` strive towards establishing the so-called *"international resource management regime"*. The Declaration of Duties and Rights of the Preliminary Draft of a World Constitution urged that, "The four elements of life - earth, water, air, energy - are the common property of humans. The management and use of such portions thereof shall be subordinated in each and all cases to the interest of the common good" [211].

According to Ely Culbertson, "To make sure that earth, water, air, and energy will become a public utility for "the common good," the founders describe a Grant of Powers to the World Government of the Federal World Republic of such sweeping nature as to dwarf the considerable grant of powers in the American Constitution. Among the powers of the World Government, there are: "The maintenance of peace; and to that end the enactment and promulgation of laws which shall be binding upon communities and upon individuals as well". Armed with this blank check, the World Government or the world dictator, with the World Government`s stooges, could most peacefully operate in any direction. Hitler made wars in the name of peace and by "promulgation of laws" [61].

As it was mentioned, the strive towards establishing the world government in the wake of World War II has been supported by politicians and intellectuals both in the United States and in Great Britain. Among the most active advocates of the world government doctrine in Britain were Earl Attlee, Lord Beveridge, Lord Boyd Orr, Lord Silkin, Sir James Pitman MP, J. Reeves MP, Henry Usborne MP and, especially, the Rt. Hon. Clement Davies MP and Gilbert McAllister. McAllister (1906-64) also served as Hon. Director of the World Parliament Association and as Secretary-general and Chairman of the Executive of the Association for World Government [273]. Outside the UK the World Parliament Association was supported by members of national parliaments.

Yet in 1945 the Parliamentary Group for World Government was founded in Britain by Henry Usborne, MP. The Group sought to introduce the ideas of globalists into national politics. To support the activities of the Group, primarily, by means of financing its permanent secretariat, the Parliamentary Association for World Government was formed in 1950. In 1951, the Group organized the first London Conference on World Government. A resolution of this meeting gave birth to the World Association of Parliamentarians for World Government. The latter received its constitution and staff from the second London Conference on World Government which took place in 1952 and in 1958.

In 1952, the conference adopted a revised constitution and changed its title to *"The World Parliament Association"* [331]. Its purpose was to co-ordinate the activities of various like-minded national federalist groups around the world. In 1963, it was renamed Association for World Government. Financial assistance to carrying out its activities was rendered upon the establishment of the One World Trust. The Parliamentary Group also intended "to advance the idea of federal administration in Britain by persuading official opinion within government circles and by influencing public opinion by propaganda" [273].

The World Parliament Association suggested to pursue the goals of the Parliamentary Group (the UK) to act as an agency for coordinating the activities of other national groups, supporting the world government doctrine, within Europe and beyond. Thus, a series of international conferences was arranged. The World Parliament Association also formulated and issued "statements of policy on world government, disarmament, the revision of the United Nations charter and on related subjects; it published, with the help of the Parliamentary Association, a regular official journal, World. During the 1950s and early 1960s it was active in pursuing its own programme, in establishing an international membership, and in maintaining relations with other organizations of similar purpose" [273].

British Prime Minister Winston Churchill has been advocating the world government doctrine since early stage of its implementation. On May 14, 1947 Churchill chaired a meeting at the Royal Albert Hall in London. At this meeting, the United Europe Movement was formally constituted. Churchill declared that, "The creation of an authoritative, all-powerful world order is the ultimate aim towards which we must strive. Unless some effective world super-Government can be set up and brought quickly into action, the prospects for peace and human progress are dark and doubtful. Without a United Europe, there is no sure prospect of world government" [292, p. 284]. The British leader further acknowledged, that "active preparations now being made for the calling of a World Constituent Assembly of representatives… to draw up the Constitution for a World Government" [70, p. 678].

In 1947, an attempt at *legitimizing the world government doctrine* was undertaken in Britain. The World Federalist Resolution was introduced to the Parliament. Henry Usborne played a key role in that regard. According to Baratta, he was a person who "gave the Chicago Committee the impetus to publish and who generally set the pace of the world government movement toward 1950" [11, p.331]. In promoting the globalists' agenda Usborne suggested to conduct "unofficial election" in the UK. He declared that if he could get one-quarter of Britain's population to vote for world government, he would have "the resultant World Charter an issue in the next parliamentary elections. Ratification then would be a "political certainty" [11, p.334].

The importance of the British ally for the U.S. plans regarding promoting the world government doctrine must be especially emphasized. Thus, according to Baratta, "Usborne [British MP] had been instrumental in hosting the 1946 Luxemburg conference, which set in motion the establishment of *the World Movement for World Federal Government* (umbrella organization of world federalist organizations in many countries) and later the European Union of Federalists (the more limited organization of European federalists). This movement is being determined today as the world government movement.

At the movement meeting, in Brussels on 4 May 1947, Usborne announced the essentials of his plan to hold an unofficial World Constituent Assembly in 1950. His Parliamentary group would lead, lending legitimacy … to what was really a revolutionary proposal. Since Britain had a population at the time of 38 million, Usborne planned a national unofficial ballot to elect 38 representatives. The United States would elect 130, and so on. These representatives then gather as a World Constituent Assembly in Geneva in the fall of 1950 to draft the world constitution [based on the paper prepared by the Chicago Committee]. Allowing time for the drafting… it was not inconceivable that world federal government would be a fact by 1955" [11, p.333-334]. However, as Baratta further acknowledged, "Usborne was ... unable *to marshal the international forces* to achieve his own greater vision" [11, p.331].

On August 17, 1947, following the foundation of the United Europe Movement more than 300 participants representing 51 organizations from 24 countries attended the Conference of the World Movement for World Federal Government that took place in Switzerland. The meeting concluded with the adoption of the Montreux Declaration - The Principles for World Federal Government. The participants of the conference considered the Covenant of the League of Nations and the Charter of San Francisco as "only steps on the path leading to... the World Federal Government" [329]. It was stated that "We fear that the UN` efforts towards peace, like those of the League of Nations, may not be successful, if the world is not willing to take this next step to World Federalist Government... Federalists in all countries of the world will try to contribute to this political evolution" [329].

On May 7, 1948, during the Congress of Europe which took place in Holland, Churchill urged that, "We must do our best to create and combine the great regional unities which it is in our power to influence, and we must endeavour by patience and faithful service to prepare for the day when there will be an effective world government resting on the main groupings of mankind" [66; 48]. Thus, Churchill advocated the same ideas that had been developed in the United States. As British professor Lee Rotherham emphasized, "The UK for its part needed to develop a form of association "without in the slightest degree weakening the sacred ties which unite Britain with her daughter States across the oceans." The Europe she would associate with would be independent but not isolationist, harmoniously fitted into *the system of world government*" [238, p. 22].

The plans of establishing the world government already in the 1950s as well as efforts to legalizing its doctrine faced opposition in the U.S. Congress as well as the lack of public support. Yet, several World Federalist Resolutions were introduced. The result was "the passage of world federalist resolutions in some 22 American States and introduction of 16 resolutions in the U.S. Congress, which led to the instructive hearings in the House of Representatives in 1948 and 1949 and in the Senate in 1950" [11, p. 300].

On February 9th, 1950, the U.S. Senate Foreign Relations Subcommittee introduced Senate Concurrent Resolution 66 which declared: "Whereas, to achieve universal peace and justice, the present Charter of the United Nations should be changed to provide a true world government constitution" [11, p. 357]. The resolution was first introduced in the Senate on September 13th, 1949 by Senator Glen Taylor. He would later suggest that each nation would "surrender ... portion of its own sovereignty which gives it the right and the power to make war" [11, p. 357]. Taylor also proposed reforming the United Nations in legislative, executive and judicial spheres. Among other active supporters of the political and legal moves to promoting the new world order agenda were Grenville Clark and the then Senator Richard M. Nixon.

On 17th February 1950 in testimony before the Senate Foreign Relations Committee James P. Warburg, the son of Council on Foreign Relations' founder and an architect of the Federal Reserve Paul Warburg, urged the United States Senate that, "We shall have world government whether or not we like it. The only question is, whether world government will be achieved by conquest or consent" [228, p. 494]. In his book "The West in Crisis" (1959) Warburg further insisted: "We are living in a perilous period of transition from the era of the fully sovereign nation-state to the era of world government" [312, p. 30].

The above facts demonstrate concerted efforts by the Anglo-American political establishment in implementing *the world government doctrine*. However, since the immediate effort to establish the "liberal" world order was opposed by the Soviet Union and lacked public support in the United States, the American foreign policy strategy was directed into the flow of the Cold War. Moreover, in the wake of World War II world public opinion did not perceive the Soviet Union – a victorious power - as a threat. That is why the role of the British ally of the United States has been important to start the ideological campaign and introduce the so-called "Soviet threat" into the public opinion domain.

Following the request of the Truman Administration, Winston Churchill delivered its notorious "iron curtain" speech in Fulton (the U.S.) on March 5, 1946. Thus, the U.S. strategy focused on subverting the USSR. Since then the "grand strategy" has been constantly changing its tactics and upgrading "images of enemy" as well as methods of strategy`s implementation. The final objective, though, that is the establishment of the world government, remained unchanged.

It must be emphasized, that since the inception of the world government movement there was a lack of consensus on which means would best suit its ends. Until now there is still a split among the supporters of the globalists ` agenda on a broader issue - "What would be the structure of world government?" Today, the World Federalist Movement declares that, "World federalism now faces the challenge of showing that it is capable of taking the lead in transitioning toward world government... During the Cold War, world government lay in the vague and distant future, but today it has become a feasible goal. World federalists take up that challenge" [329].

The "peace education" movement (i.e. the minimalists current as it was identified by Baratta) emerged in the United States mainly because the above maximalists attempt at implementing the world government doctrine, using "hard power" scenario, failed. However, the world federalists "refused to give up" and "maintained their faith across the divide of the Cold War" [11, p. 421]. They intended to further promote the new world order paradigm using "soft power" policies. The "peace education" movement was gradually introducing globalists` ideas into educational and, consequently, political agenda worldwide. Thus, the world government movement changed its tactics, but not the final objective.

In the U.S., the leader of the United World Federalists Grenville Clark has been a key figure to launch the process aimed at promoting education in global governance. Baratta acknowledged that, "The most effective of them [peace educators] was the elder statesman of the movement, Grenville Clark" [11, p. 506]. His ideas became fundamental in further implementation of the paradigm. Another founding father of the "peace education" movement, Sir Bertrand Russell explained: "Every government that has been in control of education for a generation will be able to control its subjects securely without the need of armies or policemen ..."

In 1946, a book entitled "The Teacher and World Government" was written by Joy E. Morgan, a former editor of the U.S. National Education Association (NEA). He stated: "In the struggle to establish an adequate world government, the teacher... can do much to prepare the hearts and minds of children for global understanding and cooperation...

At the very heart of all the agencies which will assure the coming of world government must stand the school, the teacher, and the organized profession."

In October 1947, similar ideas were promoted by the NEA Associate Secretary William Carr. In the NEA Journal, he argued that teachers should: "... teach about the various proposals that have been made for the strengthening of the United Nations and the establishment of a world citizenship and world government." At the same time, the American Education Fellowship, which was formerly named as the Progressive Education Association, called for the "establishment of a genuine world order, an order in which national sovereignty is subordinate to world authority."

In 1948, the *Association for Education in World Government* was founded. The Association was using Clark`s proposals for revising the UN Charter. It aimed at "collection, study and analysis of `information and facts relating to international organizations and international law` and the exploration and study of `proposed methods of achieving world government through the United Nations or otherwise" [75]. The Association considered that "the public was not prepared for a change as drastic as world government... [and] Unfortunately, the public`s reluctance to accept the idea of world governance was not the only obstacle" [75].

According to *"peace education" concept*, after World War I, then World War II, the U.S. intervention in Korea and, then, in Vietnam, "the American public had grown accustomed to war - it had become an inevitable part of reality" [75]. Therefore, the work of the "peace educators" shifted its focus "from the transformation of the UN Charter to the transformation of the public`s understanding of the problems" [75]. The key problem, thus, was how to carry out the transition from the post-World War II system to the new world order system.

In 1952, while facing the lack of public support to accept the new framework for global governance, the Association for Education in World Government changed its name to the Institute for International Government. In 1954, the latter was renamed again and became the Institute for International Order, which is today known as the World Policy Institute. According to its mission statement, "the World Policy Institute has its origins in the post-World War II movement of moderate internationalists…" [75]. Notably, in 1954 the Bilderberg group was founded.

So far, *the issue of war and peace* proves to being central in terms of evolution of the new world order paradigm. As some experts argue, "Any history of world government is necessarily a history of war and the history of efforts to abolish war" [109]. It is not surprisingly, therefore, that Clark referred to the ideas of "perpetual peace". In his own words, he "was impressed with the farseeing wisdom of Immanuel Kant, who in 1795 laid down the principle that world peace can only be secured by a great federation of peoples armed with adequate authority…" [50, p. 292]. He further stressed that, "I so clearly perceived the determining importance of the question of the precise powers to be accorded the international authority and of the related question of representation in the World Congress or Assembly" [50, p. 292].

Besides, Clark also touched upon the issue of "modification" of national sovereignty, primarily, in terms of abolishing "the right of the independent state to go to war" [50, p. 294]. He suggested that, "The question, however, is not whether sovereignty, in its normal sense, would be impaired, but whether the required modification of sovereignty is… a beneficent step which mankind has at last had the intelligence to take" [50, p. 294].

Yet at the outbreak of World War II, in September 1939 Clark focused on "the subject of world organization." He intended "to produce a plan in the shape of a proposed constitution for a Federation of Peoples" [50, p. 292]. Further in 1944 he believed that the emerging international organization in the wake of World War II would be a prototype for the world government. In his article "A New World Order - The American Lawyers` Role" he stated: "It should need no argument that we… have a vital and perhaps decisive part to play in shaping the new world organization which is to come out of this war" [50, p. 289].

In the early 1950s, Clark and Louis Sohn, a Harvard professor, started their joint enterprise on working out their own revision of the UN Charter. Then, this idea would eventually become the mainstream thought in the framework of the World Order Models Project (WOMP). The project was carried out to drafting theoretical and conceptual models for a future world order.

During their activities both Clark and Sohn urged the UN reform. They consistently challenged the UN Charter in their publications. Eventually, their joint book titled "World Peace Through World Law" (1958) suggested a "limited world government". The book proposed revising the UN Charter and establishing a world police force. It also aimed at influencing on public opinion in favour of global governance. The key objective, therefore, was to create a basis for the "*extensive discussions... required before truly effective institutes for the maintenance of peace [were] accepted by the peoples of the world*" [75].

In 1961, the Fund for Education Concerning World Peace through World Law was established (shortened to World Law Fund in 1963) as a result of concerted efforts by Grenville Clark and Harry B. Hollins, an American financier, banker, and a partner of J.P.Morgan. Both Clark and Hollins believed that "individuals had the power to influence the course of events, and would act rationally if provided the necessary information" [75]. The Fund was designed as "a world education program on the inadequacies... of the present international system and the necessity for world authority structures to deal with the world's most critical problems" [332].

The Fund was created under the sponsorship of the Institute for International Order. To start the "process of long-range education" Clark personally endowed it with about 750 000 USD [51]. In 1963, the Fund worked to promote the ideas of the above-mentioned book "World Peace Through World Law." It also published and distributed a range of educational materials on global issues, including "Legal and Political Problems of World Order" (edited by future coordinator of WOMP Saul Mendlovitz). According to Hollins, "these issues were of vital concern to all nations, and thus earned the name "World Order Studies" [75].

Finally, the Fund focused on approaching these issues from a "common-value perspective" so that "future generations would be prepared to search for solutions from a global, rather than national, perspective, and... develop acceptable solutions for an international system based on the world order values" [78]. So far, developing the so-called "common values" for a global society has been a long- lasting process which engaged joint efforts of leading think-tanks in the Unites States. The issue of their concern was creating the identity of a "global citizen", which the "peace educators" movement identified as *specie identity* whereas the proposed world state was determined as *global polity*.

Amanda Dugan, Research Consultant for the World Policy Institute (WPI), confirmed that the Fund worked on developing different models of world order as well as adapting them to the requirements of distinct cultures: "Rather than addressing individual problems that were of "vital interest" to all nations ... the Fund identified core values they believed represented the interests of the entire global community. At this point, world order studies were redesigned as the ... means of achieving four interrelated basic values": peace or war prevention, economic well-being, ecological balance, and social justice [78].

The World Law Fund "decided to promote a global educational program, its first step was to create a model that could be translated into cultures around the world. Beginning with the United States, the World Law Fund developed its "world order studies" method, a three-step process designed to transform the world. First, experts diagnose and analyze the current world problems and extrapolate the trends 20-30 years in the future; second, they pose alternative political systems designed to resolve the problems in the first step; and finally, they create and test the viability of various transition steps" [78].

During the first phase of the Fund`s activities, "all of its energy was focused on transforming American perspectives through the educational system... it was also a means to refine their program`s mission to create a model that could be translated to the "distinctive reality of each major cultural perspective..." [75]. Essentially, the overall activity of the Fund in terms of education in global governance "intended to develop requisite transitional steps for reaching a more acceptable global model" and to prepare the next generation of students to be "more sensitive to the opportunities for preparing constructively in the development of a world community" [75]. As Mendlovitz urged, "the problem was not simply how they could introduce world order studies to American schools, but how they could succeed in extending this course of study to educational systems throughout the world. This would be the Fund`s real success" [75].

Upon redefining its goal, the Fund developed a strategy that, firstly, involved establishing the Publications program to elaborate the curriculum, secondly, developing the School Program to prepare the teachers to carry out that program and, thirdly, to introduce it to universities, colleges, and schools in the United States. Thus, the Fund elaborated educational programs and curriculum for high schools and universities, aimed at teaching world order studies (i.e. *global studies*), such as the Peace and World Order Studies (curriculum guide for American universities). Although the Fund and its subsidiary programs operated independently from the Institute for International Order, the organization finally merged with the Institute for World Order (established in 1972).

The Institute`s work in the 1970s included the Public Education on Global Issues Project, and in the late 1970s the organization decided to become less theoretical and widening its focus to public policy. In 1981, Arch Gillies, a former aide to Nelson Rockefeller became the President of the Institute. In 1982, the organization was renamed again as the World Policy Institute (WPI) to reflect its shift from primarily educational focus to influencing on public policy [332]. Because of this transformation, the Institute`s World Policy Journal was founded "as a vehicle for disseminating ideas" [332].

Since then the WPI has been actively posited itself in a public policy domain. It started extending its influence towards the Soviet Union. From 1985 to 1987 the Journal`s articles were translated for Gorbachev by the Russian Institute for the US and Canadian Studies (ISKRAN). As follows from the WPI`s history overview, "The Journal`s close contacts with Russian reformists enabled it to cover the coming of Gorbachev, glasnost and perestroika, and the unraveling of the Cold War, like no other publication" [332].

During the 1980s the Security Project, implemented by the WPI, "summarized a unified economic-diplomatic-military strategy for progressives in post-Reagan America" [332]. Thus, the Institute has been influencing on both U.S. domestic and foreign policy issues. Since 2007 it has established a strategic partnership with the New York think tank Demos and expanded its networking with many like-minded groups around the world. As follows from the above, the think tank contributed to promoting *the informational dimension* of the new world order.

New World Order Doctrine

At the final stage of the Cold War the last head of the USSR Mikhail Gorbachev and the U.S. President George H.W. Bush marked *the third stage* of establishing the new world order. In their program speeches both leaders called for it to come into effect. On December 7, 1988, at the 43d UN General Assembly meeting, Gorbachev stressed, that "Two great revolutions, the French Revolution of 1789 and the Russian Revolution of 1917, exerted a powerful impact on the very nature of history and radically changed the course of world developments. Both, each in its own way, gave a tremendous impetus to mankind's progress. To a considerable extent those two revolutions shaped the way of thinking that is still prevalent in social consciousness... However, concurrently with wars, animosities and divisions among peoples and countries, another trend, with equally objective causes, was gaining momentum: the process of the emergence of a mutually interrelated and integral world. Today, further world progress is possible only through a search for universal human consensus as we move forward to a new world order" [96, p. 26]. The historical emphasis which was given by Gorbachev regarding the revolutions in France and Russia is noteworthy. The two revolutions launched the process of transforming the entire international system in line with the world revolution doctrine, thus, approaching the new world order.

Gorbachev described the emerging new world order in idealistic terms. He emphasized, that "The idea of democratizing the entire world order has become a powerful socio-political force... we must look together for ways to improve the international situation and build a new world, and, if so, we ought to agree on the basic, truly universal prerequisites and principles of such action" [96, p. 27-30]. Gorbachev further insisted on the principle of freedom of choice: "It is also quite clear to us that the principle of freedom of choice is mandatory. Its non-recognition is fraught with extremely grave consequences for world peace. Denying that right to peoples, under whatever pretext or rhetorical guise, jeopardizes even the fragile balance that has been attained. Freedom of choice is a universal principle that should allow of no exceptions" [96, p. 31]. Besides, he declared unilateral arms cut by the Soviet Union: "Within the next two years their numerical strength will be reduced by 500,000 men. The numbers of conventional armaments will also be substantially reduced. This will be done unilaterally..." [96, p. 41].

Gorbachev's liberal rhetoric and unilateral arms cuts initiative followed in conditions of growing threat of Soviet Union's power default. The U.S. subversive strategy regarding the USSR reached its apogee.

Washington had been supporting forces of disintegration in the Soviet Union. It fostered its "fifth column", dissidents as well as nationalistic movements in other countries of the Warsaw Treaty. Therefore, Gorbachev put at stake the very existence of the USSR and its state interests. This might be explained by the fact, that the speech in the UN followed unofficial meeting between Gorbachev and Bush at Governor`s Island in New York harbor on December 7, 1988. The meeting also engaged the then U.S. President Ronald Reagan who met with Gorbachev four times during his presidency (at Geneva 1985, Reykjavik 1986, Washington 1987 and Moscow 1988).

Although "freedom of choice" is, indeed, a universal idea its inaccurate application regarding the USSR triggered separatism and inter-ethnic violence which provoked regional flashpoints and, finally, led to state disintegration. The "universal principles" such as expanding democracy and liberal values worldwide were also used by the United States during NATO`s military and "humanitarian interventions" that followed the collapse of the Soviet Union in former Yugoslavia, Iraq, Afghanistan, Libya as well as in the framework of implementing the "regime change" scenarios during the so-called "colour revolutions" organized in the post-Soviet space. The process of NATO`s eastwards enlargement was carried out under the same pretext of democratizing the world and defending "human rights".

On December 2-3, 1989, the meeting between Gorbachev and Bush took place in Malta. Famous Soviet diplomat, former Minister of Foreign Affairs of the USSR, Anatoly Gromyko determined that meeting as being a "Soviet Munich". Indeed, a clear historical parallel exists between Gorbachev`s moves and geopolitical concessions that had been made by the West to Hitler in Munich in 1938. In fact, while confirming the above mentioned liberal principle of "freedom of choice" the Soviet leader also agreed not to interfere into the Soviet sphere of influence in Eastern Europe. This considerably facilitated reaching American strategic objectives.

Starting from the Baltic States the geopolitical wave of disintegration covered the entire Soviet Bloc (the importance of the Baltic States in terms of the U.S. strategy has been well documented yet by the Inquiry after the end of World War I). Because of the Malta deal, the USA focused on rendering further financial and organizational support to separatist and nationalistic movements, including, for example, "Solidarnost" in Poland. Gorbachev confirmed that, "Under the influence of Perestroika profound democratic reforms started in the countries of Central and Eastern Europe. The USSR took a firm stand of non-interference. We remained faithful to the principle of freedom of choice for all without exception" [96, p. 53].

Gorbachev's participation in the promotion of the new world order paradigm has been recognized by the international community. On October 15th, 1990, the Nobel Prize Committee awarded him a Nobel Peace Prize. In an acceptance letter Gorbachev referred to the globalists' source of inspiration, namely, the Immanuel Kant's doctrine of perpetual peace. He suggested the following option which had been raised by Kant: "either to be joined in a true union of nations or to perish in a war of annihilation ending in the extinction of the human race... In this respect, the year 1990 represents a turning point" [94].

In the early 1990s, that is half a century after the first attempt at enforcing global governance had been thwarted by Stalin's Soviet Union (in the wake of World War II), implementation of the new world order paradigm has entered its *next stage*. Gorbachev's unilateral concessions and promise of non-interference drastically differed from Kremlin's firm stand after the war. The White House compared this transformation period with the postwar stage [17, p. 42]. It was considered as being a strategic opportunity to carry out geopolitical expansion not only in Central and Eastern Europe, but also in the Middle East. Hence, the Gulf War of 1991.

On September 11, 1990 U.S. President George Bush declared: "Out of these troubled times, our fifth objective – a new world order – can emerge... Today that new world is struggling to be born, a world quite different from the one we've known... This is the vision that I shared with President Gorbachev in Helsinki" [38]. Since then Bush steadily advocated the new world order doctrine.

On January 8, 1991 Bush submitted a letter to students of the Massachusetts Institute of Technology (MIT). The U.S. President confirmed "the promise of our New World Order" [37]. As follows from the letter, the United States intended to realize this promise using the principles of "no concessions" and "no compromises". Bush urged: "If we do not follow the dictates of our inner moral compass and stand up for human life, then his [Saddam Hussein] lawlessness will threaten the peace and democracy of the emerging New World Order we now see: this long dreamed-of vision we`ve all worked toward for so long" [37].

Besides, yet in 1991 the White House applied the *factor of threat* to U.S. national interests and the concept of Weapons of Mass Destruction (WOMD) to intervene into the Middle East. Bush wrote: "Another day Saddam Hussein can work toward building his nuclear arsenal and perfecting his chemical and biological weapons capability... I ask you to ... reflect on the terrible threat that Saddam Hussein armed with weapons of mass destruction already poses to human life and to the future of all nations" [37]. However, the WOMD was not found in Iraq. Instead, this factor was used to military invade that country.

In State of the Union address on January 29, 1991, as the Gulf War and U.S. military engagement into the Middle East started, the U.S. President urged: "What is at stake is more than one small country; it is a big idea: a new world order... The world can, therefore, seize this opportunity to fulfill the long-held promise of a new world order... Yes, the United States bears a major share of leadership in this effort. Among the nations of the world, only the United States of America has both the moral standing and the means to back it up. We`re the only nation on this Earth that could assemble the forces of peace. This is the burden of leadership and the strength that has made America the beacon of freedom in a searching world."

On June 5th, 1991 Gorbachev maintained: "As to the fundamental choice, I have long ago made a final and irrevocable decision. Nothing and no one, no pressure, either from the right or from the left, will make me abandon the positions of *perestroika* and new thinking. I do not intend to change my views or convictions. My choice is a final one." He also referred to the idea of reconstructing the world: "The more I reflect on the current world developments, the more I become convinced that the world needs *perestroika* no less than the Soviet Union needs it" [95]. However, it was Gorbachev`s "fundamental choice" which became one of the key causes of breakup of the Soviet Union. In pursuing reforms, he intended to introduce "a new constitutional structure... as a genuine, free, and voluntary federation" [95]. According to the results of the referendum held in the Soviet Union on March 17th, 1991, 76, 4 per cent (out of 80 per cent of poll`s participants) voted in favour of preserving the USSR. Therefore, Gorbachev`s "choice" contradicted the will of the Soviet people.

The "perestroika" reforms in the Soviet Union influenced on the entire international system. Gorbachev declared: "Clearly, as the Soviet Union proceeds with perestroika, its contribution to building a new world will become more constructive and significant... To me, it is self-evident that if Soviet perestroika succeeds, there will be a real chance of building a new world order. And if perestroika fails, the prospect of entering a new peaceful period in history will vanish, at least for the foreseeable future..." [95]. The Associated Press article entitled "Gorbachev asks in Nobel lecture for Western aid" read as follows: "Western failure to heed his call for economic aid could dash hopes for a peaceful new world order" [31]. On December 8th, 1991, that is six months after the lecture, the Soviet Union was disintegrated.

Besides, Gorbachev called for using the UN global framework to promote the new world order paradigm. He stressed, that "We are experiencing *a turning point* in international affairs and are only at the beginning of a new, and I hope mostly peaceful, lengthy period in the history of civilization... For knowledge and trust are the foundations of a new world order. Hence the necessity, in my view, to learn to forecast the course of events in various regions of the globe, by pooling the efforts of scientists, philosophers and humanitarian thinkers within the UN framework" [96, p. 24].

Global Governance Doctrine

The United States established foundations for global governance yet in the wake of World War II. In 1944, economic foundations were settled in Bretton Woods making the U.S. dollar a world reserve currency. In 1945, political foundations were created in the face of the United Nations` system. In 1949, military foundations of Pax Americana were laid out following the creation of NATO.

After the end of the Cold War the new world order doctrine has evolved into *global governance doctrine*. Generally accepted definition of global governance can be summed up as thus: "all collective measures taken by the international community, upon consensus, to respond to new pending international issues or threats that emerge because of the advances of globalization, given the lack of a world government" [142]. Global governance envisages implementation of a mechanism for maintaining the international system. However, scholars, intellectuals and politicians suggest different approaches towards functioning of such mechanism, especially, as concerns its structure and methods of distributing world power and resources. Some might identify the prototypes for a single global authority yet in the face of the League of Nations and its successor, the United Nations. Besides, various global forums and consortiums of elites and intellectuals have been continuously promoting the global governance doctrine.

The global governance doctrine suggests ceding traditional rights of sovereignty to supranational institutions, multilateral international agencies, forums as well as nonstate actors, technologically empowered individuals and groups, which interact in solving global issues. It also includes the ideas of "shared sovereignty", creating "global regulatory regimes", "global governance networks", and "a networked world order". It implies distributing state power between international institutions and nation-states and, finally, establishing "ultimate decision-making authority" which would possess authoritative legislative, adjudicative and enforcement powers. Until now, however, there has been no consensus reached among scholars on how to exercise global governance practically and whether it is reachable at all.

In the early 1990s the lack of a deterring mechanism that could counter the U.S. geopolitical expansion embarked the United States onto the next stage of the promotion of the new world order paradigm. The Clinton Administration followed the strategic course of constructing the new world order. On November 8, 1997 Clinton confirmed: "We have to broaden the imagination of America. We are redefining in practical terms the immutable ideals that have guided us from the beginning" [52]. As it has been mentioned, Clinton declared at the Kennedy Center: "From 1945 and the end of the war through 1989 and the end of the cold war, we had a world view, Republican and Democratic presidents alike, from Harry Truman to George Bush... and after 1989 President Bush said, and it`s a phrase that I often use myself, is that we need is a New World Order" [53].

The Clinton Doctrine projected the U.S. power into the Balkans and further beyond to former Soviet Union`s spheres of influence in

Eastern Europe. As Douglas Brinkley, a historian at the University of New Orleans argued: "In August 1993, Clinton directed national security adviser Anthony Lake to come up with a single word or slogan that would do for him what "containment" had done for the Cold War presidents" [29]. With the strategy of enlargement, Brinkley outlined, Clinton hoped to go down in history "as the free trade president and the leading architect of a new world economic order" [29]. The Clinton doctrine has been based on the principle of "democracy enlargement". It also incorporated the concept of "global village". Under the same pretext of spreading democracy worldwide the United States became the driving force of globalization. The process of NATO`s eastward enlargement transferred the U.S. power as deeper into Eurasia as it had never happened before.

In 2000, U.S. National Security Advisor Condoleezza Rice, referring to the post-Cold War period, stressed that, "Yet such periods of transition are important, because they offer strategic opportunities. During these fluid times, one can affect the shape of the world to come" [229]. Rice identified the foreign policy key priorities as follows: building a military ready to ensure U.S. power, coping with rogue states, "managing" China and Russia, etc. She considered, that the next president must be comfortable with America's special role as the world`s leader. According to Rice, the Republican President should: "refocus the Pentagon`s priorities on building the military of the 21st century ... [and] should be in a position to intervene when he believes, and can make the case, that the United States is duty-bound to do so" [229]. The named priorities have been incorporated into the Bush Doctrine.

The ideological ground of *the Bush Doctrine* has been the neoconservative synthesis between ultra-right liberal values and the ideas developed by Leo Strauss (1899-1973), who was among the advocates of Trozkism. Therefore, most of the strategic documents elaborated by the Bush Administration, including the National Security Strategy (2002) and other program documents, were based on neoconservative concepts such as, for example, preemptive warfare, "regime change" concept, "humanitarian intervention", etc.

The Obama Doctrine`s key issue was how to advance U.S. national interests in such a way that would allow introducing new rules of global governance. It focused on reconstructing the post-World War II international architecture under pretext of countering new global threats.

However, the implementation of the doctrine coincided with the stage of declining American hegemony. The internal debt crisis and depletion of U.S. strategic and moral resources to further pursuing the role of the world leader made Washington redefining its foreign policy options.

Besides, the global rise of China as a new center of power in Asia as well as reviving geopolitical will of Russia challenged Pax Americana. In such circumstances, the "axis of evil" concept became obsolete. In identifying new threats to realizing its strategy the White House shifted its grand strategy`s focus from the "war on terror" to *the concept of "just war"*. The latter was announced in Obama`s Nobel Prize speech [187]. The U.S. President suggested that the "instrument of war" may be important for "keeping peace" in times of humanitarian crisis. The realization of this concept followed in the framework of NATO`s military intervention in Libya in 2012.

Yet in January 2009 Kissinger identified his vision on possible role of the Obama Administration in building the new world order as follows: "The president-elect is coming into office at a moment when there is upheaval in many parts of the world simultaneously... You have India, Pakistan; you have the jihadist movement. So, he can`t really say there is one problem, that it`s the most important one. But he can give new impetus to American foreign policy... His task will be to develop an overall strategy for America in this period when, really, a new world order can be created. It`s a great opportunity, it isn`t just a crisis" [337]. Kissinger also considered the "global upheavals" as being a "great opportunity" for world's reconstruction [337].

During the Obama Administration, the Pentagon introduced the concept of Cyber War. It stems from the Information and Psychological Warfare (IPW), which was first adopted within U.S. military doctrines [103; 118]. The Cyber War was identified in 2012 by U.S. Minister of Defence Leon Panetta. On September 11th, 2013, the U.S. Department of Defence released "The Electromagnetic Spectrum Strategy" (EMS). It was considered as being "a prerequisite for modern military operations" [80].

In 2015, the Cyber War doctrine was incorporated into U.S. National Security Strategy as a priority security issue: "As the birthplace of the Internet, the United States has a special responsibility to lead a networked world. Prosperity and security increasingly depend on an open, interoperable, secure, and reliable Internet. Our economy, safety, and health are linked through a networked infrastructure that is targeted by malicious government, criminal, and individual actors who try to avoid attribution… We will defend ourselves, consistent with U.S. and international law, against cyber-attacks and impose costs on malicious cyber actors, including through prosecution of illegal cyber activity" [182].

The Cyber War concept ensured strategic continuity in terms of the promotion of the new world order paradigm. It has been aimed, primarily, at gaining control over informational flows "in the congested and contested [electromagnetic] spectrum environment of the 21st Century" [80]. Yet in 1968 Brzezinski considered that, "The technetronic era involves the gradual appearance of a more controlled society. Such a society would be dominated by an elite, unrestrained by traditional values. Soon it will be possible to assert almost continuous surveillance over every citizen and maintain up-to-date complete files containing even the most personal information about the citizen. These files will be subject to instantaneous retrieval by the authorities" [33; 34].

According to Edward Snowden`s notorious revelations, the U.S. intelligence community created global espionage network. It used PRISM and other programs to gather sensitive and confidential information on world leaders, public activists and citizens. Washington specifically targeted those "empowered individuals" who had opposed Pax Americana (e.g. Julian Assange, Edward Snowden, Bradley Manning to name but a few).

The concepts of "non-state actors" and "empowered individuals" were identified by Harlan K. Ullman[9] in the article entitled "War on Terror Is not the Only Threat." It was published by the Atlantic Council, influential U.S. think tank[10]. Ullman advocated restructuring the Westphalian system of state sovereignty under the pretext of countering newly emerged threats: "In essence, the 365-year-old Westphalian system that placed sovereign states as the centerpieces of international politics

---

9 Harlan K. Ullman is Chairman of the Killowen Group, which advises government leaders. He has been one of the authors of the "Shock and Awe" doctrine that was used at the early stage of the war in Iraq.

10 The Atlantic Council is directed by Gen. Brent Scowcroft, former National Security Advisor under U.S. Presidents Gerald Ford and George H. W. Bush. Scowcroft has also advised the U.S. President Barack Obama.

is being tested and in some cases made obsolete by the empowerment of individuals and non-state actors. As former national security adviser Brent Scowcroft observes, global politics has entered a post-Westphalian era... September 11th could become the demarcation point of this new era much as 1648 and the Treaty of Westphalia marked the beginning of the state-centric system of the international order...." [298].

Ullman argued that, "the major enemy and adversary are no longer states.... Instead, the more immediate danger rests in the dramatic empowerment of individuals and groups... often lumped together as "non-state actors." Edward Snowden, Bradley Manning, countless `hackers` and anonymous people mailing anthrax-filled letters whose actions have indeed constituted real threats and systemic disruptions are among the former. Al-Qaida and other radical groups reflect the latter" [298]. The major cause of the empowerment has been "the diffusion of all forms of power writ large commonly called `globalization` accelerated by the information revolution and instantaneous global communications and the real and perceived fragilities and weaknesses of states to intervention, interference and disruption by non-traditional actors...." [298].

Ullman further stressed that non-state actors represent fundamental forces impeding the new world order to come into effect: "a second reality complicates taking effective action in what could truly be a `new world order`, the description coined by U.S. President George H.W. Bush after the implosion of the Soviet Union more than two decades ago. Failed and failing government from Afghanistan to Zimbabwe with Brussels and Washington in between is the largest collective impediment to the betterment of mankind. Without an extraordinary crisis, little is likely to be done to reverse or limit the damage imposed by failed or failing governance. However, the changing Westphalian system can and must be addressed if there is to be any chance of success in containing, reducing and eliminating the dangers posed by newly empowered non-state actors" [298].

Considering the beginning of "the cyber age", the cyber war doctrine replaced the concept of the war on terror: "Hence, the counter-terrorism responses have been technical and tactical rather than strategic and aren`t addressing the forces that are dramatically altering the nature of international politics" [298]. Therefore, Ullman urged reshaping and adapting the U.S. strategy: "The first step as the Westphalian system faces profound redefinition is understanding and recognizing that these shifts are under way. From that appreciation, specific concepts and ideas can be fashioned to help guide us on this journey" [298].

The concept of "global crisis" has been also elaborated in Ullman`s article: "Without an extraordinary crisis, little is likely to be done to reverse or limit the damage imposed by failed or failing governance..." [298]. That concept has been constantly applied in U.S. strategic planning along with the factor of threat. In September 1994, David Rockefeller stated at the United Nations Business Council: "We are on the verge of a global transformation. All we need is the right major crisis and the nations will accept the new world order." The U.S. think-tank Project for a New American Century stressed that there was "absent some catastrophic catalyzing event – like a new Pearl Harbor" [225]. Perhaps for this reason Ullman identified September 11th as "the demarcation point of this new era" [298].

The global governance doctrine has been supported by the U.S. traditional ally in Europe, the United Kingdom. On April 22, 1999 speaking before the Chicago Economic Club, British Prime Ministers Tony Blair (1997-2007) unveiled his "Doctrine of the International Community." The doctrine suggested principles for global governance. It called for reforming global finance and free trade system with an emphasis on international financial regulation and WTO trade rules. Blair suggested to reconsider the role of the UN Security Council, its workings and decision-making process as well as changing NATO`s structure after the military campaign in Kosovo, etc. Thus, he declared: "We are all internationalists now, whether we like it or not... The doctrine of isolationism had been a casualty of a world war, where the United States and others finally realized standing aside was not an option... We are witnessing the beginnings of a new doctrine of international community... Global financial markets, the global environment, global security and disarmament issues: We need to focus in a serious and sustained way on the principles of the doctrine of international community and on the institutions, that deliver them" [274].

In an address to British ambassadors in London on January 7, 2003 Tony Blair confirmed: "The world and many countries in it need to change... This has been understood, at least inchoately, ever since the fall of the Berlin Wall. Then the call was for a new world order. But a new order presumes a new consensus. It presumes a shared agenda and a global partnership to do it. Here's where Britain's place lies. We can only play a part in helping this - to suggest more would be grandiose and absurd - but it is an important part. Our very strengths, our history equip us to play a role as a unifier around a consensus for achieving both our goals and those of the wider world" [22].

On December 17, 2001 the UK Chancellor, Gordon Brown delivered a speech entitled "Globalization". At the Press Club in Washington DC he declared: "The war that together we are fighting against terrorism... we will win... But the question... is how we will win the peace. This is not the first time the world has faced this question – so fundamental and far-reaching. In the 1940s, after the greatest of wars, visionaries in America and elsewhere looked ahead to a new world and – in their day and for their times – built a new world order. And what they sought to create was not simply a new military and political settlement that guaranteed peace but also new rules and institutions for a new international economic and social order... Indeed, such was its scale that one of the architects of the new order - Dean Acheson - recalled that he had been present at the creation... And what they achieved as they fought their day's greatest evil - totalitarianism - is what we must seek to achieve as we fight today's greatest evil - terrorism. I want to urge that together we form a new global alliance..." [30].

At the 2009 G20 Summit in London Gordon Brown, being the UK Prime Minister, drew a historic parallel from the Great Depression into the world financial crisis that erupted in 2008, thus, suggesting a new world order: "When the Wall street crash happened in 1929. It took 15 years for the world to come together to rebuild and renew our economies. This time, I think people will agree that it is different... We are engaging in a deep process of reform and reconstructing of our international financial-system for now and for the future... This is collective-action... I think a New World Order is emerging, and with it the foundations of a new and progressive era of international cooperation... And we've agreed that in doing so we will build a more sustainable and more open, and a fairer global society" [210].

Western media's reflection on the above mentioned G20 summit has been illustrative enough. For example, the CNN stated that economic crisis may lead to new world order. It insisted that, "The U.S. and

Europe, who have dominated the G-8, now have little option too but to accept a new world order" [186]. Following this publication, the Daily Telegraph featured that "Gordon Brown announced the creation of a "new world order" after the conclusion of the G20 summit of world leaders in London" [210]. So far, the new world order paradigm has become dominant in global political agenda. Its *informational dimension* has been ensured both by politicians, experts, and the mass media.

Oddly enough, in June 2010, another typical statement regarding the promotion of the paradigm was made by the then President of Russia, Dmitry Medvedev. He advocated "liberal" ideas at XIV St. Petersburg International Economic Forum. Medvedev suggested building such new Russia that would become a "cofounder of New World Economic Order and a full-fledged member of a collective political leader in a post-crisis world". Being a participant of a "collective political leader" or any other international body consistent of powerful actors might, indeed, seem important in global world. At the same time, the above analysis of the development of the new world order paradigm demonstrates that neither strong Russia, nor powerful China and growing India had been envisaged by the transnational elites to being equal partners in the new system.

As our research has demonstrated, so far, the new world order paradigm has been based on the idea of establishing the world government. It was adopted by the "Anglo-American establishment" as a policy doctrine yet at the end of the 19th Century. During the 20th Century it was masterminded within the U.S. think tanks, starting from the inception of the Inquiry (1917), then the War and Peace Studies (1939-1945), etc. The paradigm was implemented before erupting World War I and further beyond in terms of carrying out the world revolution doctrine. Then it evolved into the world government doctrine on the eve of World War II and immediately in its aftermath. During the Cold War, the paradigm was further developed in the framework of U.S. think tank projects, including the WOMP, The 1980s, etc. In the early 1990s, it was incorporated into world's political agenda as the global governance doctrine. Thus, the new world order paradigm exerts considerable influence on the international system and defines the conduct of the U.S. foreign policy strategy.

Chapter 3
Projecting the Paradigm

Projecting the Paradigm through World War I, World War II, the Cold War

U.S. think tanks, especially, the Council on Foreign Relations (CFR) played a distinct role in the promotion of the new world order paradigm. CFR has been elaborating models for world order, specifically, through the prism of the U.S. participation in World War I, World War II, and the Cold War. The most significant projects were the Inquiry and the War and Peace Studies. During the Cold War stage, the World Order Models Project (WOMP) and the 1980s Project outlined major directions of the U.S. foreign policy strategy. Thus, the paradigm was projected.

The history of the Council of Foreign Relations[11] shows that since its inception in 1921 the CFR was and still is one of the key sources of globalists' ideas. According to Quigley, "The CFR is the American Branch of a society which originated in England, and which believes that national boundaries should be obliterated, and a one-world rule established" [98]. Peter Grosse identified the CFR as America's "foreign policy establishment". He maintained that, "The Council on Foreign Relations functioned at the core of the public institution-building of the

---

11 Council on Foreign Relations (CFR) was founded in 1921, with headquarters in New York and offices in Washington, DC. The CFR Board includes top government officials, renowned scholars, business leaders, journalists, attorneys, and nonprofit professionals. The Council Board consists of 35 Directors and the CFR President, ex officio. There are more than 4,000 members of the Council. CFR posits itself as an independent, nonpartisan think tank, membership organization, and publisher - a resource for its members, government officials, business executives, journalists, educators and students, civic and religious leaders and etc. It suggests foreign policy choices facing the United States and other countries, develops expertise in the next generation of foreign policy leaders.

early Cold War, but only behind the scenes. As a forum providing intellectual stimulation and energy, it enabled well-placed members to convey cutting-edge thinking to the public - but without portraying the Council as the font from which the ideas rose" [98].

The Council has been serving as a coordinating body for a worldwide network of intellectuals and experts specializing in a wide range of international issues related to the new world order phenomenon. From its journal *Foreign Affairs*, books and projects` publications the CFR has produced various models for realization of the U.S. foreign policy strategy, from the isolationist stage through World War I, World War II, the Cold War, and beyond into the twenty-first century`s Cyber War.

CFR`s members have been influential in both Republican and Democratic parties as well as in all administrations since Wilson`s. The Council "has the power to install its people in positions of public authority and power... [thus] it can dominate the composition of every administration since the assassination of President McKinley...Carter Administration has throughout its tenure acted exclusively based on the guidelines of the CFR`s 1980s Project" [339].

The CFR has a unique role in the U.S. politics: "Council members continued the "in-and-out" progression, established by the previous generations, through changing American administrations... But the Council, after all, had carved out a leading role in international affairs for a quarter-century before the Cold War" [98]. The Council appears as being an intellectual government of the United States, advocating the new world order to come into effect. It has been determined as an "incubator of ideas" [98].

The Inquiry, the CFR`s predecessor, was established in September 1917 as a study group to prepare materials for the peace negotiations following World War I and to draw up specific recommendations for a post-war world order. The Inquiry was composed of around 150 academics. It was directed by notorious presidential adviser colonel Edward House who would then become the head of the Council on Foreign Relations. Walter Lippmann, the author of "The American Destiny", was appointed the Head of Research at the group, but was later replaced by Isaiah Bowman. The members of the group took part in the Paris Peace Conference in 1919-1920 and coordinated the activities of the U.S. delegation.

On June 5, 1928 Sir William G. Wiseman (1885-1962), who served as head of British intelligence operations in the United States from 1916 to 1918, wrote a Memorandum on The Inquiry. It read: "From the early months of the war, allied foreign offices began to consider the terms of peace and the mechanics of the peace conference which must come some-day... Colonel House foresaw very clearly the need for preparation, and as early as the summer of 1917 suggested a plan to Wilson which at once appealed to the President`s scholarly and orderly mind. Colonel House proposed that an organization be created which was called The Inquiry, under the direction of Dr. Mezes. The best available American historians and specialists with practical experience were invited to join the staff. Dr. Isaiah Bowman became executive officer and worked out the organiza-tion of the subjects to be studied. Professor J. T. Shotwell oversaw histori-cal geography and, after the Inquiry moved to Paris, of the library. David Hunter Miller, who oversaw legal problems, later became known and respected by all the delegations in Paris as one of the ablest legal minds at the Conference. Walter Lippmann, the present brilliant editor of the New York World, was secretary. It is my impression that Lippmann fur-nished the abstract ideas which found their way into a good many of the memoranda of the American Delegation and ultimately into some of President Wilson`s public speeches... This earnest and scholarly group of men gave deep and impartial study to the tremendous and complicated problems arising from a war which shattered the remnants of the Holy Roman Empire, dissipated the dreams of Bismarck, and left the great Russian Empire chaotic and impotent" [249].

The Inquiry has been the source of globalists` ideas. It elaborated the Wilson Doctrine of universalism, which has conceptually underpinned the so-called internationalists` movement (i.e. the world government movement) evolving after World War I. Using recommendations of the Inquiry, Wilson presented his notorious speech, known as Wilson`s four-teen points, delivered to a joint session of Congress on January 8, 1918. The Fourteen Points program speech was a blueprint for the American delegation to Paris Peace Conference.

The Inquiry was influential in terms of establishing the League of Nations. In addressing the U.S. Congress Wilson called for a "general association of nations" [214]. This fourteenth point of the program was soon to become the League of Nations. The fourteen points were based on liberal ideals. However, as the U.S. Department of States' Office of the Historian indicates, "Wilson's idealism pervades the fourteen points, but he also had more practical objectives in mind: keeping Russia in the war by convincing the Bolsheviks that they would receive a better peace from the Allies" [178]. Important enough, the same geopolitical approach aimed at keeping both Russia and Germany in the war to weakening their power potentials was also applied by the United States during World War II [6].

Wilson and other members of the "Big Three," including Georges Clemenceau of France and David Lloyd George of Britain, prepared the Covenant of the League as Part I of the Treaty of Versailles [177]. British Prime Minister Lloyd George (1916-1922) identified the joint effort of the West as follows: "We are laying the *foundations of a new world*" [41]. The Anglo-American establishment intended to build such a new world with the Russian Empire split into several newly independent states or protectorates. This would actually happen exactly 100 years later - after the collapse of the Soviet Union and creation of the Community of Independent States in 1991.

The idea of a divided Russia has been a key concept wrapped in the new world order doctrine. It had been advocated in the Inquiry's document entitled "Official American Commentary on the Fourteen Points" as well as in some other documents [192; 214]. Moreover, that idea was considered during Paris Peace Conference in 1919. Section XIV (Article 116) of the Treaty of Versailles, was entitled "Russia and Russian States". It read: "Germany acknowledges and agrees to respect as permanent and inalienable the independence of all the territories which were part of the former Russian Empire on August 1, 1914" [296].

After World War II the CFR's role was very important in creating the United Nations as was the Inquiry's in incepting the League of Nations. In the aftermath of the Cold War, the Council was consistently pursuing and further developing the global agenda for a new world order tailored to adapt to the post-Cold War shift in distributing the world power. It implemented several practically oriented research projects which were focused on transforming the concept of a nation state and national sovereignty into what might be perceived as the global governance doctrine. As it has been demonstrated, the latter is an integral part of the new world order paradigm. So far, the CFR plays key role in conceptual underpinning of the paradigm.

The War and Peace Studies [290] was carried out by the Council on Foreign Relations from 1939 until 1945. It assisted in advising the U.S. Government on its policies during World War II and in its aftermath: "The men from the Council proposed a discreet venture reminiscent of the Inquiry: a program of independent analysis and study that would guide American foreign policy in the coming years of war and the challenging new world that would emerge after" [98, p. 23].

The project consisted of four functional topic groups: economic and financial, security and armaments, territorial, and political. They included over 100 members. The funding was provided by the Rockefeller Foundation. Over the course of the project its budget totaled to around 350,000 U.S. dollars. In total, there were 362 meetings of the War and Peace Studies groups. The groups produced 682 memoranda for the State Department, which were circulated among the appropriate governmental departments. The Council's wartime work was confidential.

In February 1941 Division of Special Research was created in the Department of State. The division had similar structure to the War and Peace Studies. It included Economic, Political, Territorial, and Security Sections. The Research Secretaries of the four relevant Council's groups were appointed to work in the division. Simultaneously, they continued serving as Research Secretaries at the CFR. From March 1942, the project members, namely, Hamilton Fish Armstrong (Editor of Foreign Affairs), Isaiah Bowman, Benjamin V. Cohen, Norman H. Davis, and James T. Shotwell took part in the State Department's Advisory Committee on Postwar Foreign Policy. Thus, the CFR was closely interconnected with the U.S. Department of State.

The economic and financial group produced a memo, "The Impact of War upon the Foreign Trade of the United States," already in March 1940. Yet before the attack of Japan on Pearl Harbor on December 7, 1941, the group on security and armaments, chaired by Allen Dulles, urged to allocate an American occupation force in defeated Germany. Dulles later became a key figure in the Office of Strategic Services, CIA's predecessor, which would then led by him.

The territorial group, chaired by Bowman, insisted on "open door" policy regarding China. On March 17, 1940, this group issued a memo,

"The Strategic Importance of Greenland," advising to cover Greenland, which was considered a part of the Western Hemisphere, by the Monroe Doctrine and establish U.S. military bases there. In 1944 members of The War and Peace Studies political group were active members at the Dumbarton Oaks economic conference. In 1945 this groups' representatives (43 members of the CFR) and members of Royal Institute of International Affairs (the UK) took part in San Francisco conference which established the United Nations [290].

So far, the War and Peace Studies project can be comparable with the performance of its "conceptual predecessor", the Inquiry, in terms of projecting the "liberal" matrix of the international system. Yet its role and "practical contribution to the U.S. war effort, and the political planning for the era following, remains unclear in the judgment of history" [290]. Therefore, the project requires more thorough analysis, which might become possible only upon opening access to archival resources of the U.S. State Department: "The primary function of the Council on Foreign Relations during World War II proceeded in rigid secrecy, remote from the slightest awareness of most of the Council's 663 members, who were not themselves personally involved" [290].

The World Order Models Project (WOMP) was directed by the Council on Foreign Relations [134]. It was launched in 1968 by the World Policy Institute under the auspices of the World Law Fund. The leadership of the Institute "shared a commitment to the transformation of the international system and the belief that change must be initiated by the world's citizens, not its governments" [75]. The WOMP was envisioned as a "social movement" and "an academic experiment" [77]. It was identified as being "one of the first truly global think tanks" [332].

The WOMP was financed by the Carnegie Endowment for International Peace and the Rockefeller Foundation: "Armed with this investment [with a first grant of $100,000] and the goal of creating an international network of thinkers, Mendlovitz [director of the project, a Rutgers University law professor, and a member of the CFR] began recruiting WOMP scholars" [76]. The project was recruiting scholars since the early 1960s until 1969. It sought out the type of scholars who could "clarify [their] ideas and be in touch with the people running the world before reaching out to the grassroots" [76].

Important enough, the WOMP established a link with the Soviet leadership via Gennady Gerasimov, press spokesman for Gorbachev and press secretary of the Ministry of Foreign Affairs: "[Gerasimov] had infiltration with the academic intelligentsia and media... [and] was a strong addition for WOMP" [76]. In 1991, after the collapse of the Soviet Union the WOMP separated from the World Policy Institute.

The WOMP established three task forces: Security, Disarmament and Human Rights; Science and Technology; and Global Culture" [332]. In addition, eight working groups were formed. The guiding principle of the project activities was creating a single regime for global society, including a global tax scheme and an alternative security system for the global society [165]. This envisaged dismantling the national security mechanisms in the states, establishing the international police force to settle disputes and, finally, constituting a coordinating body to ensure unity in the global structure as a prototype of the world government. Subnational level of project's implementation required engaging "a much broader range of potential actors, including world institutions, transnational actors, international organization, functional activities, regional arrangements, the nation-state, subnational movements, local communities, and individuals" [165]. Starting from the early 1990s the think tank developed various concepts, models and scenarios for carrying out the transition strategies and time framework for their implementation.

Since its inception the WOMP intended to reach the public through educational systems worldwide (i.e. *the "peace education" movement*). In the framework of the Transnational Academic Program it produced analytical and educational materials that could be used simultaneously in educational systems worldwide (e.g. a curriculum guide entitled "Peace and World Order Studies"). Under the pretext of promoting peace, education and the establishment of a just peace the project focused on elaborating the set of *global values* which would underpin the global governance doctrine. It informed the public on global issues making the public opinion ready to accept the idea of world government. Thus, it created a "transnational framework of [new] world order values, thinking, and action" [134].

The WOMP was producing the visionary thinking and, so far, designing the new world order. In 1975, the think tank published a collection of books in a series "Preferred Worlds for the 1990s." The series included the following works: "On the Creation of a Just World Order" by Saul Mendlovitz; "Footsteps into the Future" by Rajni Kothari; "The True Worlds: A Transnational Perspective" by Johan Galtung; "A World Federation of Cultures" by Ali A.Mazrui; "Study of Future Worlds" by Richard A. Falk. The World Law Fund published the book series under title "The Strategy of World Order". Besides, many WOMP Occasional Papers were published. So far, by means of its numerous publications and studies the WOMP was shaping a theoretical model of the future international system, as it was perceived by global elites. The implementation of this model was carried out in the framework of realization of the U.S. foreign policy strategy.

The think tank also established the magazine - "Alternatives: A Journal for World Policy." It organized seminars in Russia (Moscow), Japan (Yokohama), etc. The purpose of the seminars was elaborating policy guidelines for government and non-governmental bodies at the local, national and international levels. Thus, the WOMP was projecting the new world order paradigm.

According to Richard Falk, during the first stage of implementation of the WOMP it endeavored to invite renowned international scholars to contribute their ideas and "feasible utopias" in book studies to be realized by the 1990s. At the second stage, the project was to produce a set of proposals "to project preferred worlds for the 1990s" [84, p. 184]. Several of the think tank`s works appear today "as if projecting preferred futures for the 2030s, 40 years later" [84, p. 184]. Falk identified the WOMP as having "done much to shape the course of this world order journey" over the past 25 years [85, p. 3].

One of the major outcomes of the WOMP was creating the phenomenon of global governance thinking by means of establishing the set of global values. It proposed to use the globe, the species, and the planet as the single unit of analysis. Global citizenship became a key concept: "The idea of global citizenship (which was added by Mendlovitz), represented both WOMP's approach to education and policy, as well as their attempt to understand and engage the public… Thus, in promoting global citizenship, they hoped to emphasize the need for global solutions, rather than solutions based on national interest" [77]. Global citizenship was later renamed to "species identity".

In 1990, the WOMP was rewarded a UNESCO Prize for Peace Education. It stated that, "The contributions of the 'World Order Models Project' to peace education stem from a dialogue that has been established between students, specialists and activists from Eastern and Western Europe, America, Africa and Asia. Several works have been published which today are used as textbooks in universities and schools" [302, p. 19].

The following award acceptance speech by Mendlovitz, as co-Director of the WOMP, is important to demonstrate the role of the think tank in terms of projecting the new world order paradigm and, especially, in developing the informational dimension of subnational governance. According to Mendlovitz, the WOMP was an effort under-taken by "peace researchers and educators" [302, p. 34]. He stressed, that "WOMP is a participatory group of scholars and activists from all regions of the globe... Our basic achievement in this regard has been the articulation of a broad consensus about the need for a transnational, interdisciplinary perspective on the contemporary human condition. This broad perspective encompasses... a vision of the possibilities of peace, economic well-being, social justice (including participation), eco-logical stability and positive identity. These value-domains... inform an interactive matrix of our normative, analytical and policy formulations" [302, p. 29].

Mendlovitz acknowledged that, "we who believe that a peace system is possible are a relatively small minority of the human race. The question that needs to be addressed, therefore, is how to increase the numbers of human beings to come... and further to translate this realization into a significant political force... to develop a movement for a just world peace as significant as that which is calling for an environmental regime for the globe... Of course, many now claim that such a process is under way. Consider for example the recent statements by President Bush and Secretary of State Baker of the United States who have been proclaiming that a new world order is emerging" [302, p. 30].

Co-director of the WOMP emphasized that "perestroika" reforms in the Soviet Union corresponded to the priorities of the world peace move-ment in building the new world order: "Another way of reading the situ-ation... is to refer to the extraordinary events of 1989 and the present... in December 1988 Secretary-General Gorbachev gave a major address in the United Nations... Soviet Union behavior during the period 1986-1990 could fairly be interpreted as providing a substantial behavioral basis for these lofty ideals ["universal interests"]; all the more so when one reviews the remarkable set of proposals made [by Gorbachev] within the United Nations environment... it exemplifies a trend which may actually point to a new and novel world order. Indeed, if the movement for a just world peace coheres this may become a more plausible reading of the situation" [302, p. 31].

Moreover, Mendlovitz confirmed that the "*strong transnational peace movement*" has been an important mainstream within world politics: "It has called upon religious and traditional belief systems throughout the globe going back to two or three millennia. With some notable exceptions, the movement has *waxed and waned around particular wars...*" [302, p. 33]. In the same context of establishing the new world order, "non-violence activism" was emphasized as a method of achieving radical social change. Mendlovitz referred to the events at Tiananmen Square in China as well as to the Solidarity movement in Poland.

Perhaps the most important emphasis in the UNESCO Prize for Peace Education speech, in terms of our analysis, was given on the perspectives of creating a world state. Mendlovitz argued that, "processes of interdependence, integration and interpenetration are producing transnational forms and structures of economic, social, cultural and political relations that... suggest the urgent need for new forms of governance and polity" [302, p. 35]. Developments around the League of Nations and the United Nations as well as globalization processes have been restructuring the state system towards creation of the world state: "No doubt ... there is an overwhelming surge in the direction of global polity and that a world state is emerging" [302, p. 36].

According to Mendlovitz, "Indeed, some of the policy elite are beginning to discuss a single world central bank and a single currency... it behooves us to participate in the discussions, formulations and political processes that will attend this emergence. My fear is that we will be put off... 'at a local level', thus permitting the centralizing forces of the dominant states and classes to maintain control of both the transition and governance of the global polity.... Peace researchers, educators and activists should see this expansion of specie identity [i.e. global citizenship] as enhancing the vocation to which we have been called, namely, the creation of… global polity [i.e. the world state]" [302, p. 37]. In concluding, Mendlovitz mentioned WOMP's "transnational linkages of concerned intelligentsia" [302, p. 37]. He confirmed, so far, that there exists "some of the alternative interpretations and programmes of action that *the global policy elites* are promoting in their efforts to construct a new world order…" [302, p. 37].

Thus, the World Order Models Project has played a significant role in developing the idea of creating the world state. It was further promoted by transnational elites and institutions. Gorbachev served as a mouthpiece to announcing their agenda. Kerry Bolton has identified him as being "one of the globalist elite" who advocated for a new world order "in tandem with other globalist think tanks such as the Soros Foundation and Open Society Institute, etc." [23].

In 1991, *the Gorbachev Foundation* was established in pursuit of practically the same objectives that the WOMP had been focused on. Since its inception the keynote of the Foundation's activities is "Toward a New Civilization" [281]. On May 6, 1992 Gorbachev addressed a meeting of the Chicago Council on Foreign Relations stating that "the world has reversed in its move in another direction – towards new world order, towards new civilization" [93]. It might be concluded, so far, that the *ethos of the new world order paradigm* is to approach a new kind of civilization emerging in terms of approaching "technetronic age", that is, imposing global control over human development.

Since 1995 the State of the World Forum advocated *the world state concept*. Its first annual meeting was organized by the Gorbachev Foundation. The Forum's mission statement read that, "Many of the earlier civilizations which have appeared in the 6,000 years of our recorded history have largely been created by groups of so-called "creative minorities" or "sapiential circles" - independent individuals who came together to articulate and take up challenges being ignored by declining and outdated concepts, organizations and governments. The State of the World Forum seeks to address the challenge of renewal by joining with those individuals and organizations worldwide who are similarly concerned… Their results became inordinately important - they turned humanity onto new paths" [288].

At present, transnational elites urge *new global forum* which might be considered as being the prototype of the world government, to augment the United Nations [97]. Gorbachev, again, has been the mouthpiece for the promotion of their initiative. He stated, that in November 2014 "serious-minded world circles" have asked him to come up with a new platform: "It`s going to be a very big thing. There`ll be first steps and second steps, aimed for it to become a global platform for discussion of problems. It must be very representative, capable of influencing both state and international institutions, authoritative because the UN is, unfortunately, lame at the moment" [97]. Gorbachev urged, that the new global platform "would calm the world, would stop things that are going on, would rule out such bloody events" [97]. According to Gorbachev, establishing of such a platform is being promoted by "very experienced people, respected by global public opinion" [97].

The 1980s Project [247, p. 227-235] was designed in the early 1970s by Richard H. Ullman, the then director of studies at CFR, and Bayless Manning, a Council member since 1961 who became the first full-time president of the Council in 1971. The project was implemented under the auspices of the Trilateral Commission within a period of five years. Its budget totaled to $1.6 million. Ullman, appointed as project director, considered it being "the largest single research and studies effort the Council on Foreign Relations has undertaken in its…history, comparable" only to the War and Peace Studies of World War II [247, p. 225].

Notably, the CFR identified the Inquiry and the War and Peace Studies as being "predecessors" of the 1980s Project, which was aimed "to define the new issues and policy responses of an international society evolving beyond the East-West conflict" [60]. Being clearly globalist in terms of policy recommendations, the project focused on developing a post-Cold War era international scenario. The issues explored by the project started to dominate global agenda only in the 1990s: "the title of the project was a little premature; not until the 1990s did the issues explored truly dominate the international agenda. But many 1980s Project authors were by then installed in government policy-making positions, and when the Cold War came to its … end the Council had provided for the public record an impressive database for the global issues confronting coming generations" [98, p. 108; 60].

Before launching the 1980s Project, considerable preparatory activities had been carried out for four years. Beginning in mid- 1975 a group of over 300 public figures met regularly at the Council on Foreign

Relations` premises in New York [339]. Among key personalities of the 1980s Project were Henry A. Kissinger, Zbigniew Brzezinski, Joseph S. Nye, Jr., Walter J. Levy, W. Michael Blumenthal, Samuel P. Huntington, Marshall D. Shulman, Michael O'Neill, Stephen Stamas, Fritz Stern, Allen S. Whiting, Cyrus R. Vance, Leslie H. Gelb, Roger Fisher, Rev. Theodore M. Hesburgh, Robert A. Charpie, Richard N. Cooper, Harold Van B. Cleveland, Lawrence C. McQuade, William Diebold, Jr., Eugene B. Skolnikoff, Miriam Camps, James A. Perkins, Robert V. Roosa, Carroll L. Wilson, Bayless Manning, Theodore R. Marmor, Ali Mazrui, Carlos R. Diaz-Alejandro, Richard A. Falk, Edward K. Hamilton, Stanley Hoffman, Gordon J. MacDonald, Bruce K. MacLaury and others [339].

Several intellectuals mentioned above were then promoted to important positions in the U.S. government: "In January of 1977, upon the inauguration of President Carter.... all its leaders transferred to Washington, D.C. to become cabinet members of the Carter Administration. These leaders were Cyrus R. Vance, chairman of the CFR`s "Working Group on Nuclear Weapons and Other Weapons of Mass Destruction"; Leslie Gelb, chairman of the "Working Group on Armed Conflict"; W. Michael Blumenthal, head of the Central Coordinating Group for Project 1980s; Zbigniew Brzezinski, member of the Project`s governing body, the Committee on Studies. Richard Cooper, Marshall Shulman, and others were included among those who headed for Washington where implementation of their Project would be carried out" [339]. After project`s leaders moved to Washington, "the policy formulations and strategic concepts which had already been agreed upon were now distributed among various academics who were instructed to put them in writing... this phase was concluded and the manuscripts were taken to the publishers" [339].

Because of the preparatory meetings and work of special study groups, numerous policy memos, strategic projections and implementation papers were developed. The CFR confirms: "Between 1977 and 1982, the Council published nearly two dozen policy-oriented books that collectively served to define what became known as "global issues," many of them unfamiliar to conventional diplomatic thinking. With the Cold War, still the fundamental fact of international life, study groups produced monographs on the military balance, regional conflicts, and arms control, both nuclear and conventional. But fully one-third of the Council's papers dealt with economic and other issues that earlier diplomatic generations had considered beneath notice. The variety of titles revealed the broadened agenda of foreign policy: Beyond the North-South Stalemate, International Disaster Relief, Enhancing Global Human Rights, Controlling the Future Arms Trade" [98; 60].

The 1980s Project was publishing widely in order "to win over to its side people willing to put its program to work" [339]. The project produced 30 volumes on the "global issues," thus, designing the new world order. They were ranging from human rights, demographic dilemmas and world economy towards oil politics, nuclear disarmament and proliferation issues, arms trade, monetary policy, regional issues, including in Africa, the Middle East as well as on "China`s future", etc. In the foreword, which accompanied each of the 30 publications, Richard H. Ullman wrote: "The published products of the Project are aimed at a broad readership, including policy makers and potential policy makers and those who would influence the policy making process" [339].

The 1980s Project considered the poor "South" and the developing world countries as being the main threat to the liberal world order. Ullman emphasized that, "The political and economic relations between rich and poor countries promise to remain central issues on the international agenda for the indefinite future. The 1980s Project has devoted considerable attention to the likely and desirable evolution of these relations ... `North-South` issues between rich and poor societies infuse most of the Project`s work" [339]. Besides, the project promoted the concept of "limited sovereignty". Thus, it was elaborating new ideas, concepts, and scenarios to underpinning the system of global governance.

According to the CFR, "Thanks to the 1980s Project, its members and fellows were not unprepared for the intellectual demands of the post-Cold War era" [98; 60]. At present, "the Council has focused its efforts on nurturing the next generation of foreign policy leaders, expanding the Council's outreach… figuring out the rules and rhythms of foreign policy and developing new ideas for America and the international community… Building for the 21st century, the Council is pursuing a conscious campaign, extending the effort begun in the 1970s [the 1980s Project], to locate and engage the new thinkers of the next generation … they will have special insights into our new world" [60].

Incorporating the Paradigm into Global Agenda

Further to the League of Nations, the United Nations had been planned as an institutional platform aimed at establishing the system of global governance. The UN draft Charter which was suggested by the United States at the end of World War II as well as some other documents declassified in the middle of the 1990's clearly testify that yet in 1944 the United States had been aimed at creating a sub-national institutional mechanism. That mechanism had been planned to *identifying threats* for the world development and, thus, make decisions obligatory for both the UN members and non-member states on the use of military force [181]. However, the U.S. attempt to institutionalize the world government immediately in the wake of World War II failed, hence, the Cold War emerged.

Kerry Bolton put an emphasis on "America's grand new design to establish the United Nations Organization (UNO) as a world parliament, as the focus of a "new world order" as President Wilson had sought with the League of Nations after World War I" [23]. He confirmed that, "The American plan for the UNO called for power to be vested with the General Assembly and based around majority vote. The Soviet position was to make the Security Council the final arbiter of decisions with members having the right to veto… [thus] it was the USSR that rendered the UNO redundant as a method of imposing a new world order, de facto if not de jure, a situation that continues to the present time, thanks to the Soviet insistence on national – or imperial – sovereignty for itself and its power bloc" [23].

In 1949, Warren Austin, the U.S. Ambassador to the United Nations from 1946 until 1953, admitted in a publication of the UN World magazine that, "World government could not be accepted without radical change of national outlook... It will take a long time to prepare peoples and governments of most nations for acceptance of and participation in a world government… If we expect this future world government to be created by agreement and not by force or conquest, we will have to be willing to work patiently until peoples or governments are ready for it..."

The United Nations system and its agencies have played a key role in incorporating the paradigm into global agenda. The United Nations Educational, Scientific and Cultural Organization (UNESCO), for example, contributed among other to carrying out the "peace education" movement with its "global values" and, thus, establishing the *informational dimension* of the new world order. UNDP, in its turn, has added in shaping the *economic dimension* of the system of global governance.

UNESCO has been a key UN Agency created to promoting peace, education, science and intercultural understanding as well as striving "to build networks among nations that enable this kind of solidarity" [300]. At the same time, UNESCO contributed to providing institutional framework for the introduction of single standards in education and, thus, fostering the creation of the global education system.

In 1946, UNESCO's founder, Vice President of the Eugenics Society Julian Huxley referred to *the concept of eugenic policy*. The concepts of eugenic policy and population control correlate to the so-called "golden billion" doctrine suggested by the Club of Rome in 1993. These concepts, among other, constitute the core of the global governance doctrine. In a report "UNESCO: Its Purpose and Its Philosophy" Huxley stated: "Even though it is quite true that any radical eugenic policy will be for many years politically and psychologically impossible, it will be important for UNESCO to see that the eugenic problem is examined with the greatest care, and that the public mind is informed of the issues at stake so that much that now is unthinkable may at least become thinkable" [301, p. 21].

In 1968, UNESCO published a report entitled "The Right to Education. From Proclamation to Achievement 1948-1968". The document read: "We are witnessing the establishment of a new world order based upon the system of the United Nations" [287, p. 18]. The rapidly growing world population was considered as being one of the main obstacles to global governance: "not only is the population of the world increasing; it is also growing younger ... So, the first obstacle to be overcome by education is that of quantity" [287, p. 25].

On 25 September 1974, the Director-General of UNESCO, Rene Maheu, on the third session of the International Co-ordinating Council of the Man and the Biosphere Programme at Williamsburg, USA, declared: "Here in this town, two hundred years ago, a resurgent impulse towards freedom and independence led to a new approach in the form of government.... the old order, which no longer corresponded to the needs of society and to the vision of man, was being superseded by new ideals and the assertion of new rights... Similarily, the rationale behind the MAB programme is to ensure that the physical, biological and other environmental requirements of man are placed in the hands of each of us and remain under our overall control" [5, p. 1].

In his address, the Director-General of UNESCO challenged the concept of national sovereignty and advocated establishing the new world order at all levels: "Nations now act "realistically" for what they consider their own interests – which in most cases are nothing more than short-term, narrow objectives. The effects are well known: disruption of what remains of an international order, growing tension and even armed conflicts... I believe that we have now reached the point in world affairs where we must have a systematic reorganization of international relations on all levels... I wish to reiterate my firm conviction- together with my hope- that a new world order- political, monetary, economic and social- should now be established." [5, p. 2-4].

Besides, Rene Maheu identified "problems of mankind" which include "the environmental problem", "population growth and food supply", "communication between the peoples of the world" and require implementation of "world approaches and world solutions" [5, p. 4]. Indeed, these problems as well as many others are pivotal in terms of future development of mankind. Yet the approaches towards their resolution as well as the means differ drastically. Maheu confirmed: "National problems imply the use of political realism for particular ends. But the problems of mankind require very different attitudes, methods and instruments. To deal with them we need a world-wide organizational effort... and we need a universal ethic of human behavior... I certainly believe that the universal approach will sooner or later win out over the national approach... we must work for a methodological and gradual transition from the national to the universal approach..." [5, p. 4].

Under the pretext of coping with "global issues," including "climate change," "population control," "arms proliferation" (WOMD) etc., transnational elites carry out the process of establishing a centralized authority, that is, the world government. In 2004, American representative to the UN, Roger Dittmann[12], emeritus professor of physics at California State

---

12 Roger Dittman has been the U.S. Affiliate of the World Federation of Scientific Workers, UN Representative of the WFSW

University and the then President of the U.S. Federation of Scholars and Scientists made a presentation entitled "Sustainable Development, the New International Scientific Order, and UN Reform" [72]. He identified sustainable development as a remedy, which is necessary for pursuing population control.

According to Dittmann, sustainable development has been determined as follows: "Economic [and other] development that leads to reduction in population toward an optimum level for maximization of the quality of life, i.e. environmentally benign development that reduces the birth rate" [69, p. 14]. The concept of birth rate reduction corresponds to the Club of Rome "golden billion" doctrine, which was mentioned earlier. Besides, Dittmann called for *"New International Scientific Order."* He argued, "Since this is a global effort, it requires global organization, both governmental and popular.... Not only do people require organization about their (multiple) identities (including professional, scholarly, and scientific), they need international, even supranational affiliation, facing *a common adversary*" [69, p. 18].

The common adversary (enemy) is a key factor that generates the mechanism of realization of the U.S. global strategy and directs American might to establishing the new world order. *The concept of common enemy* requires establishing global institutional and organizational structures to confronting "the enemy" and, in doing so, leads the mankind towards the world government. Thus, in the Club of Rome 1993 report entitled *"The First Global Revolution"*, the think tank urges unification of mankind against a common enemy: "In searching for a common enemy against whom we can unite, we came up with the idea that pollution, the threat of global warming, water shortages, famine and the like would fit the bill. In their totality and their interaction these phenomena do constitute a common threat... All these dangers are caused by human intervention.... and it is only through changed attitudes and behavior that they can be overcome. The real enemy then is humanity itself" [278, p. 75].

The Club of Rome advocated de-centralizing state powers and transferring its competencies to *a world authority*. In "Governance and the Capacity to Govern" section, the report urges the global forum, which is the same idea Gorbachev advocated in 2014. The report claimed that, "... in the transition of the nation state towards some new kind of global system… the main issue is how to establish… a system in which there will be several layers of decision-making … For the global problems, *we need a global forum* and, at the other extreme, local matters call for a town or community meeting rather than edicts emanating from a remote and seemingly uncaring central government" [278, p. 121-122]. The first meeting of the *State of the World Forum* took place in 1995, that is, two years after the report was released.

Regarding the process of de-centralization of sovereign states or, de-sovereignization, in other words, the Club of Rome identified the following actors: "political parties, trade unions, corporations, non-governmental organizations, pressure groups of all kinds including informal groups which may be short-lived but nevertheless intense and effective in their mobilization on a particular issue. These various groups contribute to governance through their proposals and protests. Governance is no longer the monopoly of governments and inter-governmental bodies, and its effectiveness will depend on the capacity of leaders to selectively include in their decision-making process these new actors…" [278, p. 119]. Since 1990s these new actors, indeed, have become influential at the national level. Yet many of them have been eroding the sovereign state powers (e.g. various NGOs, social movements and protest groups financed by the United States' foundations in Russia and other countries worldwide).

As it was demonstrated before, the UN agencies, especially, UNESCO and UNDP contributed to creating *the informational and economic dimensions* of the new world order (accordingly). For example, UNESCO elaborated the concept of a "new world information and communication order." It was first proposed at a Meeting of Consultants which took place at UNESCO Headquarters on December 18-21, 1978. The meeting was a "practical follow-up to the resolutions of the twentieth General Conference of UNESCO" [280, p. 8].

The report of the meeting entitled "The Free and Balanced Flow of Information in a New Communication Order" read: "Fifteen consultants and observers from university and professional circles and representatives of international journalists' organizations attended this meeting. The main purpose of the meeting was to review briefly the origins of the concept of a free and balanced flow of information, to analyze the current state of discussions and the components of a new world order, together with its legal, technological and socio-economic implications, and to make suggestions and recommendations for future action by UNESCO and other international organizations" [280, p. 1]. However, since the concept of a "new world information and communication order" was not endorsed by all member States, it "was therefore considered in a very broad sense... as an attitude of mind favourable to change in the present situation and a desire for co-operation aimed at developing the communication media" [280, p. 1].

Besides, the report suggested to preparing and carrying out seminars and "pilot programmes" of education with a purpose of incorporating the above concept and its principles in the constitutions and national laws of UNESCO member states as well as inserting these principles in journalists` code of ethics [280, p. 2]. In "Status of the journalist" section, it suggested to "assess the feasibility of establishing an international code of ethics which would be adopted by journalists possessing a "universal" sense of mission, transcending their national origin in the defense of peace and fraternity" [280, p. 3]. The document insisted: "determination must be shown and sustained efforts made over an extended period so that the necessary radical changes in mentalities and structures can take place in many countries" [280, p. 3]. Therefore, a proposal was put forward to "draw up [legal] regulations relating to international mass communications" [280, p. 2-3].

In terms of establishing *the informational dimension* of the new world order, the report considered the receptiveness of the public of the information transmitted. It suggested to "study the way in which certain audiences perceive other countries through the communication media to which they are exposed, and analyse changes in their attitudes and behaviours towards those countries"; "study the interest shown by the public in news and cultural values of foreign countries"; and "analyse the conditions under which the international flow of information may impair identity and traditional cultural values" [280, p. 5].

In the section entitled "Action", the report suggested setting up global institutional infrastructure to manage dissemination of information and direct communication flows. It implied creation of "a documentation centre", "research and documentation centres on the mass media" as well as "an international institution with responsibility for co-ordinating all forms of technical or financial assistance offered by the industrialized countries and distributing such assistance to the developing countries..." [280, p. 5-6]. Therefore, the report envisaged "an international fund drawing on governmental and private contributions to provide assistance to developing countries that need to improve their communication structures" [280, p. 6].

The informational dimension of the system of global governance might be identified in the report as the "world communications network" [280, p. 7]. The document also urged setting up "World Press Council" and "World Press Institute" [280, p. 6]. This initiative might be considered as an effort to institutionalizing the world government bodies the world`s (proto-) ministry of information. Obviously, if it was established, such a ministry would have had consolidated control over global information flows. According to the well-known saying: anyone who has information owns the world[13].

UNESCO also introduced *the concept of "Gate-Keepers."* In the "Production and content of information" section, the report suggested to "Organize seminars for professionals to make them understand the need to broaden the concerns of those who, in the mass communication process, have the responsibility for selecting information, in other words, those who act as information filters (Gate-Keepers)" [280, p. 4]. The "Gate-Keepers" were to perform a distinct function of filtering and controlling the information flows in line with "liberal" values.

The report further urged to "Draw up with co-operation of peace organizations and international professional journalists` organizations, a model code of conduct for the treatment of information relating to foreign affairs" [280, p. 4]. The document advocated organizing "informal meetings between representatives from the world of journalism and officials" to explore "the peace and disarmament"; "the new international economic order"; "the education of young people," etc. [280, p. 4].

Besides, UNESCO`s report urged to "Explore the possibilities of using the communication media to help certain nations to achieve more speedily full political, economic and cultural independence" [280, p. 4]. The U.S. communication media, for example, The Voice of America, played a key role in triggering the growth of nationalistic

---

13 This saying was coined by Nathan Rothschild and later reiterated by Winston Churchill

and separatist movements within the Warsaw Pact countries. Some of the U.S.-developed means and technologies of mass communications ensured carrying out informational and psychological warfare against the Soviet Union.

On October 7th, 1983, UNESCO General Conference was held in Paris. The report by the Director-General represents another valuable source demonstrating the debate on the new world order paradigm and its evolution. The document reads: "The participants regarded the new world order as a recognized concept, developing but irreversible, which would be established stage by stage... One participant summarized the material and immaterial obstacles to the realization of a new world order and to the exercise of the right to information with particular reference to censorship" [184; p. 16]. Some participants of the conference declared that "the effort to establish a new world information and communication order in stages could not be separated from the effort to promote a new international economic order; both were perceived in terms of interdependence and interrelation..." [184; p. 10].

According to the document, "The establishment of a new world communication order appeared to one participant as a participation, a world response to the communications revolution, whereas another emphasized the importance of the word "new" in describing the concept. Some statements emphasized the importance of speaking of a new order and not the new order since the concept was steadily evolving and stressed the crucial difference between a new international order, concerned only with inter-State relations, and a new world order, which considered all communication problems in a global context. Several participants considered that the concept of a new order should be studied in greater detail. One suggested that UNESCO should try to obtain the co-operation of a group of consultants who could help it to carry out its communication research programme with reference to the new order, assess the programme and encourage its co-ordination with the research programmes and activities of national, regional and international research institutions and organizations. The group should include researchers from different disciplines and cultural regions" [184; p. 16]. Thus, the new world order paradigm appeared an important subject during the UNESCO General Conference. However, "Some participants were concerned with the terminological aspects and would have preferred to substitute for the idea of order, which could have negative connotations and which seemed somewhat inconsistent with the idea of an evolutive process, concepts or terms such as system, arrangement, environment or approach" [184; p. 16].

Another critical issue was implementing "international legal instrument" to ensure the new world order. The report confirms: "Although certain participants considered that it would be desirable and timely to proceed to the preparation of an international legal instrument designed to set down the principles of a new world order and although the United Nations Committee on Information has begun to study the possibility of defining certain concepts governing information and communication, most participants considered the suggestion of the preparation of a normative order premature or illusory. However, some participants suggested that the United Nations and UNESCO, in co-operation with the International Telecommunication Union and the other institutions concerned, should organize and encourage studies, symposia and other research activities on the fundamental principles of a new world order and the legal principles related to international communications. In this connection, stress should be laid on the fundamental principles of international law as the basis for a new world information and communication order (resolution 21 C/4.19 part VI para. b). One participant proposed that the interdependence of political, legal and ethical norms and principles in the field of international information and communication should be the subject of a study" [184; p. 18-19].

The concept of national sovereignty was also touched upon during the debate. The report reads: "Some participants proposed that the concept of sovereignty with respect to information (or informational sovereignty) should be studied, but that was opposed by several others, the representative of a non-governmental organization describing the concept as a threat to the right to knowledge which was universal, and as a form of thought control. Others suggested that UNESCO should undertake or recommended a comparative study on laws on the press, to become more familiar with the legal conditions under which the media could carry out their mission, especially in developing countries" [184; p. 19].

The role of media has been central in terms of promoting liberal values and the so-called mass culture around the globe and, thus, consolidating the informational dimension of the new world order. In "Implementation of the concept of the new world information and communication order" section of the report UNESCO acknowledged that, "New technologies have demonstrated their overwhelming power to transform the entire pattern of the exchange and circulation of information. They... bring the world nearer to a "global village" ... Some participants referred to what they called the "Americanization of the world" [184; p. 19-20]. Thus, *the concept of "global village"* was applied yet in 1983. It was incorporated into the U.S. foreign policy strategy a decade after, during the Clinton Administrations (1993-2000).

After the end of the Cold War UNESCO has been promoting the global governance doctrine. On 20 April 2009, Mr. Olabiyi Babalola Joseph Yai, Chair of UNESCO's executive board, argued that the organization was created to "think global governance." In the wake of the Global Financial Crisis of 2007-2008 he suggested to set up a "working group on global governance." He declared: "You will recall ... that I said, before Mr Ban Ki Moon, Secretary-General of the United Nations, that UNESCO's role is to think global governance. That is why the Organization was founded. We come to the rescue of the system especially when the economic machine runs out of steam, as it clearly has today. It is thus a matter of urgency to set up a long-term working group on global governance. I hope that a State or group of States will seize on this worthy proposal, and that the Organization, as of this session, will give it the attention it warrants... I consider it to be the duty of the Chair of the Board to come up with provocative ideas" [299, p. 5]. According to the Chair of UNESCO's executive board, "reflection on global governance" and "the existential crisis of UNESCO" must be the two problems that demand immediate attention regarding the future of the world and consideration of the problems and the tasks conferred upon UNESCO [299, p. 4].

On 23 October 2009 Irina Bokova, Director-General of UNESCO, confirmed: "I am convinced of the need for global governance, founded on universal ethics, to take up these common challenges" [3, p. 4]. Besides, she stated that, "With equal resolve, and at the highest levels of government and global governance, I will advocate for an increase of the share of Official Development Assistance going to education..." [3, p. 9]. Thus, one might assume a multi-level structure of the system of global governance. Its framework includes the multilateral formats of G8 and G20, global forums, media, social activism, grassroots movements, NGOs, etc.

According to Bokova, "Our mandate is so far-reaching; however, we cannot act alone. It is inconceivable that at a time when the governance of our world is being revisited the tasks entrusted to us in the Constitution will not be given their rightful place in the global framework, including in the context of the G8 and the G20. UNESCO's sphere of influence and powers of persuasion must expand. This can be done if we reach out to, and mobilize, networks and communities of practice with whom we establish innovative alliances. These could be Mayors; gender activists; youth groups and federations; the music, film and communication industries; the media; the wide world of Arts; science and scientific associations and industry" [3, p. 6]. Concerning the UN reform Bokova stressed that, "There is no alternative to forging a unified system..." [3, p. 10].

Since its inception *the European Union* has become an integral part of the system of global governance. In September 1992, the President of the European Commission Jacques Delors, being the then top European official, addressed the Royal Institute of International Affairs (the UK) with a speech entitled "The European Community and the New World Order" [4]. Delors identified "new approaches and new frameworks" of governance emerging in the world arena. He suggested to "devise the principles and rules of the new international game" [4].

Proceeding from the assumption that a post-Cold War era brought about "climate of hope," Delors stated: "now that our options are wide open again... we are at the beginning of an evolutionary trend.... we must be ready with our response" [4]. Thus, the end of the Cold War brought about a strategic opportunity to further promote the "liberal" paradigm of world order as it had happened in the wake of World War I and World War II.

In his speech, the President of the European Commission referred to the phenomenon of "universal conscience." According to Delors, "The global dissemination of information means that ideas can circulate and public opinion can adopt a common way of thinking to such an extent as to justify talk of a universal conscience" [4]. The latter implies the development of the concepts of "global values" and "global issues."

Delors urged transferring state sovereignty to a sub-national level of governance. He identified "humanitarian interventions" as a means towards that end: "International apathy about human rights violations will not be able to hide behind the pretext of immutable, inviolable national sovereignty much longer. In all the debates going on now, the moral duty to come to the assistance of peoples... despite difficulties of implementation, it [humanitarian intervention] might well become a legal duty" [4]. In this context, Delors referred to the idea of establishing the world government identifying it as a global institutional framework to which the sovereignty must be transferred. However, he assumed that establishing the global institutional framework might be a lengthy and time-consuming process: "giving birth to institutions to which sovereignty is to be transferred and which are to be given power to manage cooperation and settle disputes is a slow and arduous process" [4].

In terms of world's unification the role of the European Community was determined as a "laboratory" for the management of interdependence [4]. Delors admitted that, "The interdependence of the world's nations seems somehow inevitable ... the frontiers are coming down and we must work together" [4]. Because of growing interdependence of the world "many economists speak of the transition to a new stage - a quantum leap to a worldwide single market" [4]. Thus, globalization appears as an important stage in terms of world's unification.

At the same time, Delors called for political will to create the world government: "economic integration, unless it is backed by a strong political will, will not in itself produce stronger international institutions or help create world government. Therefore, although the need for a new world order is self-evident, our era is one of trial and error or, as the harsher critics among us would have it, of impotence, inability to take on world challenges. If we are to resist the forces of fragmentation, protectionism and exclusion, we must be more than just aware of our interdependence. We must move on and manage it, setting common objectives and applying common rules" [4].

The President of the European Commission put forward the following question: "Can the European Community ... provide a blueprint for the creation of this new world order?" In answering this question, he confirmed that, "The Community experiment in interdependence in a common framework ... must be the longest-running... it is a living process and an enriching one. In the context of a new world order it is certainly worth observing, even if the principles governing it cannot necessarily be reproduced" [4].

In concluding Delors, the top European official of that time, suggested *vesting a world power into the international organization*: "Is it possible to draw conclusions from the Community experiment, the laboratory I talked about earlier, that will help us to build a new world order?... The contribution that the Community as such can make to the new world order can, to use an image from the plant world, be considered something of a hybrid, what is produced by crossing a world power with an international organization... The conclusion... is that the Community`s contribution to a new world order is, like the Community itself, something original: a method which will serve as a reference, a body whose presence will be felt" [4].

The economic dimension of the system of global governance can be viewed in terms of the activities of TNCs as well as the Bretton Woods institutions, international banking corporations and specialized UN agencies engaged in the promotion of world`s economic interdependence, mainly, UNDP and UNCTAD. In 1992, the UN Commission on Global Governance was established to analyze global changes and opportunities that emerged in the wake of the Cold War. In 1995, the Commission produced a report "Our Global Neighborhood" [194].

The report focused on the complex and contradictory effects of globalization and outlined major transformations occurred in the second half of the 20th century, such as political, economic, military, technological, intellectual, and institutional changes. Besides, the report surveyed global issues, including ethnic conflict, environmental degradation, unemployment, and extensive population growth, that have emerged because of these transformations. It also argued, that despite the threat of nuclear war between the superpowers receded, the spread of nuclear capability and of biological and chemical weapons posed greater threats to confront world leaders. Therefore, the Commission advocated the necessity of global governance as a part of evolution of human efforts in organizing the life of mankind on the planet.

According to the report, "Governance is the sum of many ways individuals and institutions, public and private, manage their common affairs. It is a continuing process through which conflicting or diverse interests may be accommodated and co-operative action taken. It includes formal institutions and regimes empowered to enforce compliance, as well as informal arrangements that people and institutions either have agreed to or perceive to be in their interest" [194, p. 4]. The report considered global governance as the way to manage international affairs and organize a new world order. It assumed that sovereignty must be exercised collectively. Besides, the Commission urged external (humanitarian) interventions to ensure the security of people. It called for amending the U.N. Charter to permit such interventions, hence, the need for a highly trained U.N. Volunteer (military) Force [194, p. 4].

In 1994, the UNDP issued the annual Human Development Report, which suggested endorsing "a new development paradigm" and "a new framework of global governance" [113, p. 5, 11]. The report advocated restructuring specialized organizations within the UN system as well as the Bretton Woods institutions to cope with new challenges to human security: "The edifice of global governance was last rebuilt in the 1940s after the Second World War... The institutions of global governance created in the 1940s (UN, World Bank, IMF, GATT) have played a key role in the past five decades in keeping the world at peace and in accelerating global economic growth and trade liberalization. They certainly succeeded in avoiding any recurrence of the experience of the pre-1940s.... The United Nations, for its part, started with enormous promise but was never allowed to play its role as the fourth pillar of development" [113, p. 82]. The report further urged that, "The need for strengthened institutions of global governance is much greater today than ever before. Markets have become globalized... Nation-states are weakening as decision-making becomes either local or global. In such a milieu, the long-term perspective for global governance needs to be re-examined" [113, p. 83].

The UNDP considered starting a creative debate on the shape of global institutions for the 21st century. It suggested to transforming the IMF into a World Central Bank and expanding WTO into a World Production and Trade Organization (WPTO): "A World Central Bank is essential for the 21st century... It will take some time-and probably some international financial crisis-before a full-scale World Central Bank can be created. In the meantime, four steps could convert the IMF into an embryonic central bank... And for the future, one could think of expanding a WTO into a WPTO-a world production and trade organization" [113, p. 84, 87]. The report emphasized that it "has included just a few of the institutions that the world is likely to need in the 21st century. Some people may consider them overly ambitious, but others may consider them timid" [113, p. 88].

Moreover, the UNDP advocated *the world government doctrine*. The report stated that, "we need nothing less than a world government… This may appear to be totally utopian today. But he [Jan Tinbergen, the first Nobel Prize winner in economics in 1969] points out: "The idealists of today often turn out to be the realists of tomorrow" [113, p. 88]. In a special contribution to the section of the report entitled "Global governance for the 21st century" Jan Tinbergen suggested institutional framework for the world government, including establishing the world ministries.

The Nobel Prize winner wrote that, "Mankind`s problems can no longer be solved by national governments. What is needed is a World Government. This can best be achieved by strengthening the United Nations system. In some cases, this would mean changing the role of UN agencies from advice-giving to implementation. Thus, the FAO would become the World Ministry of Agriculture, UNIDO would become the World Ministry of Industry, and the ILO the World Ministry of Social Affairs. In other cases, completely new institutions would be needed. These could include, for example, a permanent World Police which would have the power to subpoena nations to appear before the International Court of Justice, or before other specially created courts… Other institutions could include an Ocean Authority (based on the new Law of the Seas), and an analogous Outer Space Authority, to deal with matters such as outer space, aviation and information satellites. But some of the most important new institutions would be Financial - a World Treasury and a World Central Bank. The World Treasury would serve as a world ministry of finance. Its main task would be to collect the resources needed by the other world ministries through one or more systems of global automatic taxation… In addition, there should be a World Central Bank based on a reformed IMF to deal, among other things, with monetary, banking and stock exchange policies… there should be a corresponding "world financial policy" to be implemented by the World Bank and the World Central Bank… As the world economy becomes increasingly integrated, so the redistribution of world income should become similar to that within well-governed nations. Some of these proposals are, no doubt, far-fetched and beyond the horizon of today's political possibilities. But the idealists of today often turn out to be the realists of tomorrow" [113, p. 88].

The UNDP also considered the growing power of transnational corporations: "Transnational corporations (TNCs) control more than 70% of world trade and dominate the production, distribution and sale of many goods from developing countries, especially in the cereal and tobacco markets. An estimated 25% of world trade is conducted as intrafirm trade within TNCs. These corporations thus have great power, which, if harnessed for sustainable human development, could be of great benefit... There is a growing consensus that governments and TNCs should work closely together to promote national and international economic welfare" [113, p. 87].

Finally, the UNDP report produced *"a world social charter"*, which was determined as being a social contract at the global level just as previous social charters emerged at national levels in 1930s and 1940s (the New Deal in the United States and the Beveridge Plan for the welfare state in the United Kingdom) [113, p. 48-50]. The world social charter considered building "a new global civil society, based on the principles of equality of opportunity, rule of law, global democratic governance and a new partnership among all nations and all people" [113, p. 6]. Thus, the charter might be perceived as an attempt to introduce a conceptual model for the world constitution, comparable to the Draft produced by the Chicago Committee in 1948.

Projecting the Paradigm beyond the Cold War

Since the Inquiry the Council on Foreign Relations has been a mastermind projecting the new world order paradigm. After the end of the Cold War, the CFR has launched various programs to engage expertise from around the world in the process of frame working the system of global governance. Thus, it adapted the paradigm to the profound changes within the international environment. Although discussions at the CFR's premises and many of its research efforts remain confidential some of the studies related to global governance have been partially published.

In 2000, the Study Group on New World Order was established under the auspices of the Council on Foreign Relations' David Rockefeller Studies Program. It operated from July 1, 2000 until June 30, 2004. According to the CFR, "The activities carried out under this study group during previous years have supported the development of the project director's [Michael Mandelbaum] recently published book, *The Ideas that Conquered the World: Peace, Democracy, and Free Markets in the Twenty-first Century...* Following this book promotion, the project director will begin research on a new book, building on the first, related to America's role in the world" [268]. Records of the study group meetings were not for attribution.

At U.S. State Department's Open Forum discussion, which took place on September 18, 2002 on the release of the book, Mandelbaum confirmed that its purpose, hence the objectives of the Study Group on New World Order, was to provide an overview and a replacement to the foreign policy framework that existed during the Cold War years and extend it beyond into the 21st century: "We had such a framework during the Cold War years. The Cold War itself provided a context for almost everything that happened in the world, which either derived from or could be related to that great conflict between East and West. Since the collapse of Communism and the end of the Cold War, we've been without such a framework. The purpose of this book is to provide a replacement" [168]. In an effort to creating such a framework the book focused on the so-called "liberal theory of history." This theory involved three ideas synthesized in the Wilson doctrine at the end of World War I, firstly, the primacy of free markets as the economic engine for global economy, secondly, the promotion of democracy as a form of governance, thirdly, peace as a method of organizing international relations [168].

According to Mandelbaum, "The purpose of *The Ideas That Conquered the World* is to provide a context into which to fit the disparate events that preoccupy all of us and that are of professional concern... [such as] issues from terrorism to globalization, from Chinese succession politics to the Argentine economic crisis. The purpose of the book is to provide a framework, an overview, and *the big picture*" [168].

As Fareed Zakaria, editor of Newsweek International observed, "Michael Mandelbaum stepped back from the crises of the moment to look at *the big picture.*"

In the context of Mandelbaum's book, the "big picture" might be identified as being an interconnection between major events of the past, including the French Revolution, World War I, World War II, the Cold War, and the promotion of liberal ideas with the purpose to implement an ancient pattern (paradigm) for the new world order and, thus, establish the world government. In this connection, the liberal ideas played a pivotal role. The term "liberal" was used in the book in its original 19th century's sense, meaning, *"for liberty"* [168]. It is under this pretext of struggling "for liberty" that the model of global governance has been projected. Mandelbaum argues that, "the extent to which they [liberal ideas] were established and did expand, the extent to which they followed *the pattern, as old as human history...* would be the measure, in the twenty first century, of what the end of the Cold War made possible: a new world order" [169, p. 375].

The concept of Mandelbaum's book advocated the world government. It considered that during the past centuries "there was no world government to keep order or to act as a global monetary authority" [169, p. 374]. Therefore, it urged a "global sovereign" to be endorsed in response to challenges and threats to the liberal order: "To perform, effectively and reliably, the tasks of global regulation... would require something that remained beyond the range of even serious discussion at the outset of the twenty first century: *the creation of world government"* [169, p. 395].

Leslie H. Gelb, President on the Council on Foreign Relations, has noted that "The Ideas That Conquered the World" is the most important work thus far on what's new and what's old about the post-Cold War world, about the forces and ideas that will do battle in the future..." According to Walter Russell Mead's Foreign Affairs review, one of the most important questions facing policymakers is whether liberal politics and liberal economics will dominate the twenty-first century. Mandelbaum concludes that the new century will be continuing the advance of liberal order [175]. Taking the above into consideration, it might be assumed that the promotion of the liberal order envisages establishing the world government.

On May 1st, 2008, the CFR launched the International Institutions and Global Governance program (IIGG),[14] a comprehensive five-year program on international institutions and global governance. This program was designed to make the CFR "a center of excellence in thinking about global governance, and a repository of useful knowledge and lessons learned" [285]. According to the concept document of the program, one of its key purposes was to explore the institutional requirements for world order in the twenty-first century. It also aimed to assess existing regional and global governance mechanisms and offer concrete recommendations for U.S. policymakers on specific reforms needed to improve their performance.

The IIGG program proceeded from a consideration that the international order, which was established in the aftermath of World War II, has become obsolete as if it did not keep pace with fundamental changes in the system, including but not limited to globalization: "The point of departure for the program is a recognition that the world of 1945 has evolved dramatically, fundamentally, and irrevocably. New rules and institutions of global governance will need to consider several fundamental changes in world politics" [285].

The program considered several challenges for a new system, including an ongoing shift in global power to non-Western countries due to the change in global distribution of power (political, economic, demographic, technological, and military) driven by the rise of China, India, Brazil, and other nations of "developing world". In addressing these challenges, the CFR`s major assumption has been that the war between great powers "will always be possible in a system of sovereign states" [285]. Thus, the issue of war and peace has remained central to projecting the new world order paradigm into the 21st century.

The IGG program suggested three options for updating the existing framework of global governance, firstly, by means of promoting *an organization with universal membership*, secondly, a regional or sub-regional organization, thirdly, informal and narrower coalition of like-minded countries; or combination of all three. The program acknowledged that, "the creation of new frameworks for global governance will be a defining challenge for the twenty-first century world… The need for a reformed,

---

14 The program drew on the resources of CFR's David Rockefeller Studies Program

robust system of multilateral cooperation has never been more obvious" [285].

The program further maintained that existing multilateral institutions provided insufficient and inadequate foundations for addressing current global threats and opportunities for advancing U.S. national and global interests. Therefore, the CFR sought to identify, firstly, weaknesses in the existing frameworks for multilateral cooperation, secondly, propose specific reforms tailored to new global conditions and, thirdly, promote U.S. global leadership in building the capacities of existing organizations and in sponsoring new, more effective regional and global institutions and partnerships [285].

The IIGG program suggested a new paradigm (pattern) for global governance in the 21st century. The emphasis in elaborating such pattern has been given on the increasing role of *transnational government networks* and a growing importance of coalitions of the "like-minded countries". It considered that, in the previous decades, the process of multilateral cooperation and its law-making tended to be formal, hierarchical and centralized, involving high-level national delegations. On the contrary, in the new century, multilateral cooperation would imply a distributed and networked character through interaction between *transnational networks of government officials* from various state agencies and authorities [285].

Another important change in the political process that shapes establishing "liberal" world order has been the U.S. growing reliance on building coalitions, which consist of like-minded countries (e.g., the Proliferation Security Initiative etc.). Therefore, an ongoing dilemma for the U.S. strategy is to exploit the capabilities of such coalitions. Special emphasis in developing the new concept of global governance has been given to "long-term U.S. national interests" as well as the country's "long-standing tradition of liberal "exceptionalism" [285]. In this context, the IIGG program viewed the United States as "the world's most prominent actor at least until 2050... since it serves as the ultimate custodian and guarantor of world order" [285].

The program declared that, "The United States and its partners have a critical window of opportunity to update the architecture of international cooperation to reflect today's turbulent world. The creation of a more effective framework for global governance will depend on a clear and mutual understanding among the world's major nations of the new dynamics and forces at play in world politics... It will also depend on the willingness of the United States to exercise the same creative, enlightened leadership that it exercised in the mid-twentieth century, when it chose to champion and defend new forms of international cooperation" [285]. The IIGG program also admitted that, despite "tremendous changes in the context, content, and conduct of international relations, there has been no "act of creation" analogous to the burst of international institution building that occurred in the 1940s and early 1950s.

The program considered that, "states disagree over how to reallocate power and authority in existing organizations and bring old rules in line with new realities. The world community thus makes do with creaky institutional machinery that is increasingly obsolete, ineffective, and unrepresentative, and which makes few allowances for the potential role of the private sector and global civil society in shaping and addressing the global agenda. As hard as it is to create rules of global governance, it is even harder to re-write them when institutions already exist" [285]. At the same time, the CFR confirmed that, "Over the past six decades, the United States has benefited tremendously from this architecture, which has helped to legitimate U.S. global leadership... and permit the joint pursuit of shared objectives across a wide range of countries" [285].

Due to the global shift in the international system the IIGG program intended "to assist the architects of U.S. foreign policy and their counterparts in other countries and in regional and global organizations in drafting the blueprints for new structures of international cooperation" [285]. It suggested reforming "bedrock institutions of world order", including the United Nations, regional organizations, and major ad hoc groups: "wherever such reforms are recommended, the Council will include a plausible strategy for winning international backing for this new governance framework" [285].

The principal areas of reforms have been identified as follows: the composition of the Security Council, the G-8, NATO, and the Bretton Woods institutions. Major regional organizations, such as the European Union (EU), the Association of Southeast Asian Nations (ASEAN), the African Union (AU), and the Organization of American States (OAS) have been also in the focus of the CFR`s reforming agenda. Besides, in developing the new model for global governance, the CFR abided by the following principles of the U.S. foreign policy strategy: "*Consistency with U.S. interests and values*, including whether the proposed framework promises to advance U.S. national security and welfare, legitimate U.S. purposes abroad, and resonate with the democratically-expressed will of the American people." In developing the named framework, the program also considered a diverse "array of frameworks - formal and informal, universal and regional, and functional - to address particular tasks." The IIG program maintained that, "In some cases, effective governance may require public-private partnerships involving a range of stakeholders, including private corporations and non-governmental organizations." [285].

It must be noted that, *the "big picture"* issue was also considered in terms of implementing the IIGG program and developing the new model of global governance for the 21st century. In the conditions of changing global environment the program determined *"three big picture issues"* as follows: "the changing nature of sovereignty in an age of globalization; the challenges of accommodating non-state actors in global decision-making; and the preconditions for democratic accountability in multilateral institutions" [285]. Thus, at the modern stage of projecting the new world order paradigm the concept of national sovereignty seems to be incompatible with the U.S. "visionary thinking" on the principles of global governance.

The CFR suggested replacing the nation state doctrine and, instead, applying the emerging doctrine of "contingent sovereignty" as well as other concepts limiting traditional state power: "Where appropriate, the Council will also explore the potential for global governance arrangements that are less state-centric" [285]. For this reason, perhaps, the program advocated multilateralism as a cornerstone for the new international order: "Regardless of whether the administration that takes office… Democratic or Republican, the thrust of U.S. foreign policy is likely to be multilateral to a significant degree" [285].

At present, projecting the new world order paradigm and transforming the post-World War II system of international order requires "achieving consensus at the United Nations (UN) and other inclusive institutions on important political and security challenges [which] will be difficult" [147, p. 1]. Therefore, the IIGG program challenged the UN system and sought to establish alternative mechanisms for global governance and policy coordination. In undertaking this effort, the Strategic Policy Planning Dialogue (SPPD) was launched.

The SPPD constituted of nine participating states such as Australia, Canada, France, Germany, Italy, Japan, South Korea, the United Kingdom, and the United States. In 2008, its policy planning directors gathered in Toronto to launch a series of official dialogues on global security issues. Subsequent meetings of the SPPD took place in Washington and Seoul annually. During the meetings, a range of long-term strategic challenges were discussed "from Afghanistan and North Korea to the security implications of climate change and the role of Russia and China in the international order" [147, p. 17].

The Council emphasized that, "The successful establishment of this framework and its continuity from the Bush administration into the Obama administration demonstrates that it is feasible even with today's emphasis on greater cooperation with emerging powers to launch a new mechanism for coordination among traditional allies" [147, p. 17]. Thus, the concept of a *new mechanism for world governance* was incorporated into the global agenda. It seems to be another important "big picture issue" in addition to those mentioned above.

On January 2013, the CFR released a working paper of the IIGG program entitled "Like-Minded and Capable Democracies: A New Framework for Advancing a Liberal World Order" [147]. The document suggested establishing a "Democracies 10" group, or D10, with the SPPD as a foundation but with the inclusion of the EU. The document stated that, "While other states, particularly in Europe, might arguably meet these criteria, such a framework would need to be narrowly constituted to maximize its effectiveness. The larger the group, the more formal its proceedings and the more difficult and time consuming it could become to forge consensus. The inclusion of the EU provides a way to bring in other capable European states while keeping the size of the group small. The ten participants proposed here would represent a geographically diverse group of like-minded partners that are all members of the G20 and play an influential role on global issues" [147, p. 1].

According to Ash Jain, the author of the document and a former member of the State Department's policy planning staff, founding a group of like-minded democracies is aimed at constituting a powerful and compelling mechanism to advance a liberal international order [147,

p. 1]. The primary mission of this mechanism, as the program document further reads, would be to establish *a new framework for global governance* through strategic cooperation between the D10 member states on global politics and security issues and, thus, to advancing the norms and values of a liberal world order. In pursuing these objectives, the D10 group would perform three primary functions: strategic consultation, policy coordination, and crisis response.

So far, the CFR suggested rearranging the UN-centered framework of world order. It considered the D10 as *a new model of global governance* which would bring together a group of like-minded states that account for more than 60 percent of the world's GDP and more than three-fourths of its military expenditures [147, p. 11]. In contrast to NATO, a new framework has been planned to be "limited to a small number of *strategically like-minded* and highly capable states" [147, p. 1]. The U.S. intended to further promote its "robust global leadership role" by means of implementing "a holistic strategy of engagement" which would "add a new framework aimed at deepening strategic cooperation with like-minded allies to advance the norms and principles of a liberal international system" [147, p. 19].

In creating such new framework for global governance, the CFR perceived that, "The D10 would not require a secretariat, a permanent staff, or an actual physical location. Instead, like the G8 and G20, states could rotate hosting meetings. Moreover, while summit meetings of D10 leaders could be scheduled from time to time if deemed useful, such meetings would not be essential to the success of this framework. The goal would be to avoid an emphasis on high-publicity leaders' summits and joint communiqués, focusing instead on *facilitating behind-the-scenes strategic and policy coordination* across diplomatic channels, with foreign ministers providing overall guidance and direction… While it may seem anachronistic to refocus on engagement with long-standing allies, it is an approach grounded in the reality of today's world – a world that may end up converging around a set of global economic norms, but one that remains stridently divided on many political and security issues that are at the core of a liberal world order… But they are missing a crucial element for success: a collective institutional vehicle for strategic coordination" [147, p. 19].

To institutionalizing the D10 network as a model of global governance, the CFR considered the following challenges to U.S. interests. Firstly, China`s role as a rising global power as well as its regional activities in the South China Sea. Secondly, the future of political Islam in the wake of the events on the Middle East caused by the Arab Spring. Thirdly, the promotion of democracy in "an increasingly difficult Russia" and, finally, the protection of Internet freedom [147, p. 11].

Besides, the Council identified new global threats the U.S. should be countering with and, thus, further promoting the paradigm. It argued that, "Today, the threats to a liberal world order are much more diffuse. They include outlier regimes seeking to acquire nuclear weapons; Islamic extremists attacking the West and western interests while forcing radical ideologies on their own people; dictators trampling on human rights and committing violent atrocities; and great power autocracies seeking to extend spheres of influence... Effective multilateral cooperation remains essential to addressing these challenges. Yet the like-minded lack a collective institutional entity through which they can collaborate in the face of these challenges" [147, p. 8].

In the context of the above, it might be assumed that *Russia and China*, which have been considered by the CFR as being the "great power autocracies", impede the promotion of the "liberal" world order. The CFR argued that, "Russia and China are at odds with the West over fundamental objectives relating to the expansion of a liberal international order... neither Russia nor China is a revisionist power, and neither is seeking to undermine the Westphalian system of state sovereignty or reorganize global institutions in which they have privileged status" [147, p. 3]. According to the CFR, Russia and China "remain fundamentally opposed to the expansion of many of the liberal norms and principles long championed by the West particularly when they require involvement in the internal affairs of other states. Concerned about the legitimacy of their own autocratic regimes, Russia and China have sought to counter what they view as a U.S.-led effort to constrain their influence and reshape the global environment at their expense" [147, p. 3]. Moreover, Russia and China have been viewed as opposing powers in terms of reversing the "democratic" color revolutions in Georgia, Ukraine, and Kyrgyzstan; applying the veto in the UN Security Council vote during the crises in Kosovo, Sudan and Syria and abstaining on a

UN Security Council resolution on Libya; opposing Washington efforts regarding Iran and North Korea, and from Sudan to Zimbabwe to Venezuela [147, p. 3].

The above program document claims that Russia opposes the establishment of foreign military bases in the CSTO member states, including Armenia, Belarus, Kazakhstan, Kyrgyzstan, and Tajikistan. Similarly, China has clearly demonstrated its privileged status in its own regional neighborhood as well as its stance towards U.S. political and military ties to Taiwan, and warning the United States against interfering in disputes with Malaysia, the Philippines, and Vietnam over the rich resources of South China Sea, where Beijing claims "indisputable sovereignty." The document reads that, "First, Russia and China have sought to frustrate U.S. attempts to expand democracy... and criticizing Western attempts to promote democracy from Syria to Belarus.... Second, Russia and China have rejected Western efforts to intervene against governments perpetrating violence against their own civilians... both countries have vociferously defended the sanctity of national sovereignty against any outside interference... Third, Russia and China have opposed Western efforts to isolate outlier regimes that have violated accepted norms of international behavior ... Finally, Russia and China diverge from Western powers in claiming the right to maintain what Russian prime minister Dmitry Medvedev has called "privileged" spheres of influence" [147, p. 3-4].

According to the CFR, Russia and China would find it difficult to create "a more hard-edged anti-Western bloc". Yet, the Council considered that as if "both countries engaged in their own rivalry for geopolitical influence". It also urged that the two powers "*lack a long-term vision of the world*" that could facilitate the emergence of a coalition between them and "a more unified effort in this regard" [147, p. 15]. Furthermore, "China has resisted Russia's attempts, for example, to build the SCO into a quasi-military alliance that could counter NATO, seeing it instead as primarily a vehicle for expanding Chinese economic interests. At the same time, rising democracies eager to maintain their balanced diplomatic approach and cooperative relationships with all major powers will be reluctant to bandwagon against the West in any new political bloc. The BRICS summits, for example, while highlighting statements of shared concerns in protecting sovereignty and noninterference, have been unable to translate these concerns into any common policy framework to address major challenges, such as Iran or Syria" [147, p. 15].

As concerns the perspectives of the so-called "rising democracies" - India, Brazil, South Africa, Turkey, Indonesia, and others - to support the expansion of the liberal world order, the CFR maintained that the West has increasingly appealed for such a support. Yet those countries hesitate "particularly when it requires using coercive diplomacy, economic sanctions or, especially, the use of force" [147, p. 4]. The CFR identified the named countries as if being "caught in between." Therefore, it suggested to implement *"the like-minded alternative" scenario*, that is, to focus on the D10 to achieve the U.S. long-term strategic objectives.

In our view, however, the CFR underestimated the role of the BRICS as well as the all-encompassing partnership and strategic cooperation between Russia and China. As far as fruitful cooperation between the BRICS member states demonstrates, this group of indeed like-minded countries tend to become the key power pillar around which the new world would be evolving. This new scenario would eventually replace what used to be Pax Americana.

The CFR has been also active in developing various concepts urging *the UN reform agenda*. This agenda might be considered as being a part of the overall process of establishing the world government. In 2012, during the 67th UN General Assembly meeting the CFR organized an expert roundup "The United Nations and the Future of Global Governance". Some of the participants argued that, "the world must be governed as a whole" having the UN as "the necessary mediator for this global management." CFR`s experts also stressed that the UN must be adapted to the realities of a rapidly changing world by means of reforming, as if, its "unaccountable and anachronistic Security Council"; an institute of "a papal election" of Secretary General; and various UN agencies of "questionable utility" such as ECOSOC, UNESCO and the Human Rights Council [289].

To undertake the UN reform, *the concept of minilateralism* was proposed instead of multilateralism: "Universal entities like the UN need minilateral groups of key countries that can work together across regional boundaries to achieve results that can be commended to the membership at large. The G-20 is one such minilateralist invention... But G-20 leaders could help the international community bring UN architecture and processes into the twenty-first century. Areas in need of most reform include the outdated membership configuration of the Security Council and the selection process (and empowerment) of the secretary general" [289]. In general, the U.S. concept of "minilateralism" corresponds to the D10 initiative mentioned above as well as other concepts of the type which aim at centralizing the world power by "like-minded countries."

Besides, *the concept of global social contract* was raised during the discussion forum. It was identified as being "a universal social contract, governed by the UN" [289]. As some experts put it, "There is no other way to transform the jungle of states into a society … [therefore] The concept of state building must evolve into society building" [289]. In our view, however, the named concepts of "a universal social contract" as well as "society building" at a global level, generally, underpin the implementation of the world government doctrine. Altogether, they foster the idea of adopting a world constitution as a global policy framework.

As follows from the above, the CFR has strengthened a global networking of "like-minded" transnational elites in their striving towards new world order. The Council explains, "The Council on Foreign Relations is no longer unique in its purpose. A dozen or more research institutions around the world attempt to analyze the changing global scene… with a clear focus on the policy implications for their respective governments. They publish rich and admirable journals that expand the understanding of their populace, just as the lonely voice of Foreign Affairs set out to do 75 years ago. Study and discussion groups among experts and concerned citizens, which the Council pioneered in the 1920s, are now commonplace - in university research institutes, on television and the Internet, forums that the founders could not have begun to contemplate in their dedication to spreading public understanding of complex matters of diplomacy" [98].

Chapter 4
Implementing the Paradigm

Origins of the Paradigm within U.S. Foreign Policy Strategy

Since its inception, the new world order paradigm implies gaining world hegemony. In the 13th century, after plundering the Byzantine Empire during the Four Crusades the West accumulated considerable financial and economic might that predetermined rising of the Anglo-Saxon civilization and its expanding around the globe. Thus, at the end of the 19th century the "Anglo-American establishment" emerged as an influential international subject influencing mainstream international processes and social movements to attain the above-mentioned objective.

During the periods of Pax Britannica and Pax Americana a world-wide network emerged encompassing transnational elites, political and business leaders, mass media and intellectuals advocating the new world order. Carrol Quigley, famous American historian and mentor of U.S. President Bill Clinton, acknowledged: "There does exist and has existed for a generation, an international network which operates, to some extent, in the way the radical right believes the Communists act. In fact, this network, which we may identify as the Round Table Groups, has no aversion to cooperating with the Communists, or any other groups, and frequently does so. I know of the operations of this network because I have studied it for twenty years and was permitted for two years, in the early 1960s, to examine its papers and secret records. I have no aversion to it or to most of its aims and have, for much of my life, been close to it and to many of its instruments. I have objected, both in the past and recently, to a few of its policies, but in general my chief difference of opinion is that it wishes to remain unknown, and I believe its role in history is significant enough to be known" [223, p. 950].

As it has been mentioned, origins of the paradigm can be traced back to Ancient Egypt where the idea of "novus ordo seclorum" emerged.

In the late 18th century this core idea, which had been aimed at gaining world hegemony, was incorporated into U.S. foreign policy concepts and doctrines. Evolution of that idea can be visible in terms of Manifest Destiny, Pax Americana (American Century), American Destiny, American Dream, New American Century, "New American Moment", and other concepts. Altogether they have established ideological and philosophical basis of the U.S. foreign policy strategy.

The doctrinal basis of the U.S. "grand strategy" was laid out in presidential doctrines (starting with the Monroe Doctrine and continuing with the Truman Doctrine, the Reagan, the Bush, the Obama Doctrines, etc.) and principal foreign policy documents (e.g. NSC 20/1, NSC 20/4, NSC-58, NSC-68, etc.). Each doctrine represented a combination of political, ideological, economic and military factors that shaped the strategy at a certain stage of its implementation. Yet, the key strategic objective, that is the establishment of the new world order, remained constant.

The named concepts and foreign policy doctrines have been fostering a subnational elitist ideology which underpins the process of establishing the system of global governance. Being one of the mainstream thoughts within the U.S. political establishment, the new world order paradigm was projected by think tanks and organizations of transnational elites, including the CFR, the Bilderberg Group, the Trilateral Commission, The Club of Rome as well as many other influential world forums and organizations. The U.S. "grand strategy" has been shaped as a means of implementing the paradigm.

The U.S. Department of State interprets the Latin phrase "novus ordo seclorum" as being "a new order of the ages". It heralded the beginning of the "new American era" in 1776 [282, p. 6; 283]. In the late 18th century the U.S. Founding Fathers adopted that idea as a cornerstone for U.S. development. In 1782, the term "novus ordo seclorum" appeared on U.S. Great Seal, and in 1935 it was added to U.S. dollar bill. During the 20th century and onwards both terms - "a new order of the ages" and "a new world order" - have been applied by the U.S. political establishment in terms of realization of the American foreign policy.

In 1940, Theodore Roosevelt appealed to "a new order of the ages" in a program speech. He posited this concept as a "philosophy of orderly government" [236]. In 1971, Richard Nixon stated that, "we must rise to build a new world order in the spheres of political, diplomatic, economic, financial, and monetary activity" [215, p. 1167]. In 1990, George H. W. Bush addressed the U.S. Congress urging, that "a new world order - can emerge" [38]. These political statements, to name but a few, identify the promotion of the new world order paradigm.

Bill Clinton admitted: "From 1945 and the end of the war through 1989 and the end of the cold war, we had a world view, Republican and Democratic presidents alike, from Harry Truman to George Bush... and after 1989 President Bush said, and it`s a phrase that I often use myself, is that we need is a New World Order" [53]. In 2005, George W. Bush confirmed in his inaugural address: "When our Founders declared a new order of the ages ... they were acting on an ancient hope that is meant to be fulfilled." In 2009, Barack H. Obama declared: "In words and deeds, we are showing the world that a new era of engagement has begun" [307].

Since early history of the American republic the U.S. «grand strategy» implies the concept of Manifest Destiny. This concept explains to a considerable extent continuous determination of the United States to lead the world and accept its "burden of responsibility". Yet in the beginning of the 20th century the U.S. President Theodore Roosevelt stated: "If we stand idly by... if we shrink from the hard contests... then the bolder and stronger peoples will pass us by, and will win for themselves the domination of the world" [10, p. 14]. In 2000, Project for the New American Century urged: "If we shrink our responsibilities [of world leadership], we invite challenges to our fundamental interests" [225].

In 2014, U.S. President Barack Obama determined the American exceptionalism as follows: "So the United States is and remains the one indispensable nation. That has been true for the century passed and it will be true for the century to come... The question we face; the question you will face; is not whether America will lead, but how we will lead... America must always lead on the world stage. If we don't, no one else will" [189]. Such an intention to be a world leader has embodied the U.S. foreign policy doctrines, National Security Strategies, and program speeches.

Manifest Destiny stems from the so-called American (liberal) exceptionalism, that is, the idea that the United States had been destined to expand democracy and liberal values around the globe. The CFR, for example, acknowledged "the country's longstanding tradition of liberal `exceptionalism`" [285]. Christopher Layne, American professor and a member of the CFR, emphasized that, "many Americans, particularly among the elites, have embraced the notion of American exceptionalism with such fervor that they can`t discern the world transformation occurring before their eyes" [141]. Thus, the phenomena of Manifest Destiny and American "exceptionalism" have focused the U.S. foreign policy strategy on attaining the world hegemony.

The idea of Manifest Destiny secularized from a Puritan belief in establishing a "City on a Hill." As Dr. Gavin Finley put it, "They sailed from England with a dream. Their Puritan vision was for the New World to be a `city set upon a hill`, and a light to the world. This later overflowed into a sense of `manifest destiny` and a belief that America will lead the world into a new era of peace and security... A vision of a just and pious "Nation under God" still remains in America today" [87].

In its theological meaning Manifest Destiny suggested that the United States had been destined by God to expand "liberty" beyond its borders. In this context, *the concept of liberty* might be considered as being, also, a religious vision of freedom which has been granted to a people by an external control. Indeed, since the times of the first settlers in North America religion has played a key role in American politics. The notions "God Bless America" and "In God We Trust" have become symbolical. As CFR`s member Walter Russel Mead explains, "Religion has always been a major force in U.S. politics, policy, identity, and culture. Religion shapes the nation`s character... and influences the ways Americans respond to events beyond their borders. Religion explains both Americans` sense of themselves as a chosen people and their belief that they have a duty to spread their values throughout the world" [174].

The term "manifest destiny" was coined by New York journalist John L. O'Sullivan in 1845. In an editorial in the *New York Morning News* he attempted to justify America`s claim to new territories: "And that claim is by the right of our manifest destiny to over spread and to possess the whole of the continent which Providence has given us for the development of the great experiment of Liberty and federated self-government entrusted to us. It is right such as that of the tree to the space of air and the earth suitable for the full expansion of its principle and destiny of growth" [28, p. 352]. In 1935, Albert K. Weinberg defined Manifest Destiny as being "in essence the doctrine that one nation has a preeminent social worth, a distinctively lofty mission, and consequently, unique rights in the application of moral principles… [and] a firmly established article of the national creed" [313, p. 53].

According to *Encyclopedia of the New American Nation*, "The idea of manifest destiny is one of the clearest expressions of the belief in the exceptional nature of the United States. Territorial expansion was justified by Americans because they believed theirs was a special nation chosen by Providence to spread its virtues far and wide… American expansion was also thought to be divinely blessed because it would cause the extension of democracy and freedom. Americans argued further that they should expand because they would use the land in ways more beneficial to and desirable for the progress of humankind than could its often sparsely distributed existing inhabitants" [82].

Manifest Destiny is a key concept identifying the process of establishing the new world order. Michael T. Lubragge considered this concept as being "a philosophy that created a nation". He wrote: "Manifest Destiny was the driving force responsible for changing the face of American history… Manifest Destiny existed and still exists as the philosophy that embraces American history as a whole. Manifest Destiny is an intangible ideology that created American history. In its simplest form, Manifest Destiny can be defined as, "A Movement." More specifically, it would be the systematic body of concepts and beliefs that powered American life and American culture… Manifest Destiny became the rallying cry throughout America. The notion of Manifest Destiny was publicized in the papers and was advertised and argued by politicians throughout the nation. The idea of Manifest Destiny Doctrine became the torch, that lit the way for American expansion… Although the movement was named in 1845, the philosophy behind Manifest Destiny always existed throughout American History… Manifest Destiny conveyed the idea that the rightful destiny of the US included imperialistic expansion. This idea certainly contributed to several wars… The notion of Manifest Destiny… exemplified America's ideological need to dominate from pole to pole… To some, the Manifest Destiny Doctrine was based on the idea that America had a divine providence. It had a future that was destined by God to expand its borders, with no limit to area or country" [153].

The roots of many international conflicts can be identified, to a certain extent, in terms of the promotion of Manifest Destiny. As Lubragge wrote: "Manifest Destiny... also created the dark side of American History, non-darker than the plight of the American Indian... negative side was the belief that the white man had the right to destroy anything and anyone... who got in the way. Tracing the path of Manifest Destiny across the West would highlight mass destruction of tribal organizations, confinement of Indians to reservations, and full-blown genocide... In the name of this doctrine, Americans took whatever land they wanted... With this said, America would not be America without the phenomenon of Manifest Destiny. The philosophy that built American history was the rationalization that expansionists everywhere used to justify territorial growth... Americans used Manifest Destiny as their proclamation of superiority and insisted that their conquests merely fulfilled the divine mission that man is impelled by forces beyond human control... Without it, American territory would be as big as the property surrounding its first settlement... Because of the notion of Manifest Destiny, America's drive to explore and conquer new lands will never die" [153].

Manifest Destiny influenced the U.S. evolution into a world power. It has been realized in terms of constant territorial and geopolitical expansion as well as establishing the American "spheres of influence" around the globe. The expansion has been conceptually underpinned yet in the so-called Frontier Thesis presented by historian Frederick Jackson Turner to a special meeting of the American Historical Association at the World's Columbian Exposition on July 12, 1893, in Chicago.

In the *Frontier Thesis* Turner argued that, "The existence of an area of free land, its continuous recession, and the advance of American settlement westward, explain American development... So long as free land exists, the opportunity for a competency exists, and economic power secures political power. But the democracy born of free land, strong in selfishness and individualism, intolerant of administrative experience and education, and pressing individual liberty beyond its proper bounds, has its dangers as well as its benefits" [297]. Turner also urged that the United States no longer had a discernible frontier in its traditional sense of a line of demarcation. Moreover, he justified the American expansion from historical and economic perspectives: "In this advance, the frontier is the outer edge of the wave - the meeting point between savagery and civilization. Much has been written about the frontier from the point of view of border warfare and the chase, but as a field for the serious study of the economist and the historian it has been neglected. The American frontier is sharply distinguished from the European frontier - a fortified boundary line running through dense populations" [297].

Implementation of Manifest Destiny can be visible since Spanish-American War of 1898. In the aftermath of the war, the U.S. military occupation of the Philippines (1899-1902) followed with an estimated 34,000 to 220,000 Filipino casualties. These events were a landmark in terms of U.S. transition towards an imperial power.

On November 21, 1899 at the meeting with the General Missionary Committee of the Methodist Episcopal Church, which took place in the White House, the U.S. President William McKinley told that his inspiration and the decision for military occupation of the Philippines came in a dream from God: "The truth is I didn`t want the Philippines, and when they came to us, as a gift from the gods, I did not know what to do with them… I walked the floor of the White House night after night until midnight; and I am not ashamed to tell you, gentlemen, that I went down on my knees and prayed Almighty God for light and guidance more than one night. And one night late it came to me this way - I don`t know how it was, but it came… that there was nothing left for us to do but to take them all, and to educate the Filipinos, and uplift and civilize and Christianize them… the next morning I sent for the chief engineer of the War Department (our mapmaker), and I told him to put the Philippines on the map of the United States…" [239, p. 17].

On September 16, 1898 Albert J. Beveridge, U.S. Senator from 1899 to 1911, advocated American expansion in his political campaign speech: "And, now, obeying the same voice that Jefferson heard and obeyed, that Jackson heard and obeyed, that Monroe heard and obeyed, that Seward heard and obeyed, that Grant heard and obeyed, that Harrison heard and obeyed, our President today plants the flag over the islands of the seas, outposts of commerce, citadels of national security, and the march of the flag goes on! Distance and oceans are no arguments… The ocean does not separate us from lands of our duty and desire… Cuba not contiguous? Porto Rico not contiguous! Hawaii and the Philippines no contiguous! The oceans make them contiguous. And our navy will make them contiguous…" [19].

Beveridge further urged overseas interventions as if they corresponded to fulfilling the divine Providence and countering tyranny and anarchy: "Think of the thousands of Americans who will pour into Hawaii and Porto Rico... Think of the tens of thousands of Americans who will invade mine and field and forest in the Philippines... Think of the hundreds of thousands of Americans... in Cuba, when a government of law replaces the double reign of anarchy and tyranny! ... Fellow Americans, we are God`s chosen people... We cannot fly from our world duties; it is ours to execute the purpose of a fate that has driven us to be greater than our small intentions. We cannot retreat from any soil where Providence has unfurled our banner; it is ours to save that soil for Liberty and Civilization. For Liberty and Civilization and God`s promise fulfilled, the flag must henceforth be the symbol and the sign to all mankind - the flag!" [19].

On January 9, 1900 in an address entitled "In Support of an American Empire", which was delivered before the U.S. Senate, Beveridge confirmed Manifest Destiny: "Mr. President, this question is deeper than any question of party politics; deeper than any question of the isolated policy of our country even; deeper even than any question of constitutional power. It is elemental. It is racial. God has not been preparing the English-speaking and Teutonic peoples for a thousand years for nothing but vain and idle self-contemplation and self-admiration. No! He has made us the master organizers of the world to establish system where chaos reigns. He has given us the spirit of progress to overwhelm the forces of reaction throughout the earth. He has made us adepts in government that we may administer government among savage and senile peoples. Were it not for such a force as this the world would relapse into barbarism and night. And of all our race He has marked the American people as His chosen nation to finally lead in the regeneration of the world. This is the divine mission of America... We are trustees of the world`s progress, guardians of its righteous peace. The judgment of the Master is upon us: "Ye have been faithful over a few things; I will make you ruler over many things" [342]. In concluding his address before the Senate Beveridge referred to "manifest duty" of the United States [342].

Since then many American politicians and statesmen had been endorsed with a strong belief in Manifest Destiny. For example, the U.S. President George W. Bush has applied that concept to launch military interventions into Afghanistan and Iraq. Four months after the US-led invasion of Iraq in 2003, Bush declared: "I am driven with a mission from God" [162; 129].

At the end of 19th century, *the "open door" concept* was incorporated into the U.S. «grand strategy». Initially, it was developed as a statement of principles suggested by U.S. Secretary of State John Hay in a series of diplomatic notes circulated in 1899-1900 to Great Britain, Germany, France, Italy, Japan, and Russia. The so-called "Open Door Notes" expressed the view that the whole of China should be opened to foreign trade. The notes attempted at establishing American "spheres of influence" in China and sharing equal privileges between the dominant powers: "The notes thus represent imperialist economics in the guise of anticolonialism" [122, p. 32]. According to the U.S. State Department, "the "Open Door" became the official U.S. policy towards the Far East in the first half of the 20th century" [176].

The "open door" has been a key concept within the Wilson doctrine. The doctrine was proclaimed at President Wilson`s address to the U.S. Congress on April 2, 1917. Considering the American "manifest duty" to spread liberty and democracy across the world Wilson declared: "The world must be made safe for democracy. Its peace must be planted upon the tested foundations of political liberty... We are but one of the champions of the rights of mankind. We shall be satisfied when those rights have been made as secure as the faith and the freedom of nations can make them... God helping her [America], she can do no other" [319].

The Wilson Doctrine marked United States` entering World War I. It symbolized the end of the U.S. policy of isolationism, which had been carried out since the adoption of the Monroe doctrine in 1823, and the beginning of the era of globalism. The Wilson doctrine advocated liberalism as if it was a universal value essential for the mankind. It implied opening the entire world to American interests.

Geopolitical Imperatives of the Strategy

The U.S. foreign policy strategy has been a geostrategy in its essence. It constitutes many geopolitical concepts advanced by founding fathers of the Anglo-Saxon geopolitical thought, namely, Alfred T. Mahan, Frederick J. Turner, Halford J. Mackinder, Nicholas J. Spykman. Therefore, most of the U.S. Presidential doctrines implied geopolitical considerations of the named scholars, which required the American power to expand. Starting from the Monroe Doctrine that declared Western hemisphere as being a sphere of American interests and further to the Truman Doctrine, the Bush Doctrine, and beyond the strategy identified the most important regions of the globe as being the U.S. "spheres of vital interests". This fact has been especially obvious during the post-World War II period when the United States sought to establish its dominance in three regions of crucial importance in Eurasia: Western Europe, the Middle East (Persian Gulf) and East Asia. Thus, the composition of liberalism combined with geopolitical requirements of the "sea power" to establish the new world order shaped the U.S. «grand strategy».

The "Anglo-American establishment" has been primarily concerned about the possibility of formation of a consolidated power center in Eurasia, which might challenge its striving towards world hegemony. Such an approach suggested weakening the Eurasian power centers, including Russia, Germany and China to decreasing the force of their geopolitical gravity. Since the end of World War II one of the main geostrategic imperatives of the United States` foreign policy has been preventing the possibility of unification of the Eurasian geopolitical landmass and blocking the emergence of a potential competitor to the United States, whether in the face of a state or a group of states, that might counter Pax Americana. Walter Rostow, Henry Kissinger and Zbigniew Brzezinski, to name but a few, also advocated such a policy about potential geopolitical rivals emerging in Eurasia [237, 136; 36].

Yet in the late 19th century American Rear Admiral Alfred T. Mahan designed *the principle of "Anaconda"*. This principle was applied regarding northerners in the civil war in the United States (1861-1865). It suggested depleting the power of a potential enemy by blocking its territory from the sea and coastlines. On a global scale, Mahan`s theory considered suffocating continental masses in the rings of "anaconda" and deriving them from a possibility to controlling the coastal areas and blocking their outlets to the sea territories. Realization of this principle can be visible at the Cold War stage, particularly, in terms of the U.S. "strategy of containment". It had been used to isolate the Soviet Union and seal it off by means of creating military and political blocs such as NATO, CENTO, ANZUS and ASEAN. Although the geopolitical concept of Mahan was not officially recognized by Washington as being the cornerstone of its geostrategy, his ideas influenced Henry Lodge, an American Senator and historian, as well as U.S. Presidents William McKinley and Theodore Roosevelt. The latter considered himself being a disciple of Mahan, especially, as concerns the idea of creating a "big navy" [18].

In the beginning of the 20th century *the Heartland theory* by Halford J. Mackinder explained the importance of Eurasia as being a center-stage in terms of reaching world hegemony. In 1904, the British Royal Geographical Society published Mackinder`s notorious article entitled "The Geographical Pivot of History", in which he formulated that theory. Mackinder identified the northern-central core of Eurasia as the "pivot region", and viewed this geopolitical space as a potential seat for a world empire (although the term "Heartland" was not yet applied) [164; 309].

In 1919, Mackinder presented one of his major works entitled "Democratic Ideals and Reality: A Study in the Politics of Reconstruction." Mackinder suggested a famous geopolitical dictum that determined Eurasia as being a World Island crucial for attaining world dominance: "Who rules East Europe commands the Heartland; Who rules the Heartland commands the World Island; Who rules the World Island commands the World" [163]. This postulate was composed on the eve of the Paris Peace conference. Thus, the idea of creating a strip of buffer states between Russia and Germany emerged. It intended to preventing synergy and mutual strengthening of the two countries after World War I.

In 1938, Nicholas J. Spykman determined pivotal role of geographic factors in terms of foreign policy planning: "Because the geographic characteristics of states are relatively unchanging and unchangeable, the geographic demands of those states will remain the same for centuries…" [259, p. 29]. Considering the geographic location of the United States, he proposed to "develop a *grand strategy* for both war and peace based on the implications of its geographic location in the world" [258, p. 8].

Important enough, Spykman viewed national spirit as being one of the crucial factors of a state power along with the size of a territory; population; the amount of raw materials; economic and technological development; the stability of political system; military power; and the power and military might of its potential enemies [258]. Indeed, the collapse of Soviet Union demonstrated that undermining state`s national spirit along with other power pillars might eventually cause weakening and disintegration of a country.

In 1944, Spykman elaborated the concept of *Rimland* as if it was a key to global control: "Who controls the rimland rules Eurasia; who rules Eurasia controls the destinies of the world" [260, p. 43]. Rimland included Western Europe, the Middle East, southwest Asia, China and the Far East. These regions, if combined with the offshore islands of Britain and Japan, wielded both land and sea power [248]. Thus, in our view, Spykman extended the "anaconda" principle further to the countries of Africa and Asia, including India and China.

Besides, he advanced the *concept of prevention* of the rise of competitors to the United States: "our constant concern in peace time must be to see that no nation or alliance of nations is allowed to emerge as a dominating power in either of the two regions of the Old World from which our security could be threatened" [260, p. 34]. The principle of prevention underpinned the U.S. Cold War "strategy of containment". For this reason, perhaps, Spykman has been known as the "godfather of containment", described in this manner by, among others, George F. Kennan [131].

According to Spykman, the biggest threat to U.S. security "has been the possibility that the rimland regions of the Eurasian land mass would be dominated by a single power" [260, p. 44]. He further claimed that the United States was "obliged to safeguard her position by making certain that no overwhelming power is allowed to build itself up in these areas [the Rimland regions of Europe; the Middle East, and the Far East]" [260, p. 51]. Therefore, blocking U.S. geopolitical competitors and preventing the rise of the new rivals has been the requirement of the process of establishing Pax Americana. This fundamental geopolitical approach has been unchanged until the present.

Spykman determined what might be categorized today as being the phenomenon of *geopolitical gravity* which evolves around the great powers. He argued that, "The realm of international politics is like a field of forces comparable to a magnetic field. At any given moment, there are certain large powers which operate in that field as poles. A shift in the relative strength of the poles or the emergence of new poles will change the field and shift the lines of force" [261, p. 395].

Spykman also considered shifts in the post-war balance of power. Regarding Russia he stated that, "Russian state from the Urals to the North Sea can be no significant improvement over a German state from the North Sea to the Urals" [258, p. 460]. As concerns the Asia-Pacific region, he believed that China would emerge as a "continental power of huge dimensions," and this will force the United States into an alliance with Japan to preserve the Asian balance of power [258, p. 469]. Notably, the Obama doctrine aimed at "re-balancing" China and, in doing so, establishing closer alliance with Japan.

From a geopolitical perspective, Russia has been a key to establishing the new world order. It represents one of the world's largest centers of geopolitical gravity, which is cable to consolidate an independent power center in Eurasia, engage other influential Eurasian players into the Eurasian integration process and, thus, neutralize the very idea of gaining the global control over the mankind. The Ex-Soviet KGB Foreign Intelligence Service Chief Leonid Shebarshin explained that the very existence of Russia with her enormous power capacity in Eurasia makes impossible neither establishing any kind of power monopoly in the world, be it military, political or economic, nor dominance of any coalition [253]. Therefore, he concluded that the West needs only one thing from Russia - it is Russia that does not exist [252]. Yet, another notorious saying holds that to dominate the world one needs to control Russia [46].

Indeed, Russia's overwhelming territory in Eurasia, her vast natural resources and spiritual power explain to a considerable extent why most of the attempts at gaining world hegemony had been aimed at conquering the country, especially, those undertaken during the 20th century. Such attempts included Napoleon's Russia campaign in 1812; World War I prompted by Western intention to split and divide the Russian Empire; Bolshevik's coup d'etat in 1917 aiming at inciting the world revolution in the long run; Hitler's pursuit of "new order" and wakening World War II; the Cold War against the Soviet Union and the U.S. attempt at imposing a unipolar world in its aftermath [201]. Therefore, Russia has been a central figure in terms of the grand geopolitical chess play. Nikolai Starikov compared Russia with a "White King". He urged that those who used to play black would never retreat provided they "mate" Russia [262, p. 14].

From a theological perspective, Russia possesses the orthodox legacy of the Byzantine Empire. According to Christian tradition, it might be associated with the "Katehon" which has been destined to generate a divine force to counter the emergence of a secular world order and, eventually, deter the "world evil" in the face of the Antichrist. In this connection, perhaps, Brzezinski identified Russian Orthodox creed as an "enemy". In 1999, he declared in L'viv (Ukraine) that under U.S. hegemony the new world order must be built against Russia, at the expense of Russia, and on the remnants of Russia.

Kerry R. Bolton explained: "Russia has never fitted well into the plans of those seeking to impose a uniform system upon humanity. Russia has remained untamed in terms of the sophisticated Western liberals seeking to establish a unipolar global world, as were Afrikaners, Iraqis, Iranians, Serbs, et al. The difference is that Russians continue to constitute a significant opposition, which therefore requires subverting" [23].

Being the main geopolitical impediment to the new world order, Russia has been constantly perceived as if it was a threat to "free" and "liberal" world. It has been considered as such being a monarchy, the Russian Empire, and then during the Bolsheviks' rule under the communist doctrine. The same effort to "demonizing" Russia followed regarding Stalin's Soviet Union. In the early 1980s the Reagan administration determined the USSR as "evil empire".

Although "New Russia" emerged as a follow up of market reforms under the guidance of American advisors in the 1990s, it was still considered as being the "under-democratized country". In 2006, the CFR produced a special report entitled, "Russia's Wrong Direction: What the United States Can and Should do" [242]. So far, even after the end of the Cold War the U.S. political establishment continued to viewing Russia as a "geopolitical rival" (e.g., in the words by U.S. Presidential candidate Mitt Romney, and others). The Soviet communism was considered equal to Hitler's Nazism. Finally, the Obama administration compared a perceived Russian "threat" with that of the Islamic State movement (IS, formerly ISIS/ISIL). Obviously, "the globalist hopes for Russia were yet again dashed with the advent of Putin" [23].

As follows from the above, it is primarily Russia's deterring power as well as her uniting capabilities (i.e. geopolitical gravity) that have been challenging the implementation of the new world order paradigm. Historically, therefore, the global elites intended to divide the country into several parts and, thus, establish control over her territories. That is why the U.S. strategy regarding Russia incorporated the well-known principle "divide and rule". Hence, several attempts to divide the country followed. These attempts coincided with waging World War I, World War II, and the Cold War.

The first attempt at splitting Russia into several newly independent states (protectorates) was undertaken in the wake of World War I as, for example, the "Official American Commentary on the Fourteen Points" testifies. This document was developed by The Inquiry [214; 192]. Yet, in September 1918 Edward House, the then head of The Inquiry, considered dividing Russia into four independent territories [250, p. 348; 144, p. 219].

House suggested to establish Provisional Governments in the former Russian Empire and develop policy approaches regarding Siberia, the European Russia, the "Mohameddan Russia" (Central Asia), and The Caucasus. He wrote: "As for Great Russia and Siberia, the Peace Conference might well send a message asking for the creation of a government sufficiently representative to speak for these territories... The essence of the Russian problem then in the immediate future would seem to be: 1. The recognition of Provisional Governments. 2. Assistance extended to and through these Governments. The Caucasus should probably be treated as part of the problem of the Turkish Empire. No information exists justifying an opinion on the proper policy regarding Mohammedan Russia - that is, briefly, Central Asia. It may well be that some power will have to be given a limited mandate to act as protector. In any case the treaties of Brest-Litovsk and Bucharest must be cancelled as palpably fraudulent... the Peace Conference will have a clean slate on which to *write a policy for all the Russian peoples*" [250].

As it was mentioned before, members of The Inquiry comprised the U.S. delegation at the Paris Peace Conference in 1919. The Inquiry developed Wilson`s Fourteen Points as the basis for negotiating the Treaty of Versailles. Section XIV (Article 116) of the Treaty of Versailles was entitled "Russia and Russian States". It read that, "Germany acknowledges and agrees to respect as permanent and inalienable the independence of all the territories which were part of the former Russian Empire on August 1, 1914" [296].

The second attempt to weaken and divide Russia was undertaken during World War II. Yet on June 24, 1941 U.S. President H. Truman declared: "If we see that Germany is winning we ought to help Russia and if Russia is winning we ought to help Germany, and that way let them kill as many as possible..." [6]. Subsequently, the plans of war against the USSR were elaborated already in spring of 1945.

Winston Churchill's War Cabinet drew up a plan to invade the Soviet Union within days of the defeat of Germany in 1945. The plan, codenamed "Operation Unthinkable", recommended re-arming of 100,000 German troops to help British and U.S. armies fight their erstwhile wartime ally; and was presented to Churchill on May 22, 1945. The "Operation Unthinkable", however, was rejected after a secret meeting between Field Marshall Bernard Montgomery and U.S. General Dwight Eisenhower. This was mainly due to the success of the Soviet Army during the Berlin Operation and the fall of the Third Reich, which demonstrated Soviet military capability to potentially invade Europe up to the Atlantic (in case the USSR was attacked by its former war-time allies).

After the U.S. atomic bombing of Japan in August 1945 the United States elaborated numerous plans of nuclear strikes against the USSR. Such plans existed already in September 1945. However, the then quantity of the American nuclear weapons was insufficient to cover the vast territory of the Soviet Union.

The above geopolitical analysis of waging World War I and World War II demonstrates that the process of implementation of the new world order paradigm suggests *clashing the Eurasian power centers* with each other to weakening their geopolitical gravity and, thus, preventing the rise of a competitor in Eurasia powerful enough to impede the named process. In line with such policy Germany and Russia were undermined twice in the 20th century: "clashing of two continental geopolitical powers of Eurasia in the first half of the 20th century (Russia/USSR and Germany) occurred twice (in 1914 and 1941) during realization of the Anglo-American geopolitical concepts. And both times, which is also generally known, the main financial and political prize belonged to Washington. The third time the USA received that prize in 1991 after the end of the Cold War, which they conducted jointly with Western Europe, having incorporated the neutralized power center of Germany into the latter" [138, p. 58]. At the modern stage, another attempt at clashing European power centers followed during the U.S.-supported civil war in Ukraine in 2014. Under the guise of the crisis the United States have been increasing NATO`s military presence in Eastern Europe and the Baltic States.

The third attempt to divide and control Russia was undertaken during the Cold War. Since its inception the U.S. "strategy of containment" sought to "foster the seeds of destruction within the Soviet system" [185]. The strategic objective was subverting the Soviet system from inside and imposing the new world order in the long run by means of incorporating Russia into "liberal" system of global governance. Genesis of such policy can be seen in psychological and information warfare against the USSR. As Gregory Mitrovich demonstrated drawing on recently declassified U.S. documents, through the aggressive use of psychological warfare, the U.S. officials sought to provoke political crisis among key Soviet leaders, incite nationalist tensions within the USSR, and to trigger unrest across Eastern Europe [179]. This eventually occurred with Gorbachev`s rising to power.

Since 1948 the Harvard Project on the Soviet social system was carried out by the Center for Russian Studies at Harvard University. According to Vladislav Shved, it was "one of the most ambitious political-sociological studies conducted on Soviet society" [255]. The Harvard Project continued after the collapse of the Soviet Union or, in other words, splitting the latter. In August 1997, the Harvard Institute informed about inception of a New Harvard Project [284]. This endeavor has been also known as the Harvard-Houston project. At the end of the 1980s the Soviet intelligence gathered information confirming that the ultimate goal of the project was splitting Russia and establishing control over its resources [88, p. 3-4; 254].

It is believed that Brzezinski has been among the members of the project. Therefore, perhaps, Brzezinski`s program book "The Grand Chessboard" considered Russia as if it was a "black hole" in Eurasia after the collapse of the Soviet Union. The book advocated the idea of decentralizing (dividing) the country and making it a "free confederation" consisting of three parts: the European part of Russia, the Siberian Republic and the Far Eastern Republic [36, p. 241].

So far, the U.S. "grand strategy" has a permanent objective of splitting Russia`s largest territory in Eurasia. In this context it must be noted, that yet in 1950 Russian philosopher Ivan Il`yn warned that the attempts by the West to split and divide Russia might cause another World War due to the inevitable clash, if so, between world powers over the vast Russian resources and their consequent struggle to dominate in Eurasia [117].

The possibility of *erupting World War III* must be considered in terms of the current U.S. attempt to isolating and undermining Russia and, thus, transforming the international system. J. Baratta emphasized as if the predictability of World War III. He stressed that, "The prediction that mankind faced a choice between either world government or world war has not been realized to date…" [11; p. 330].

Baratta noted that, "… when open East-West war broke out in Korea, many in the world federalist movement felt that the long-predicted World War III was at hand…" [11; p. 330]. He concluded that, "If [next] world war comes, the survivors will grimly acknowledge the truth of the [Chicago] committee`s prediction" [11; p. 330]. So far, there might be the interconnection between realization of the world government doctrine and possible eruption of another world war. Indeed, it is assumed that the new world order had been planned in the remote past to bring about somewhat (i.e. "order"; government) *emerging out of chaos* (Ordo Ab Chao – lat.).

After the end of the Cold War the U.S. strategy focused on preventing the reemergence of a rival to Pax Americana or an alliance having the power capacity comparable to that of the former Soviet Union. In 1992, the draft Defense Planning Guidance (DPG) or, the so-called Wolfowitz Doctrine, was prepared by the then members of the U.S. Department of Defense, namely, I. Lewis Libby, Paul Wolfowitz, and Zalmay Khalilzad under the auspices of the Defense Secretary Dick Cheney. The discussion of the document engaged influential figures within the neoconservative circles of the U.S. government, including Richard Perle, Albert Wohlstetter (former mentor to Perle and Wolfowitz), and Andrew Marshall, head of the Pentagon`s Office of Net Assessment.

The Defense Planning Guidance, which was partially declassified but had its original draft redacted, argued for prevention of "the reemergence of a new rival". The document read: "Our first objective is to prevent the reemergence of a new rival. This is a dominant consideration underlying the new regional defense strategy and requires that we endeavor to prevent any hostile power from dominating a region whose resources would, under consolidated control, be sufficient to generate global power. These regions include Western Europe, East Asia, the territory of the former Soviet Union, and Southwest Asia. There are three additional aspects to this objective: First the United States must show the leadership necessary to establish and protect a new order that holds the promise of convincing potential competitors that they need not aspire to a greater role or pursue a more aggressive posture to protect their legitimate interests. Second, in the non-defense areas, we must account sufficiently for the interests of the advanced industrial nations to discourage them from challenging our leadership or seeking to overturn the established political and economic order. Finally, we must maintain the mechanisms for deterring potential competitors from even aspiring to a larger regional or global role" [73].

Although the Defense Planning Guidance as a whole was rejected by the White House, many of the ideas contained in the draft were widely regarded as an early formulation of the neoconservatives' post-Cold War global agenda. Their ideas served as an overall framework for implementing the U.S. «grand strategy». Thus, *the concept of preemptive warfare* evolved into President George W. Bush's 2002 National Security Strategy [73].

Members of the PNAC, who had advocated U.S. invasion of Iraq, were installed at important positions at the Bush Administration. They considered the role of the Defence Planning Guidance in shaping the U.S. foreign policy strategy as follows: "The Defense Policy Guidance (DPG) drafted in the early months of 1992 provided a blueprint for maintaining U.S. preeminence, precluding the rise of a great power rival, and shaping the international security order in line with American principles and interests. Leaked before it had been formally approved, the document was criticized as an effort by "cold warriors" to keep defense spending high and cuts in forces small despite the collapse of the Soviet Union; not surprisingly, it was subsequently buried by the new administration.

Although the experience of the past eight years has modified our understanding of military requirements for carrying out such a strategy, the basic tenets of the DPG, in our judgment, remain sound" [225].

Since the beginning of the 21st century the U.S. intention to preserve its world`s dominating position persisted. The concept of preventing the rise of geopolitical competitors who might challenge Pax Americana has remained unchanged. PNAC confirmed, "At present the United States faces no global rival. America's *grand strategy* should aim to preserve and extend this advantageous position as far into the future as possible" [225].

"Big Picture"

Despite several attempts aimed at gaining world or regional dominance had been undertaken by the empires of the past, it was only since plundering the Byzantine Empire during the Four Crusades in the 13th century when the West accumulated considerable financial and economic might that underpinned the promotion of the "liberal" model of world order[15]. As it was demonstrated before, at the end of the 19th century the so-called "Anglo-American establishment" emerged as an influential international subject engaged in projecting the paradigm [222]. During the periods of Pax Britannica and Pax Americana this subject expanded its influence around the globe.

The Anglo-American establishment supported both Bismarck`s and Hitler`s rising to power [262]. The strategic purpose was to direct the

---

15 As a result of World War I and, especially, in the wake of World War II the Anglo-Saxon civilization consolidated its overwhelming financial, economic and military might. In 1922, the gold belonging to the former Russian Empire, which had totaled to more than 1500 tons in 1914, was transferred from Russia, mainly, to England. It is noteworthy in this context, that the wealth of the Byzantine Empire which had been plundered by the West during the Four Crusades could hardly be estimated at all. In the aftermath of World War II the United States accumulated almost two thirds of the world gold reserves. It had been transferred to the U.S.` Fort Knox during the war according to military contracts as well as in the framework of the American Lend-Lease Program. Furthermore, as a result of the Cold War and market reforms carried out in the post-communist Russia under the guidance of American advisors, the gold reserves of the country decreased, dramatically, to 240 tons in 1991, compared to 2300 tons in 1990.

Second Reich and then the Third Reich against Russia. According to John Loftus and Mark Aarons, the Nazis could have remained a small political party in a weak and unarmed Germany, which lacked financial resources, provided that powerful investments of foreign capital had been arranged from overseas to support Hitler`s rising to power. This became possible because of an alliance that was established between the American oil concerns and the companies belonging to Saudi Arabia.

By the 1930s, the first Saudi king Ibn Saud and famous British diplomat and adventurers Jack Philby had organized financial support of the Nazi rising to political power in Germany. Particularly, the above authors claim that G.H. Walker & Co., American investment banking and brokerage firm, "was one of Hitler's most powerful financial supporters in the United States. The relationship went all the way back to 1924, when Fritz Thyssen, the German industrialist, was financing Hitler's infant Nazi party... there were American contributors as well" [152]. It must be also emphasized that G.H. Walker & Co. was founded in 1900 by George Herbert Walker, grandfather and great-grandfather of U.S. Presidents George Herbert Walker Bush and George Walker Bush [91].

Hitler`s rising to power was financed by a combination of major German, British, and American banks and industrial companies. This fact has been well documented, for instance, in the book that Fritz Thyssen wrote himself entitled "I Paid Hitler" (1941) [293]. Allen Dulles (the then corporate lawyer for Sullivan & Cromwell and the future head of U.S. intelligence) as well as Averill Harriman (another important figure in the U.S. establishment and head of W. A. Harriman & Company) were linked with Thyssen. Since 1924 they invested in Germany through the Union Banking Corporation.

The U.S. industrial monopolies and concerns which possessed, perhaps, the best technologies of that time, had been active especially in those industrial areas of Kaiser`s Germany that eventually influenced on the growth of Nazi`s military machine. As a result, before World War II broke out Nazi Germany had launched the production of new types of weaponry, including tanks and airplanes. Moreover, the U.S. industrial concerns continued oil supplies for the needs of the Nazi military machine until the second front, that is, the Western front of the European theatre of World War II was open in 1943. The apogee of the Western policies that were leading towards the clash between the Third

Reich and the USSR was the so-called appeasement of Hitler. The policy of appeasement was reflected in the decisions taken in Munich in September 1938.

The process of implementation of the new world order paradigm demonstrates the "big picture" of history. It has a wide historical framework spanning thousands of years. Therefore, the "big picture" can be perceived only from a panoramic perspective. In this regard, Natalia A. Narochnizkaya, famous Russian scholar and politician, explains that exploring historical and political processes from a panoramic perspective, that is, in terms of continuous world development is important to understand that every major geopolitical shift in history had been caused by deeper trends than conventional interstate rivalry [181; p. 14].

Vasily V. Bartold (1869-1930), Russian academician, considered that the main task of a historian is to construct the overall [big] picture of facts in their causal connection" [12, p. 6]. Lenin, the leader of the Bolshevik Revolution in Russia, argued: "While trying to solve specific questions, but leaving broad questions unsolved, we will drop across those broad questions again and again" [257]. This saying might be paraphrased as follows: either we perceive the "big picture" or we will always come across its details.

The "big picture", so far, can be figuratively compared to a historical puzzle which consists of major historical events, including wars, revolutions, etc. Establishing cause and effect connection between these developments might add to understanding their driving forces as well as fundamental trends within world political and historical processes both in the past and at present. The "big picture", so far, is a necessary prerequisite to viewing human history as an integrated whole rather than observing its fragmented parts.

Since the Treaty of Westphalia of 1648 the promotion of sub-national system of global governance challenged the principle of state sovereignty. The Revolution of 1789 subverted the monarchy in France and created preconditions for carrying out Napoleon's military campaign into Russia in 1812. It also laid the ground for eruption of the European Revolutions of 1848. The Revolution of 1917 overthrew the monarchy in Russia and aimed at igniting the "world revolution". Finally, the "colour revolutions" and the Arab Spring inspired social unrests globally, thus, bringing about *the global revolution*.

In the "big picture`s" view, World War I led to the collapse of the Russian Empire and other European empires. As it has been demonstrated, in the aftermath of the war the United States undertook the first attempt at establishing a subnational authority in the face of League of Nations. Despite that first global institution failed to exist the United States followed the same sub-national agenda in the wake of World War II.

After World War II the U.S. carried out a historic breakthrough towards gaining world hegemony: "Global in scale and in its repercussions, World War II created a new world at home and abroad" [276]. In its aftermath, the U.S. emerged as a global power having overwhelming economic, financial, and military might. American economic power totaled to more than 50 per cent of world`s GNP. The U.S. collected 70 per cent of world`s gold reserves.

The end of World War II and, as a result, the power vacuum in the world arena shaped an unprecedented opportunity for the United States to use its power capabilities and, particularly, economic and military might for the attainment of strategic objectives. The main objective was to become a 'preponderant power', and, thus, establish the new world order. The Soviet Union and the expanding influence of communism (e.g. in Eastern and Central Europe, China, Italy, France) represented the major obstacle for the U.S. hegemony. Therefore, the United States directed all its resources to "contain" communism and subvert America`s only geopolitical competitor.

To gain public and Congressional support for the implementation of the strategy, American policy makers used the challenge from communism. In this regard, the factor of "Soviet threat" created an ideological basis for starting the strategy, and getting funds for its realization. The "Soviet threat" justified "crusade" against the Soviet Union, and allowed to implement economic diplomacy, which included programmes of economic and military aid. This was initially reflected in the Truman Doctrine and the Marshall Plan.

By means of the economic diplomacy the U.S. transferred the excessive dollar reserves and imports to Western Europe. As a result, Western European countries benefited economically, but were engaged into the "open door" system. Washington, in its turn, abolished influence of communists in European politics, and created a cohesive and powerful

Western bloc to counter the USSR. Therefore, in taking these actions Pax Americana emerged.

In the context of the above it must be noted that it was Stalin who, indeed, foiled the establishment of the world government (i.e. the new world order) twice in the first half of the 20th century. Firstly, he undermined Trozky`s plans to trigger a "world revolution" in the wake of Bolshevik`s Revolution in Russia (new evidence demonstrates that such plans constituted a sub-national agenda) [251]. Secondly, Stalin subverted realization of the world government doctrine in the aftermath of World War II. Bolton confirms: "it was the USSR under Stalin that thwarted a world order, without which we would have very possibly been subjugated by a global central authority immediately following World War II" [23]. Therefore, the West proclaimed the "iron curtain" and adopted the "strategy of containment" to isolate the USSR, its economic development and ideological influence. Thus, the Cold War burst out.

So far, the implementation of the new world order paradigm represents a constant warfare and a chain of interconnected events. It incorporates, among other, the Four Crusades, World War I, World War II, the Cold War, the War on Terror, and the ongoing Cyber War. These events have been the important milestones and consistent stages forging ahead the system of global governance. The periods of transformation of the international system, which followed in their aftermaths, provided wide strategic opportunities to "shaping events". As Samuel P. Huntington acknowledged, "The West won the world not by the superiority of its ideas or values or religion [...] but rather by its superiority in applying organized violence. Westerners often forget this fact; non-Westerners never do" [114].

William J. Astore, a retired lieutenant colonel (USAF), argues that, "If one quality characterizes our wars today, it`s their endurance. They never seem to end. Though war itself may not be an American inevitability, these days many factors combine to make constant war an American near certainty" [8]. This consideration also reminds a well-known thesis advanced by Carl von Clausewitz, German general and military theorist, who stressed that, "War is the continuation of Politik by other means".

It is obvious, therefore, that there is a correlation between the implementation of the new world order paradigm and carrying out the U.S. foreign policy strategy. This becomes visible through the prism of the following *mechanism of strategy`s realization.* The mechanism consists of three components: informational, economic, military and political. It extrapolates the American might around the world to establish global control over international development.

The mechanism has been driven by the factor of threat. It implies the so-called "image of enemy" which has been stimulating the defense of U.S. national interests, mobilizing public opinion in accordance with U.S. foreign policy objectives and, thus, favoring American geopolitical expansion. Such threats were identified in the face of the Soviet communism (the "Soviet threat"), then the Islamic radical movements (the "terror threat") and, finally, by non-state actors and "empowered individuals" (the Cyber threat). In confronting these threats, the U.S. power has been extrapolated around the globe.

In this context, World War I, World War II, the Cold War, the War on Terror, and the Cyber War have been strategically linked. The *process of constant warfare* has been transforming the international system into the system of global governance. Thus, proclamation of the "iron curtain" and "evil empire" in the face of the Soviet Union directed the process of creation of Pax Americana into the course of the Cold War. Declaring "rogue states", "axis of evil" and the "terror threat" established a strategic framework for carrying out the "War on Terror". After the 9/11 the neocons managed to transform the stated factor of threat and applied it to the Islamic terror. This has been crucial for maintaining the strategic continuity of the U.S. foreign policy strategy and enhancing the U.S. geopolitical expansion within the Greater Middle East region.

As follows from the above, the "big picture" or, in other words, the process of the implementation of the new world order paradigm has been *constant warfare* promoting the geopolitical expansion by the West. This process had been triggering crises to transforming the world system. Carrying out the warfare (i.e. the issue of war and peace) has been inherent in the paradigm. Indeed, the existing systems of international relations such as the Westphalian system of 1648, the Versailles and Washington sub-system of 1918, the Yalta and Potsdam sub-system of 1945 and, currently, the post-Cold war system have been transformed because of the named wars.

The above mechanism of U.S. foreign policy strategy`s realization has been shaping dimensions of the new world order, namely, informational, economic, military and political. *The informational dimension* implies the promotion of liberal and secular values by means of global media, applying modern communication technologies, including information and psychological warfare's technologies, propagating the "mass culture", etc. Besides, this dimension has been underpinned by various social and grassroots movements, including "human rights" movements, the LGBT movement, etc. Many of them penetrate traditional cultures, especially, within multiethnic and multinational states. This process of informational penetration of "the global values" can be figuratively compared to an Opium War in which "liberal" information and "freedoms", if the being considered as a policy of all-permissiveness, play a key role in eroding the national sovereignty doctrine.

The economic dimension of the new world order emerged because of creation of the "open-door" world of free trade and global market economy. It was ensured, primarily, by the might of U.S. dollar in the global finances. It has comprised transnational corporations (TNCs) [305], multilateral organizations and institutions such as GATT (WTO), the International Monetary Fund (IMF), the World Bank, Bank for International Settlements (BIS), the International Bank of Reconstruction and Development (IBRD), forums (The World Economic Forum, G8/7, G20), etc. These institutions have shifted economic processes to a sub-national level and fostered global market economy with a dominant role of the United States.

The military and political dimension emerged in the framework of NATO enlargement, creating the Anti-Missile infrastructure in Eurasia, and expanding U.S. military bases in key geopolitical and strategic regions in the world. For example, the Middle East was defined as being the U.S. "sphere of vital interests" yet in the aftermath of World War II. Since the "greater Middle East" concept was adopted it comprised the Arab world, Iran, Israel, and Turkey plus the Horn of Africa, the Trans Caucasus, western Central Asia, and South Asia [130]. The "Greater Middle East" includes the energy-rich Caspian Basin countries with the Arabian Peninsula, Iran, Turkey, and Iraq. It produces a "strategic energy ellipse" with over 70 percent of the world's proven oil reserves.

Despite Western assurances of not expanding NATO eastwards in the 1990-s, 10 countries of Central and Eastern Europe as well as the Baltic States have joined the Alliance since 1999. Croatia and Albania have applied for membership in 2008. Finally, on April 2, 2012 NATO Secretary General declared that the Alliance is moving towards a profound transformation. Its new strategic purpose was identified as to become a central pole in the American-dominated security network spanning globally. This demonstrated NATO`s bid for global military control. The political spectrum of the military dimension might be identified in terms of numerous statements on the new world order agenda made by politicians and intellectuals both in the United States and around the globe.

Besides, the military and political dimension can be visible in terms of U.S. military interventions around the globe. During the Cold War the interventions included, first, American military engagement in regional conflicts in Korea, Vietnam and, indirectly, in providing weaponry to Mujahideen extremists in Afghanistan fighting against the USSR, etc. After the collapse of the Soviet Union the U.S.-led NATO military interventions were carried out in former Yugoslavia, Iraq, Afghanistan, and Libya. Washington also supported realization of "colour revolutions" and "regime change" scenarios on the post-Soviet space, particularly, in Georgia, Kyrgyzstan, Ukraine and, concurrently, in the Middle East during the Arab Spring as well as in terms of social unrests in many countries.

In "big picture`s" view, so far, the evolution of the United States from an isolated state in the 18th century towards the only superpower at the end of the 20th century and a mastermind for the new world order has passed through the strategic stages of isolationism (starting from the Monroe Doctrine in 1823 until the beginning of World War I), globalism (starting from the Truman Doctrine in 1947 until the end of the Cold War) and hegemonism (starting from the Bush Doctrine in 2002). Throughout these periods the American power has laid informational, economic, and military and political foundations (dimensions) of the new world order. Thus, the inception of the Truman Doctrine marked the beginning of the Cold War. The Bush Doctrine was an important milestone in terms of launching the War on Terror. The Obama Doctrine signalized the beginning of the Cyber War. However, following the world financial and economic crisis of 2008 Pax Americana entered the stage of decline.

It appeared, however, that the U.S. political establishment did not accept the very fact that the American hegemony has waned. Many of its political figures still advocate active global engagement of the United States. Thus, on September 8, 2010 the then-U.S. Secretary of State Hillary Clinton claimed at CFR`s premises that "a new American moment" began: "a moment when our global leadership is essential, even if we must often lead in new ways… For the United States, global leadership is both a responsibility and an unparalleled opportunity" [1]. Clinton urged that, "The United States can, must, and will lead in this new century" [1]. She further maintained that the Obama Administration has started to build "a new global architecture" [1].

On October 12, 2011 Hillary Clinton addressed the audience at White House with a speech "American Global Leadership at the Center for American Progress" [54]. In the introductory note to the speech a moderator stressed that, "Secretary Clinton reasserted and redefined Americans' - America's global leadership and secured it for the 21st century. She saw sustained American leadership as a key to advancing our interest and values and creating a world where more people can live up to their God-given potential, what we at home still call the American dream" [54].

The U.S. continuous intention to lead the world in the 21st century follows in line with Manifest Destiny. In a State of the Union address, delivered on January 24, 2012, U.S. President Obama stressed that, "Anyone who tells you that America is in decline or that our influence has waned, doesn't know what they're talking about" [191]. The U.S. National Security Strategy 2015 suggested "to seize the opportunities of a still new century." It argued that, "Any successful strategy to ensure the safety of the American people and advance our national security interests must begin with an undeniable truth - America must lead. Strong and sustained American leadership is essential to a rules-based international order that promotes global security and prosperity as well as the dignity and human rights of all peoples. The question is never whether America should lead, but how we lead" [182].

Despite such a rhetoric, it is obvious that Pax Americana has come to its end. The new geopolitical center of gravity, the Eurasian Alliance, has been emerging in the framework of the Eurasian integration process. It ushers the world into a new era – the era of united Eurasia.

Chapter 5
Creating New System of International Order

Cold War Stage

The first attempt at alternating the Anglo-Saxons' model of global governance and creating new system of international order instead of Pax Americana was undertaken by the Soviet Union. Since late 1940s Stalin promoted an idea to create economic and political alliance consisting of non-Western governments. The strategic goal of the USSR was to establish an international trade and economic organization as a viable alternative to the Bretton Woods institutions dominated by the U.S.

The *Stalin plan* implied that the new alliance (organization) would use regional currencies in developing mutual trade and, thus, decrease the dominant role of the U.S. dollar. This idea stemmed from Stalin's last book entitled, *Economic Problems of Socialism in the USSR* (1952). The Soviet leader urged establishing the economic and political block of like-minded countries during his meetings with the Ambassadors of China, India, Argentina, Finland, Ethiopia. He promoted the same idea in several interviews with the press [9]. Notably, since 2008 the United States focused on similar idea of creating a free trade zone in the Asia-Pacific region, yet, the negotiations on the Trans-Pacific Partnership have been kept secret (initially, the TPP project was launched in 2003 by New Zealand, Singapore, and Chile).

In 1951, Ministry of Foreign Affairs of the USSR and Ministry of External Affairs worked out proposals to promote equal international and regional trade by means of creation of a free trade zone in the Asia-Pacific region. Negotiations on this issue were planned to be held in the middle of March-beginning of April 1952 at the international conference to be summoned in Moscow. As a result, on April 3rd-12th, 1952, the International Economic Conference took place in Moscow.

Drawing on new evidences from Russian and Western archives, Russian scholar Mikhail Lipkin testifies that, "The story of the Moscow International Economic Conference of April 1952 is wrongly forgotten. Meanwhile, despite the pressure and information boycott from the West, it managed to get together 450 representatives from 47 countries of the world, including the well-known capitalist countries. In the West, this event was blackmailed as one more chain in soviet propaganda. In the East, an attitude was much more complex" [148]. Thus, Moscow International Economic Conference was the first undertaking by Stalin`s Soviet Union to create a new free trade system with a key role of national currencies.

Many of the participating countries at the Moscow conference supported the Soviet initiative. As Lipkin further argues, "In addition to the plans of opening an iron curtain, materials of the conference demonstrate that the idea of peaceful coexistence and economic cooperation was at first voiced by Stalin - not by Khrushchev. And one of the results of the Conference was a decision to establish the Committee for the promotion of international trade. Its major aim was to prepare a secondary International Conference on Trade, to promote the results of the first one and to transfer a Resolution of the Moscow Conference to the UN General Assembly calling for the convocation of the Intergovernmental Conference on the promotion of the world trade. But suddenly [due to Stalin`s death] the USSR has lost its interest..." [148].

The Intergovernmental Conference was, indeed, planned as a follow up of the Moscow conference with a purpose to establish an international organization as an alternative to the Bretton Woods institutions. However, the Stalin plan was not realized at that time. As historian and publicist Nikolay Dobryukha urges, the Kremlin archives contain documented evidence proving that Stalin was poisoned [245; 321].

In the framework of realization of the Stalin plan the Soviet Union also initiated organizing the Conference of the United Nations Economic Commission for Asia and the Far East (ECAFE). The ECAFE was established in 1947 in Shanghai, China, with the purpose to encourage economic cooperation among its member states and assist in post-war economic reconstruction. Its first conference was held in the Philippines`` capital Manila from 23 February until 4 March 1953.

The Conference was supported by China, India, Iran, Mongolia, Indonesia, Burma and Northern Vietnam. The USSR suggested creating a system of interstate reciprocal payments in national currencies and withdrawing restrictions in mutual trade. One of the results of the conference was resuming bilateral trading contacts between China and Japan. The first post-war trade agreement between the two countries was signed in June 1952 in Beijing. Then it was regularly extended.

The second attempt at alternating the Bretton Woods system was initiated by the developing countries in the UN. In 1974, they put forward a set of proposals entitled, *New International Economic Order*. It was meant to be a revision of the economic foundations of the international system in view of growing disparities in the world trade, aggravating "North-South" issues, and considering the needs of the "Third World" countries.

On 1 May 1974, the United Nations' General Assembly Resolution 3201 (S-VI) adopted a Declaration on the Establishment of a New International Economic Order which, among other, called for "the reformed international monetary system" [227]. Besides, on 12 December 1974 a Programme of Action and a Charter of Economic Rights and Duties of States were adopted. These documents, along with the Declaration, suggested restructuring world's economy to ensure balanced development and equal participation by developing countries in the international trade system.

Firstly, the Declaration appealed to creation of the new international economic order based on the principles of national sovereignty and interdependence: "our [developing countries'] united determination to work urgently for the Establishment of a New International Economic Order based on equity, sovereign equality, interdependence, common interest and cooperation among all States, irrespective of their economic and social systems which shall correct inequalities and redress existing injustices, make it possible to eliminate the widening gap between the developed and the developing countries and ensure steadily accelerating economic and social development and peace and justice for present and future generations...» [227].

Secondly, the Declaration demonstrated the existing disparities in international development and the growing gap between rich and poor countries: "The benefits of technological progress are not shared equitably by all members of the international community. The developing countries, which constitute 70 per cent of the world's population, account for only 30 per cent of the world's income. It has proved impossible to achieve an even and balanced development of the international community under the existing international economic order. The gap between the developed and the developing countries continues to widen in a system which was established at a time when most of the developing countries did not even exist as independent States and which perpetuates inequality" [227].

Thirdly, considering a series of grave crises that the world economy experienced since 1970 and had severe repercussions on the developing countries due to their vulnerability to external economic impulses, the Declaration stated: "The present international economic order is in direct conflict with current developments in international political and economic relations" [227]. The Declaration considered that, "irreversible changes in the relationship of forces in the world necessitate the active, full and equal participation of the developing countries in the formulation and application of all decisions that concern the international community" [227].

Finally, the Declaration stressed interdependence of all members of the international community and called for equal and just cooperation between them: "a close interrelationship between the prosperity of the developed countries and the growth and development of the developing countries, and that the prosperity of the international community as a whole depends upon the prosperity of its constituent parts. International co-operation for development is the shared goal and common duty of all countries. Thus, the political, economic and social well-being of present and future generations depends more than ever on co-operation between all the members of the international community based on sovereign equality and the removal of the disequilibrium that exists between them" [227].

In constructing the new system of international order the Declaration suggested implementing the following *principles*: the principle of abiding by the international law; respecting of sovereignty, equality and territorial integrity of all states; non-interference in the internal affairs of other states; equal participation of all countries in solving world economic problems in the common interest of all countries; the right of every country to adopt the economic and social system that it deems the most appropriate for its own development.

The Declaration stated full permanent sovereignty of every state over its natural resources and all economic activities, including the right to nationalization or transfer of ownership to its peoples as well as "promoting the transfer of technology" to the developing countries. The document also requested "regulation and supervision of the activities of transnational corporations by taking measures in the interest of the national economies of the countries where such transnational corporations operate based on the full sovereignty of those countries" [227].

Moreover, the developing countries suggested establishing "just and equitable relationship between the prices of raw materials, primary commodities, manufactured and semi-manufactured goods exported by developing countries and the prices of raw materials, primary commodities, manufactures, capital goods and equipment imported by them with the aim of bringing about sustained improvement in their unsatisfactory terms of trade and the expansion of the world economy" [227]. Obviously, the implementation of the above principles and regulations, if realized, might undermine the overwhelming influence of Western corporations in the international trade.

On 2-3 April 1979, the international expert meeting took place in Vienna to discuss the subject of "The New International Economic Order - Philosophical and Socio-cultural Implications." The meeting was organized by the International Progress Organization. It was held under the auspices of the President of the Republic of Austria.

The expert meeting was attended by representatives of the United Nations, the United Nations Educational, Scientific and Cultural Organization (UNESCO), the Arab League's Educational, Scientific and Cultural Organization (ALECSO), the United Nations Industrial Development Organization (UNIDO), the Organization of the Petroleum Exporting Countries (OPEC), the Independent Commission on International Development Issues (ICIDI), and by a number of experts from the Arab region, Europe, Africa, and Asia.

Because of the meeting a Communique was adopted stating that, "The principles as expressed in the resolution of the United Nations concerning the establishment of a New International Economic Order should not only be discussed in an abstract and formal manner. Those principles should be transformed into rules of international law. Special emphasis should be given to the recognition of the fundamental social rights - as part of the system of human rights -, not only on a national level, but as guiding rule of the transnational responsibility of states" [120]

In the 1970s and 1980s, the above-mentioned principles were not supported by the West. The Soviet Union, in its turn, was distracted from their implementation with the advent of Gorbachev and the beginning of "perestroika". However, those principles are important to consider in terms of promoting the *concept of the new international order* at present.

Modern Stage

The *third attempt* at reshaping the U.S.-dominated system of global governance has been undertaken at the apogee of the Cold War, and is still under way. This attempt has both economic and geopolitical perspectives. From an economic perspective, it has been aimed at, firstly, switching the oil trade into a new currency, instead of the U.S. dollar (i.e. euro, "golden dinar", "sucre", etc.) and, secondly, introducing a new world's reserve currency. Notably, yet in 1989 Alfred Herrhausen[16], Chairman of Deutsche Bank, suggested to establish a currency union between Germany and the Soviet Union.

From a geopolitical perspective, the process of the Eurasian integration has been waning Pax Americana. This process evolved from the idea of creating Eurasian Union of States, which was first suggested by the President of Kazakhstan Nursultan Nazarbaev. It was then conceptualized, among other, within the articles written by the Presidents of Kazakhstan, Russia, and Belarus in 2011 [158; 183; 216]. Finally, the BRICS and the Eurasian Economic Union emerged as being the geopolitical pillars for the new international order. It must be noted, that yet in 1998 the Russian Prime Minister Yevgeny Primakov put forward a concept of creating a strategic triangular, that is, the geopolitical pivot Moscow-Delhi-Beijing. This model might be considered as being a prototype of the BRICS.

---

16 Alfred Herrhausen was assassinated in Frankfurt on November 30, 1989.

In 2000, the ex-President of Iraq Saddam Hussein declared an intention to switch Iraqi`s oil export into euro: "In October 2000 Iraq insisted upon dumping the US Dollar - `the currency of the enemy` - for the more multilateral euro" [83]. Indonesia, Malaysia, and several other countries in Asia might have followed the suit: "Pertamina, Indonesia`s state oil company, dropped a bombshell recently. It`s considering dropping the U.S. dollar for the euro in its oil and gas trades. Other Asian countries may not be far behind any move in Indonesia to dump the dollar. The reasons for this are economic and political, and they could trigger a realignment that undermines U.S. bond and stock markets over time" [15].

Therefore, "Operation Iraqi Freedom" (Second Persian Gulf War) started in 2003 under the false pretext of Iraq`s "imminent threat" - as if it possessed weapons of mass destruction. Charles Recknagel emphasized: "Saddam sealed his fate when he decided to switch to the euro in late 2000 (and later converted his $10 billion reserve fund at the U.N. to euros) - at that point, another manufactured Gulf War become inevitable under Bush II... *Big Picture Perspective:* Everything else aside from the reserve currency and the Saudi/Iran oil issues (i.e. domestic political issues and international criticism) is peripheral and of marginal consequence to this [Bush] administration. Further, the dollar-euro threat is powerful enough that they will rather risk much of the economic backlash in the short-term to stave off the long-term dollar crash of an OPEC transaction standard change from dollars to euros. *All of this fits into the broader Great Game that encompasses Russia, India, China*" [226].

In 2002, Colonel Mummar Ghadaffi, the President of Libya, challenged Pax Americana. Ghaddafi initiated an idea of refusing from dollar and euro and introducing a new regional currency, namely, "golden dinar". He also suggested uniting the African states into a federation allegedly called "The United Africa" with 200 million of population and its own army [24]. Obviously, Mummar Ghaddafi intended to repeat the plans of General De Gaulle. He urged refusing from dollar and start using gold coins instead, that is, resetting the "golden standard". This would lead to the inevitable collapse of the Federal Reserve System.

Russian businessman and social figure German Sterligov commented: "In 2002 Malaysian Prime Minister Muhammad together with Mummar Ghaddafi proposed initiative to launch golden dinar. At the beginning this idea was approved by Iraq, Sudan and Brunei, next year Indonesia, United Arabian Emirates and other countries joined to it… There were some sessions of Ministers of Finance of these countries and the project about refusing from dollar and euro and using golden dinar began to be transferred to life. There was a pilot project where golden coins were already minted and it began to be used in Malaysia, Indonesia and Iran…" [265].

Sterligov further stressed: "psychological effect of idea by Ghaddafi (one of main Muslim leaders) to start using golden dinar was stunning… A substantial number of countries would follow him. This project was prepared very actively for many years, Ghaddafi made African countries to unite together into powerful state and to start use golden coins. Egypt was ready to take part in it, that`s why revolutions started there and CIA interfered to break the plans about getting out from international bank system… He [Ghaddafi] applied to China, India and Russia - these countries who may be ready to start using gold coins. Especially China, which announced about using of golden yuan soon… If Mummar Ghaddafi found time to launch golden coins before the war started, not only Muslim countries would follow him. There would be many countries, including maybe even Germany" [265].

In 2010, the *Ghaddafi initiative* of using one golden currency and uniting Africa`s countries into a powerful federative state was approved by many Arabian countries and almost all African countries except for Republic of South Africa and the head of League of Arabian states. The initiative was negatively estimated by the West. According to former President of France Sarkozy (2007-2012), Libyan people caused a threat for financial security of mankind [265]. Therefore, in 2011 the U.S.-led NATO intervention into Libya followed. The military operation "Odyssey Dawn" brought about the "regime change" and plunged that country into the abyss of chaos.

Clive P. Maund explains the U.S. tactics about any country which tries to refuse from American dollar: "Any state that moves to opt out of using the dollar as a medium of exchange is dealt with, forcibly if deemed necessary. The tactics are threefold – economic blockade (sanctions), the funding of an internal revolution, perhaps assisted by US special forces, and an outright military invasion, or perhaps a combination of the three. This is what happened in Iraq and Libya, both of which planned to trade their oil in currencies other than the dollar. Perhaps the greatest irony of all is that the world's savings, via the Treasury market, are used to fund the vast US military machine with its hundreds of bases spread across the world which forcibly makes sure they stay yoked to this system" [172].

In 2005, Hugo Chavez, the ex-President of Venezuela, in his address to the 60th UN General Assembly Meeting highlighted the importance of the 1974 UN Declaration and suggested to implement its principles into global agenda. Thus, Chavez declared: "What we need now more than ever… is a new international order…. we need to retake ideas that were left on the road such as the proposal approved at this Assembly in 1974 regarding a New Economic International Order. Article 2 of that text confirms the right of states to nationalizing the property and natural resources that belonged to foreign investors. It also proposed to create cartels of raw material producers. In the Resolution 3021, May, 1974, the Assembly expressed its will to work with utmost urgency in the creation of a New Economic International Order based on… the equity, sovereign equality, interdependence, common interest and cooperation among all states regardless of their economic and social systems, correcting the inequalities and repairing the injustices among developed and developing countries, thus assuring present and future generations, peace, justice and a social and economic development that grows at a sustainable rate. The main goal of the New Economic International Order was *to modify the old economic order conceived at Breton Woods*… But it is also urgent a new international political order" [45].

Besides, Venezuela under the regime of Hugo Chavez began to carry out barter deals with neighboring countries to exchanging oil for goods and, thus, excluding the U.S. dollars from the transactions. Moreover, to countering the American initiative of a free economic zone of the Americas, the Bolivarian Alliance for the Americas (ALBA) was established in 2004 at the initiative of Fidel Castro and Hugo Chavez [166]. The member states of ALBA are Bolivia, Chile, Cuba, Ecuador, Nicaragua, Dominica, Antigua and Barbuda, Saint Vincent and the Grenadines. The purpose of the ALBA has been promoting trade and cooperation between its members as well as introducing a single currency for all countries of ALBA.

Thus, Chavez[17] put forward the idea of creating a supranational currency for South America to create the Sucre zone (ALBA) as being the analogue of the euro area (EU). The new currency, namely, "sucre" (SUCRE - Sistema Unico de Compensación Regional - One regional system of settlements) was planned to be introduced from January 2010. Initially, "the sucre" was intended to be a virtual currency in non-cash transactions between participants of ALBA and, consequently, serving as a single currency drawing from the experience of euro as the EU`s single currency[18].

At present, Russia`s and China`s efforts to refuse from dollar`s hegemony represent a threat to Pax Americana: "Enter Russia (and China), the biggest threat yet to dollar dominance. These large powerful neighbors have entered into various major currency and trade agreements in the recent past that do not involve the dollar, and therefore pose a serious threat to the dollar's reserve currency status that left unchallenged would bring it to an end" [172].

The End of Pax Americana

On November 18, 1957, Mao Zedong declared at the Moscow Meeting of Communist and Workers` Parties: "It is my opinion that the international situation has now reached a new turning point. There are two winds in the world today, the East Wind and the West Wind. There is a Chinese saying, "Either the East Wind prevails over the West Wind or the West Wind prevails over the East Wind." I believe it is characteristic of the situation today that the East Wind is prevailing over the West Wind. The forces of socialism have become overwhelmingly superior to the forces of imperialism" [200]. This statement has proved to being true until now.

---

17 After his sudden illness Hugo Chavez declared: "I am far from delusions of persecution, but the fact remains - the murder as a way of removing unwanted politicians has been always practiced by the Empire (USA). I have no proof, and yet it is obvious that there is something strange with progressive politicians in Latin America."

18 The policy of abandoning the dollar in trade policies of ALBA member states and introducing "sucre" was interrupted due to the sudden illness and, consequently, passing away of Hugo Chavez in 2013.

The implementation of the new world order paradigm by the Anglo-American establishment, from one side, and promotion of the Eurasian integration process by the BRICS group, from the other side, suggest two opposing scenarios for future world development. Clive P. Maund confirms: "We are witness to the greatest struggle of our age – the battle to maintain global dollar hegemony, and with it US economic, military and political dominance of the entire planet – and this struggle is now coming to a head" [172].

Russia and China, being the driving forces of the Eurasian integration process, resist implementation of the new world order paradigm. They have jointly challenged the dominance of the U.S. dollar: "Russia, in alliance with China, is threatening to bring an end to the dollar as the global reserve currency, which would mean the end of the American empire" [172]. Therefore, "colour revolution" efforts have been undertaken in Russia and China (e.g. events in Hong Kong in 2014; street protests in Russia at "Bolotnaya square" in 2011-2013). Nikolai Patrushev, Russian Security Council Secretary, and a former Director of the Russian FSB, the successor organization to the KGB, confirmed that the United States try to split the Muslim world and, simultaneously, weaken Russia and China [306].

The Eurasian integration threatens the promotion of the Anglo-Saxon "liberal" matrix of world order. Therefore, the United States` foreign policy strategy has been focused on impeding that process. On December 6, 2012 former U.S. Secretary of State Hillary Clinton acknowledged that the United States "…. are trying to figure out effective ways to slow down or prevent it [the Eurasian Union]" [27].

Elena Ponomareva, professor of Comparative Politics at the Moscow State Institute of International Relations, explained the negative attitude of the United States` political establishment about creation of the Eurasian Union. In an article, *The Eurasian Project: A Threat to The New World Order*, Ponomareva put forward the following question: "But why does the West perceive Putin`s recent Eurasian integration proposal as a threat? Why are we seeing Cold War-style headlines crop up in Western media? The reality of the matter is that - if implemented - the plan would pose a geopolitical challenge to the new world order under the dominance of NATO, the IMF, the EU and the US. Russia`s increasing assertiveness suggests that it is ready to start building an inclusive alliance based on principles which provide a *viable alternative to Atlantism* and neoliberalism" [203].

Therefore, several "regime change" scenarios had been supported by Washington in Eurasia, such as the so-called "tulip revolution" in Kyrgyzstan in 2005, "rose revolution" in Georgia in 2003, "orange revolution" in Ukraine in 2005 which evolved into the humanitarian crisis in that country after the consequent "regime change", the so-called "Euromaidan" of 2014. According to U.S. Department of State, the United States invested 5 billion dollars in the promotion of democracy in Ukraine. Washington also suggested investing up to 10 million USD for establishing of a nationalistic political party in Ukraine based on the so-called "Right sector" extremists` group that advocated fascist ideology. In his interview with CNN U.S. President Obama admitted that the United States "had brokered a deal to transition power in Ukraine" [338].

In the above context, the title of Reuters` article, *Ukraine Holds Key to Putin`s Dream of a New Union*, appears symbolical. Notably, the article identified Ukraine as being "the cradle of Russian civilization" [105]. The second "regime change" in Ukraine happened just on the eve of signing of the Treaty on Creation of the Eurasian Economic Community on May 29, 2014. Therefore, the civil war in Ukraine can be explained in a wider geo-political, geo-economic and historical context of establishing the new world order - as an integral part of a global scenario leading the mankind towards what might, indeed, result in "clash of civilizations".

According to Clive P.Maund, "The US searched for a geographic doorway through which to attack Russia – the North and east routes don't work because they are either ocean or China, countries like Poland in Europe wouldn't do either, because they are firmly in the Western camp now, but the Ukraine was perfect for the job because of its being a large country on the SW flank of Russia that is torn in two directions, having old loyalties and blood ties to Russia, and aspirations to a closer union with Europe – the perfect place to foment a pro-Western revolution and perhaps a civil war that would draw Russia in and could then be used as an excuse to implement sanctions. That is exactly what has happened" [172].

Russia and China appear key competitors of the United States in Eurasia. Yet in 1959 the term *"Sino-Soviet threat"* was used. The report,

The Mid-Century Challenge to U.S. Foreign Policy, argued: "What we can know for certain is that we shall be much preoccupied over the coming decade with the relations between the two great communist powers [USSR and China]. For the present we must avoid, wherever possible, courses of action which seem to drive China closer to the Soviets; and be prepared for new situations as relations between these two massive powers undergo change. We must, above all, give sympathetic and imaginative consideration to the problems and the hopes of the countries around the rim of Asia" [233, p. 36].

Already at the beginning of the 21ˢᵗ century China has been viewed as American potential rival [225, p. 4]. The neoconservative elites acknowledged the geopolitical power shift from the West to the East. PNAC`s report admitted: "During the Cold War, the main venue of superpower rivalry, the strategic "center of gravity," was in Europe... and with Europe now generally at peace, the new strategic center of concern appears to be shifting to East Asia" [225, p. 3]. Such an approach regarding China has become dominant in subsequent Presidential administrations in the United States as well as among the grand strategists. The Obama administration`s "Asia pivot" focused on deterring the growing influence of China. Thus, it might be perceived as being an updated version of the *"strategy of containment"* but regarding China.

In an article tellingly entitled, *The End of Pax Americana: How Western Decline Became Inevitable,* Christopher Layne argues: "The United States and China now are competing for supremacy in East and Southeast Asia... and many in the American foreign-policy establishment view China`s quest for regional hegemony as a threat that must be resisted. This contest for regional dominance... possibly could lead to war. In geopolitics, two great powers cannot simultaneously be hegemonic in the same region. Unless one of them abandons its aspirations, there is a high probability of hostilities. Flashpoints that could spark a Sino-American conflict include the unstable Korean Peninsula; the disputed status of Taiwan; competition for control of oil and other natural resources; and the burgeoning naval rivalry between the two powers" [141].

Wang Jisi, Director of the Center for International and Strategic Studies and Dean of the School of International Studies at Peking University, and Kenneth Lieberthal, who has been national-security director for Asia during the Clinton administration, argue that strategic distrust between the United States and China has grown to a worrisome degree. They emphasize that, `mutual cooperation` that both countries admit as being important has different perspectives if being viewed from Washington and Beijing. The Chinese side believes to replace the United States as the world's predominant power. Washington, instead, is working out strategic instruments to prevent such a rise of China. Yet, many in the U.S. government consider that China views bilateral relations with the United States in terms of a zero-sum game in its striving towards world hegemony [146].

The U.S. government attempted at engaging China into its grand strategy. Washington suggested Beijing to "sharing the burden of world leadership" with the United States. Thus, yet in 2009 the Obama administration suggested China to establish G2 or a "Group of Two" formula. Simultaneously, the U.S. establishment attempted to "reload" its relations with Russia.

However, after the U.S. failure to engage China into a G2 strategic format, and the end of "perezagruzka" with Russia, a new multilateral framework was required to advance the liberal order. In the conditions of declining American hegemony and lack of resources for unilateral deployment of power around the world Washington focused on defining various formats of interaction, primarily, with its traditional democratic allies.

In doing so, the United States incepted the mentioned *Trans-Pacific Partnership* (TPP) program to re-balance the Asia-Pacific region. The TPP suggests establishing an international trade and economic organization which would join 12 countries in Asia-Pacific region, including Japan [7]. The TPP is an allegedly free-trade area stretching from Chile to Japan that could encompass 800 million people and 40 percent of world`s GDP - but would exclude China. China, from its side, has been countering the U.S. "pivot" by means of promoting its "Asia-Pacific dream". As Xi Jinping declared: "We are duty-bound to create and fulfill an Asia-Pacific dream for our people" [68; 47].

In 2009, the United States attempted to launch its own version of the New Silk Road. It was elaborated by the influential think tank - Center for Strategic and International Studies. Strategic aims of the project were weakening Russia`s geopolitical influence in Central Asia, deterring the growth of China and blocking the emergence of alternative geopolitical configurations and alliances in the region capable to challenge Pax Americana. Moreover, the American version of the New Silk Road corresponded to Washington's strategic concept of Greater Central Asia which, in its turn, has been connected with the concept of Greater Middle East. Realization of both concepts aimed at consolidating American geopolitical and geoeconomic control in Eurasia.

Since the U.S. foreign policy strategy has been focused on preventing the rise of global competitors as well as alliances between power centers in Eurasia, one might assume that the U.S. would further attempt at impeding the conduct of the Eurasian integration process, having the BRICS as its driving force, by means of constructing "sanitary cordons" between power centers in Eurasia, first, China, Russia and Germany. In view of the pending withdrawal of U.S. troops from Afghanistan as well as current escalation of violence in Iraq and the entire Middle East, securing geopolitical interests of both China and Russia along the New Silk Road and creating the economic belt of prosperity, as it was suggested by the President of China Xi Jinping, seems especially important to ensure international security. Therefore, destiny of the Eurasian integration and, more specifically, realization of both Russian Dream and Chinese Dream have been closely connected. In this regard, joint efforts of the two countries and their allies, particularly in terms of crises resolution in Ukraine and Syria, are important to deter the expansion of global chaos from the Middle East across Eurasia.

It cannot be excluded, therefore, that the U.S. would further attempt at realizing its subversive policy regarding the Eurasian integration process by triggering centrifugal forces and igniting the existing sources of violence in the region, exploiting ethnic and territorial controversies in Eastern Europe (Ukraine), Central Asia and Asia-Pacific regions. Thus, the Arab spring-alike scenarios, growth of drug trafficking and increase in international terror activities might follow the U.S. "on the ground" military presence in the Middle East – after the withdrawal from Afghanistan.

Potential expansion of the global chaos through the Middle East further into Eurasia requires deepening joint strategic and security cooperation, first, between Russia, China, India, Pakistan and Iran. In this regard, regional organizations such as the Shanghai Cooperation

Organization (the SCO) and the Collective Security Treaty Organization (the CSTO) may play a key role in securing the Eurasian integration process. Currently, the effective cooperation between Russia and China might serve as a prerequisite for establishing a Eurasian-centered global partnership network to balance the world system.

Despite the U.S. continuous attempts at creating the new world order, supporting "freedom fighters" in Ukraine, Syria and other regional flashpoints, introducing shortsighted sanctions against Russia, deterring China`s growing influence in the Asia-Pacific region, it also appeared that the global leader eventually overstrained itself. Washington`s influence in Eurasia and around the globe obviously decreases. Thus, at the modern stage Pax Americana has been coming to its end.

The signs of declining American hegemony are the U.S. "bubble economy", weakening positions of the U.S. dollar in world`s mutual payments and in the global financial and economic system, the biggest external debt of the United States which exceeded 17 trillion USD in 2014, etc. Clive P. Maund put it more bluntly: "Notwithstanding its undeniably great accomplishments of the past hundred years, the relationship of the United States to the rest of the world is parasitic. This is because it creates money and debt instruments out of nothing, requiring virtually no effort, which it then swaps for goods and services with other countries. Because the US dollar is the global reserve currency, it can rack up astronomic deficits that would be untenable for any other country. US debts are now at such levels that if the US dollar loses its reserve currency status, the United States economy will implode and it will quickly be reduced to the status of a banana republic – hence the sense of urgency in the face of growing threats" [172].

According to the report by U.S. National Intelligence Council, "with the rapid rise of other countries, the "unipolar moment" is over and Pax Americana - the era of American ascendancy in international politics that began in 1945 - is fast winding down" [92]. The end of American hegemony has been acknowledged by many authors and experts around the world, including Kissinger and Brzezinski. Persuasive arguments on that regard have been presented, for example, in the mentioned article by Christopher Layne [140; 141].

Layne emphasized: "The Euro-Atlantic world had a long run of global dominance, but it is coming to an end... That era of American dominance is drawing to a close as the country`s relative power declines, along with its ability to manage global economics and security" [140]. He further argued that the collapse of the Soviet Union "filled the American consciousness with powerful notions of national exceptionalism and the infinite unipolar moment of everlasting U.S. hegemony. But most discerning Americans know that history never ends, that change is always inevitable, that nations and civilizations rise and fall, that *no era can last forever*" [140].

The end of Pax Americana creates global whirlpool and a geopolitical "black hole" in the world arena causing multiple international security dilemmas. This has become obvious, especially in view of American geopolitical and strategic failures in Afghanistan and the Middle East causing the expansion of the global chaos. On March 18, 2015 President Obama claimed the rise of the Islamic State movement as if it was "unintended consequence" of the U.S. invasion in Iraq in 2003. In particular, he confirmed that, "Isis is a direct outgrowth of al-Qaeda in Iraq that grew out of our invasion. Which is an example of unintended consequences" [212]. Notably, former U.S. Secretary of Defense Robert Gates admitted, that "the greatest national security threat to this country [the USA] at this point is the two square miles that encompasses the Capitol building and the White House" [90].

In our view, the stated "unintended consequences" correspond to carrying out the so-called *managed chaos doctrine*. It might be assumed that Washington declared the War on Terror in pursuit of somewhat that had been identified as being "order out of chaos" ("Order Ab Chao" – lat.). Indeed, the U.S. global engagement from a position of military strength provoked imbalances in the international system, radicalization of Islam, especially, in the regions of American direct military interventions, globalization of terrorism, escalation of inter-ethnic and inter-religious controversies, rising of separatists` and nationalists` movements, etc.

As a result of applying "hard power" tools, supporting "freedom fighters" who then, in many cases, tend to be identified by Washington as "terrorists", inspiring "color revolutions" and ignoring the international law the so-called "three evil forces" of separatism, extremism and terrorism were triggered bringing about the expansion of global chaos. The latter, if not deterred, might cause dramatic consequences for the whole mankind. As Brzezinski urged: "It's going to be tough. It's going to be dangerous and destructive... I think we're sliding in an *era of great confusion and prevailing chaos*" [32].

So far, in terms of declining Pax Americana, the U.S. strategic objective in Eurasia has been to prevent further economic integration processes between Europe and Asia by means of carrying out the *managed chaos doctrine*. As Nikolai Starikov put it, "In order to survive and preserve its leading role on international stage, US desperately needs *to plunge Eurasia into chaos*, to cut economic ties between Europe and APR (Asia-Pacific Region). The States need to turn the territory that lies between them (Russia, Central Asia, Middle East) into a zone with local armed conflicts, falling economies, deficient governments and general instability. Middle East is already very close to a state of total chaos, US-created ISIL is working to further complicate the situation in that region. Central Asia is a potentially very unstable region and it has been "farmed out" to the revived Taliban, but so far it has kept the appearance of stability. Russia is the only territory (country) within this potential zone of instability that is capable of resistance. It is the only state that is ready to confront the Americans. Undermining Russia's political will for resistance, shifting its foreign policy – is a vitally important task for America" [263; 318].

Meanwhile, the end of Pax Americana shapes a strategic opportunity for beginning of a new era of world development - *the era of United Eurasia*. Implementation of the Eurasian integration scenario requires introducing a *new matrix of global governance*. Firstly, it suggests the promotion of an alternative economic pattern to the existing neoliberal doctrine and, therefore, establishing new world reserve currency. The new pattern might be based on Chinese model of socially oriented market economy. Secondly, creation of the new system of international order implies a global partnership network to promoting the concept of shared leadership and mutual responsibility in compliance with the international law.

Finally, the new system of international order involves creation of subnational analytical and research think tanks that would underpin realization of the Eurasian integration process conceptually as well as increasing public awareness regarding the new world order doctrine. Such think tanks might be founded based on the Shanghai Cooperation

Organization, similarly to the SCO Business Council, and/or the BRICS. Only thus the new power center emerging in the world arena will be capable to alternate what used to be Pax Americana and its core geo-economic foundation - the Bretton Woods model of global governance with a dominant role of the U.S. dollar.

The Beginning of the Era of United Eurasia

The ongoing Eurasian integration process represents irreversible historical and geopolitical trend aimed at re-balancing the international system and transforming the unipolar world into what might evolve into the era of United Eurasia. The emerging Eurasian Alliance has been based, mainly, on power pillars established in the framework of the activities of the BRICS, the Eurasian Union, the SCO, the CSTO, ASEAN as well as other institutional platforms. Thus, its driving force has been generated, mainly, because of joint strategic cooperation between Russia and China.

In 2007, President of Russia Vladimir Putin delivered his notorious speech at the 43rd Munich Conference on Security Policy. The so-called *Munich speech* might be considered as being an epoch-making in terms of creating the new system of international order. It has been the first effort made by the Russian President to demonstrate an independent stance of Russia in pursuit of its own state interests. Before that, Russia had been following the policy course established in the framework of the pro-Western "Kozyrev diplomacy" (named after Russian Foreign Minister Kozyrev) and carrying out liberal reforms in compliance with U.S. interests of incorporating Russia into the new world order. Indeed, "the brief drunken interregnum of Yeltsin must have seemed as though Russia was at last about to come into the globalist fold" [23].

The *Munich speech* was a landmark in modern history of Russia when the concept of a unipolar world order was openly criticized by the Russian leader. Vladimir Putin declared: "a unipolar world... refers to one type of situation, namely one center of authority, one center of force, one centre of decision-making. It is world in which there is one master, one sovereign. And at the end of the day this is pernicious not only for all those within this system, but also for the sovereign itself because it destroys itself from within... And this certainly has nothing in common with democracy... I consider that the unipolar model is not only unacceptable but also impossible in today's world. And this is not only because if there was individual leadership in today's – and precisely in today's – world, then the military, political and economic resources would not suffice. What is even more important is that the model itself is flawed because at its basis there is and can be no moral foundations for modern civilization. Along with this, what is happening in today's world... is a tentative to introduce precisely this concept into international affairs, the concept of a unipolar world" [221].

Firstly, the President of Russia confirmed that the implementation of the *unipolar world order concept* implies eruption of permanent conflicts: "Unilateral and frequently illegitimate actions have not resolved any problems. Moreover, they have caused new human tragedies and created new centres of tension... Today we are witnessing an almost uncontained hyper use of force – military force – in international relations, force that is plunging the world into an abyss of permanent conflicts... We are seeing a greater and greater disdain for the basic principles of international law... the United States, has overstepped its national borders in every way. This is visible in the economic, political, cultural and educational policies it imposes on other nations... this is extremely dangerous. It results in the fact that no one feels safe... Of course, such a policy stimulates an arms race" [221].

Secondly, Vladimir Putin emphasized the necessity to abide by the rule of international law: "I am convinced that the only mechanism that can make decisions about using military force as a last resort is the Charter of the United Nations... The use of force can only be considered legitimate if the decision is sanctioned by the UN... Otherwise the situation will simply result in a dead end... Along with this, it is necessary to make sure that international law have a universal character both in the conception and application of its norms" [221].

Thirdly, Putin claimed that NATO`s eastward enlargement contradicted to the assurances made by the West in 1990 before the collapse of the Soviet Union: "NATO expansion does not have any relation with the modernization of the Alliance itself or with ensuring security in Europe. On the contrary, it represents a serious provocation that reduces the level of mutual trust. And we have the right to ask: against whom is this expansion intended? And what happened to the assurances our western partners made after the dissolution of the Warsaw Pact? Where are those declarations today? No one even remembers them. But I will allow myself to remind this audience what was said. I would like to quote the speech of NATO General Secretary Mr. Woerner in Brussels on 17 May 1990. He said at the time that: "the fact that we are ready not to place a NATO army outside of German territory gives the Soviet Union a firm security guarantee". Where are these guarantees?" [221].

Moreover, already in 2007 Putin emphasized the importance of uniting Eurasia and establishing *interconnections between power centers* such as Russia, China, India and Brazil. He considered that economic potentials of the named countries would inevitably convert into multipolarity: "The combined GDP measured in purchasing power parity of countries such as India and China is already greater than that of the United States. And a similar calculation with the GDP of the BRIC countries – Brazil, Russia, India and China – surpasses the cumulative GDP of the EU. And according to experts this gap will only increase in the future. There is no reason to doubt that the economic potential of the new centres of global economic growth will inevitably be converted into political influence and will strengthen multipolarity. In connection with this the role of multilateral diplomacy is significantly increasing" [221].

In conclusion Vladimir Putin emphasized "the need for principles such as openness, transparency and predictability in politics" to construct just world order. He confirmed the intention of Russia to pursue an independent foreign policy in constructing a just world order: "Russia… has practically always used the privilege to carry out an independent foreign policy… we would like to interact with responsible and independent partners with whom we could *work together in constructing a fair and democratic world order* that would ensure security and prosperity not only for a select few, but for all" [221]. The Munich speech might be considered as being a breakthrough towards creating the Eurasian Union and, thus, approaching the *era of a united Eurasia*.

In 2011, the mentioned article by Vladimir Putin, *A New Integration Project for Eurasia: The Future in the Making*, was published [219]. The President of Russia emphasized that the Eurasian Union was intended to become a "powerful supra-national union" of sovereign states based on the EU model. It will serve as a bridge connecting European Union and the Asia-Pacific as well as become a geopolitical pole on an equal footing with the United States and China. Therefore, the Eurasian Union will unite its members' economies, legal systems and customs services, as well as ensure military coordination between them.

The article stated: "We suggest a powerful supranational association capable of becoming one of the poles in the modern world and serving as an efficient bridge between Europe and the dynamic Asia-Pacific region. This project also implies transitioning to closer coordination in economic and currency policies in the Customs Union and CES and establishing a full-fledged economic union. Its natural resources, capital, and potent reserve of human resources will combine to put the Eurasian Union in a strong competitive position in the industry and technology race, in the struggle for investors, for the creation of new jobs and the establishment of cutting-edge facilities. Alongside other key players and regional structures, such as the European Union, the United States, China and APEC, the Eurasian Union will help ensure global sustainable development" [219].

The role of the Eurasian Union in creating *just, equitable and peaceful world order* was further promoted at the Valdai International Discussion Club held in Russia on 19 September 2013. President Putin confirmed that the Eurasian Union will link the Eurasian power centers and, also, serve as a bridge between the East and the West: "The 21st century promises to become the century of major changes, the era of the formation of major geopolitical zones, as well as financial and economic, cultural, civilizational, and military and political areas. That is why integrating with our neighbors is our absolute priority. The future Eurasian Economic Union, which we have declared and which we have discussed extensively as of late, is not just a collection of mutually beneficial agreements. The Eurasian Union is a project for maintaining the identity of nations in the historical Eurasian space in a new century and in a new world. Eurasian integration is a chance for the entire post-Soviet space to become an independent centre for global development, rather than remaining on the outskirts of Europe and Asia" [217].

Besides, Vladimir Putin stated that the Eurasian integration process implies *the principle of diversity* and suggests making a joint contribution of all interested parties into sustainable world development: "This is a union where everyone maintains their identity, their distinctive character and their political independence. Together with our partners, we will gradually implement this project, step by step. We expect that it will become our common input into maintaining diversity and stable global development" [217].

On October 24, 2014 Vladimir Putin confirmed the intention of Russia to participate on equal footing in constructing the new system of international order. At the meeting of the Valdai International Discussion Club's XI session, which theme was, *The World Order: New Rules or a Game without Rules*, he declared: "We have an integration-oriented, positive, peaceful agenda; we are working actively with our colleagues in the Eurasian Economic Union, the Shanghai Cooperation Organization, BRICS and other partners. This agenda is aimed at developing ties between governments, not dissociating. We are not planning to cobble together any blocs or get involved in an exchange of blows. The allegations and statements that Russia is trying to establish some sort of empire, encroaching on the sovereignty of its neighbors, are groundless. Russia does not need any kind of special, exclusive place in the world… While respecting the interests of others, we simply want for our own interests to be taken into account and for our position to be respected" [218].

The new model of international order, which is emerging in the framework of the process of the Eurasian integration, suggests creation of "a common space for economic and humanitarian cooperation stretching all the way from the Atlantic to the Pacific Ocean" [218]. It requires strengthening new power centers in Eurasia by means of implementation of the so-called *"integration of integrations" principle*. According to Vladimir Putin, "This is particularly relevant given the strengthening and growth of certain regions on the planet, which process objectively requires institutionalization of such new poles, creating powerful regional organizations and developing rules for their interaction. Cooperation between these centres would seriously add to the stability of global security, policy and economy" [218].

In concluding Vladimir Putin declared: "building a more stable world order is a difficult task. We are talking about long and hard work. We were able to develop rules for interaction after World War II, and we were able to reach an agreement in Helsinki in the 1970s. Our common duty is to resolve this fundamental challenge at this new stage of development" [218].

Therefore, following the Russian endeavor to alternate the existing "liberal" model of global governance the West introduced economic sanctions regarding Russia. The policy of sanctions was imposed by the United States. At the Congress of Federation of Independent Trade Unions of Russia, which was held on 7 February 2015, Vladimir Putin pointed out: "There is, however, an attempt to restrain our development by different means, an attempt to freeze the world order that has taken shape in the past decades after the collapse of the Soviet Union, with one single leader at its head, who wants to remain an absolute leader, thinking he can do whatever he likes, while others can only do what they are allowed to do and only if it is in this leader's interests. Russia would never agree to such a world order. Maybe some like it, they want to live in a semi-occupied state, but we will not do it. However, we will not go to war with anyone either, we intend to cooperate with everyone" [220].

China, from its side, being the first world's largest economy and a power center in East Asia has made a solid input into the creation of the new system of international order. On January 30, 2012 "People's Daily", the Communist Party of China mouthpiece, published an article entitled, *China and Russia should Create the Eurasian Alliance* [67]. The article emphasized that the American strategy of world domination has been focused on Eurasia, where China and Russia have been identified as the last strategic objectives. In this connection, the article called for the two countries acting jointly to deter the "imperial ambitions" of the United States. The interaction between China and Russia will contribute not only to enhancing security but also involving other countries in Eurasia, including Iran and Pakistan, to infringe the strategic plans of the U.S. in the region [67].

On September 7th, 2013, a historic speech followed from Chinese President Xi Jinping. The President of China presented a strategically powerful initiative to restore the Silk Road, which would connect the Pacific and the Baltic Sea and, thus, become the New Silk Road. Xi also announced launching the 21st Century Maritime Silk Road (i.e. The "Belt and Road" initiative). According to Xi Jinping, "The proposed economic belt along the Silk Road is inhabited by close to three billion people and represents the biggest market in the world with unparalleled potential" [334].

The New Silk Road concept envisages closer integration between the SCO member states starting from individual areas and linking them over time to cover the whole Eurasian region. The Chinese initiative also aims at promoting the establishment of the SCO Development Bank and ensuring financial flows and payments in local currencies, thus, replacing the U.S. dollar. Besides, China has established a Silk Road Fund (40 billion USD) to finance a network of railways and airports linking China with Central Asia.

On October 13, 2013 Xinhua News Agency called for "de-Americanizing the world" [151]. Being a mouthpiece of Chinese government, the Agency stated: "Such alarming days when the destinies of others are in the hands of a hypocritical nation have to be terminated, and a new world order should be put in place, according to which all nations, big or small, poor or rich, can have their key interests respected and protected on an equal footing" [151]. Xinhua urged that, "several corner stones should be laid to underpin a de-Americanized world" [151]. Therefore, it has called all nations, firstly, to abide by the basic principles of the international law, including respect for sovereignty; secondly, recognize the authority of the United Nations in dealing with global hotspot issues; thirdly, to reform the world`s financial system and its major international financial institutions. The Chinese side suggested introducing *a new international reserve currency* as a key instrument to reforming world`s financial system.

In addition to the New Silk Road concept, the overall strategy of China`s development as a great power implies realization of the *Chinese dream*. This concept has been put forth by Chinese President Xi Jinping in November 2012. The meaning of the Chinese dream has been explained as building a moderately prosperous society and realizing national rejuvenation. Xi emphasized that the Chinese dream is a dream for peace, development, cooperation and mutual benefit for all. It is connected to the beautiful dreams of the people in other countries. The Chinese dream will not only benefit the Chinese people, but also people of all countries in the world [42].

The *Russian dream* of creating a harmonious community of economies from Lisbon to Vladivostok and the emerging Eurasian Union, from one side, and the Chinese dream of achieving national rejuvenation, building a moderately prosperous society and constructing the New

Silk Road economic belt expanding from China via Central Asia into Western Europe, from the other side, have contributed significantly to the unification of the Eurasian continent. Because of this process a new geopolitical center of gravity, the Eurasian alliance, is being formed.

According to Li Hui, Chinese Ambassador to Russia, Chinese dream is in accord with Russian dream: "China is devoted to realizing the great rejuvenation of the Chinese nation, and Russia is also striving to regain its national strength. The Chinese dream is in accord with the Russian dream. The two countries maintain their determination to choose development paths suited to their own national conditions, and have set clear strategic goals for national rejuvenation. China and Russia offer each other mutual opportunities and are each other's priority partners for cooperation, which has laid a solid foundation for political trust and strategic and practical cooperation between the two sides. The three-pronged Sino-Russia relationship is at a historic point of strength." [150; 199].

The *Indian dream* was proposed by Jawaharlal Nehru (1889 – 1964). Being the first Prime Minister of India and a central figure in Indian politics for much of the 20th century, he wrote a book titled, *The Discovery of India* (1951). Nehru's consideration of India as "a potential great nation and strong country" constitutes the core of the Indian dream.

The national dream concepts, namely, the Russian dream, the Chinese dream, the Indian dream, are creative and complimentary ideas capable to ensure synergy, which is necessary to carrying out vital process of the Eurasian integration. The Chinese dream and the Indian dream are also complimentary: "China and India are both developing countries with the arduous task of rapidly developing their national economies, improving their people's livelihood and moving out of poverty. As close neighbors, the two countries should respect and trust each other, stay on friendly terms with and learn from each other and give full play to their complementarity in the pursuit of their respective dreams" [161].

Informational and ideological basis for the new system of international order constitutes the national dreams mentioned above. Their implementation implies all-encompassing Greater Eurasia doctrine. It can be developed by means of ensuring complementarity between the Russian dream, the Chinese dream, and the Indian dream. The idea of elaborating the Eurasian doctrine was first put forward by the Russian school of thought in geopolitics yet at the end of 19th century. In 1845, the Russian Geographical Society was founded in Saint Petersburg. The so-called "Evraziyzi" or Eurasian-minded elites and scholars in Russia elaborated the concept of Greater Eurasia. This concept required strengthening Russia as being a center of geopolitical gravity in Eurasia and, thus, creating preconditions for unification of the whole continent on equal footing.

Further elaboration of the Greater Eurasia doctrine requires implementation of the following *principles*: achieving unity through diversity; promoting "integration of integrations"; creating synergy in geopolitical, economic, cultural, and other fields. Besides, the doctrine suggests supporting for generally recognized principles and norms of international law, as well as rejection of power politics and politics infringing on sovereignty of other states. Thus, the principles of openness, pragmatism, solidarity, non-bloc character and nonaggressive nature regarding third parties would facilitate the rapprochement of the participating states in carrying out the Eurasian integration. The latter fosters inter-civilizational and inter-religious dialogue between major civilizations and cultures in the world.

Achieving unity through diversity means that nations and ethnic groups that form multinational and multiethnic states would be affiliated with greater cultures and civilizations, for example, Russian civilization, Chinese civilization, Indian civilization, Western European (Latin) civilization rather than identifying themselves as being independent entities per se. The promotion of national unity and integrity is important to protecting minorities` and ethnic groups` cultures from negative effects of globalization. In this regard, Chinese *"Grand Unity under Heaven" doctrine* and the concept of succession in country`s historical development are important.

Promoting "integration of integrations" suggests creating global partnership networks between major integrational units in the world such as the EU, the Eurasian Union, the BRICS, ASEAN, NAFTA, MERCOSUR as well as engaging respective regional organizations and forums, including the SCO, the CSTO, G20, CICA etc., into this process. Geopolitical networking between these units would integrate the potentials of the main Eurasian power centers, including Russia, China, India and, possibly, Pakistan and Iran in the not too distant future. Thus, "integration of integrations" principle mostly concerns creating synergy between integrational units as well as establishing shared leadership and responsibility in addressing global issues.

Synergy (geopolitical, geoeconomic, philosophical, cultural etc.) between ancient civilizations and power centers in Eurasia can be achieved in the framework of the Eurasian integration process. It contributes to unification of the whole continent and creating the "*community of common destiny*" based on respective national dreams. Although such an idea of a united Eurasian continent might seem a utopia at first sight, it tends to be a viable alternative to the expanding global chaos.

On October 18th, 2013, South Korean President Park Geun-hye delivered a speech at the conference "Global Cooperation in the Era of Eurasia". She has declared: "The creation of such a new Eurasia is not simply an ideal and a dream but a viable goal to achieve... To this end, I want to propose a Eurasian Initiative, a set of directions for making Eurasia into a single united continent, a continent of creativity and a continent of peace..." [197].

Geopolitical basis of the new system of international order emerges, as it has been mentioned, due to carrying out the Eurasian integration process to a larger extent. Currently, this process has two geopolitical pillars, namely, the BRICS (Brazil, Russia, India, China, South African Republic) and the Eurasian Union (Russia, Belarus, Kazakhstan, Armenia – and other countries currently applying for membership). Besides, MERCOSUR, ALBA, ASEAN, and other integrational alliances and regional units, including the EU and NAFTA, might contribute to establishing the new system of international order.

The Concept of participation of the Russian Federation in BRICS confirms "a common desire of BRICS partners to reform the obsolete international financial and economic architecture" [58]. The BRICS is a key element of a new international system: "subject to a firm political will on the part of governments of the participating states to deepen cooperation, the association can potentially become a key element of a new system of global governance, first, in the financial and economic areas" [58]. In that regard, Delhi Declaration, which has been adopted on 20 March 2012 at the BRICS Summit, called for the new world financial system, reforming the Bretton Woods system and replacing the U.S. dollar with a new reserve currency.

The Eurasian integration process began, primarily, due to the global rise of China, the Asian dragon, and the revival of geopolitical power of Russia, which can be figuratively compared to the Phoenix. The Russian phoenix re-emerged again from the ashes of liberal reforms which had been carried out in Russia in the wake of the Cold War under the guidance of Western advisors. Contrary to the Anglo-Saxon doctrine of global governance both China and Russia share traditional values. They support carrying out the Eurasian integration geopolitical projects in pursuit of their national dreams and state interests.

The Eurasian integration transforms world's geopolitical and geoeconomic landscape. It modifies current "liberal" system of global governance in many ways: through the bilateral activities of the BRICS member states and of the Eurasian Union; at the Shanghai Cooperation Organization (the SCO) and the Collective Security Treaty Organization (the CSTO); through implementation of the New Silk Road concept; at the Association of Southeast Asian Nations (ASEAN) and the Conference on Interaction and Confidence Building Measures in Asia (CICA); inside the G20; and via the 120-member-nation Non-Aligned Movement (NAM), etc.

Many sectors of economy of BRICS' participating states are complimentary [58]. Their economic models differ from the U.S.-promoted model of neoliberalism. The BRICS demonstrates dynamic trade and development of multiple projects in different areas. At present, in total, there are more than 20 formats of cooperation within the BRICS which are intensively developing; and 11 prospective directions of scientific and technical cooperation, from aeronautics to bio- and nanotechnology. Financial pillars of the economic cooperation develop through the activities of the BRICS Stock Alliance, the BRICS Development Bank[19], the Eurasian Development Bank, and the Asian Infrastructure Development Bank (AIIB)[20] – a China-led financial institution that might challenge the World Bank. These newly established financial and economic institutions are capable to finance large infrastructural projects and, thus,

---

19 BRICS Development Bank is an alternative to the World Bank. It was created at BRICS Summit held on 27 March 2013.

20 The Asian Infrastructure Investment Bank (AIIB) was established in Beijing on October 24, 2014. Initially, 42 countries had joined or applied to join the AIIB as founding members.

create *economic foundations* of the new system of international order. Further economic integration would inevitably imply enhancing security of the participating countries, which might lead to establishing a kind of *Eurasian military and political alliance* as an alternative to NATO.

The strategic potential of the BRICS integrates 42 percent of the world's population and about a quarter of the world's economy, which makes this bloc of states an important global actor. It represents a huge market with a human potential of 3 billion people and vast natural resources. Besides, the BRICS countries are politically like-minded in terms of supporting the principles of international law, the central role of the UN Security Council and the principles of the non-use of force in international relations. That is why they are so actively performing in the sphere of settling regional conflicts.

Creation of the Eurasian Union contributed to ensuring geopolitical synergy in Eurasia. The cumulative economic effect of the Eurasian Union might total to 900 million U.S. dollars by 2030. If Ukraine joined the project economic benefits would had accounted for more than 1 trillion U.S. dollars.

So far, the Eurasian Union and the New Silk Road economic belt are mutually interconnected geopolitical projects that forge ahead stable, balanced and equitable world order. These two projects, along with the BRICS, might be viewed as being integral parts of each other. Indeed, since the New Silk Road economic belt has been planned to extend between China, Russia and Germany, it will thus connect the East and the West, namely, the Asia-Pacific region and the European Union via Central Asia and Russia.

The New Silk Road will extend from Chongqing in China via Astana, Moscow, Minsk, Warsaw, Berlin to Duisburg in Germany. Therefore, geopolitical platform of the Eurasian Union is complimentary to the New Silk Road. Although the Eurasian Union and the New Silk Road projects might slightly differ in nuances they do not contradict each other in terms of balancing the world order and promoting the unification of the Eurasian continent.

As a result of BRICS` activities, creation of the Eurasian Union, and realization of the New Silk Road concepts a new geopolitical configuration of powers, *the Eurasian Alliance*, emerges. It empowers financial, economic, energy and security potentials of the BRICS participating states. The new configuration of powers - which can be figuratively determined as being *Pax-BRICSannica* - is capable to balance the international system.

The Eurasian Alliance is potentially capable to deter centrifugal forces within the international system caused by implementation of the new world order paradigm. Russia, China, India and, possibly, Pakistan and Iran in the foreseeable future, can further develop their geopolitical gravity to consolidating the Eurasian Alliance, ensuring stability in the world`s pivotal region and, thus, bringing about *the era of united Eurasia*.

Conclusion

"Ideas can only be neutralized by ideas"
Honoré de Balzac

The new world order paradigm represents *a multifaceted phenomenon,* which emerged yet in Ancient Egypt. Firstly, it originated as being a form of sub-national elitist philosophy and system of beliefs underpinning the idea of gaining world`s hegemony. Since then this idea underpins "liberal" matrix of governance. The matrix has been promoted by the Anglo-Saxon civilization already upon plundering the Byzantine Empire in 13th century. It led the world through the periods of Pax Britannica, Pax Americana and beyond.

Secondly, the paradigm has been incorporated into the U.S. "grand strategy" in terms of the following concepts: Manifest Destiny (1898), American Dream (1931), American Destiny (1939), American Century (1941), New American Century (2000), New American Moment (2010), etc. The doctrinal basis of the "grand strategy" constitutes the world (global) revolution doctrine, the world government doctrine, the new world order doctrine, and the global governance doctrine - each corresponding to a certain stage of realizing the "grand strategy".

Thirdly, the paradigm might be perceived as being a long-lasting subnational project. During the 20th century The Council on Foreign Relations (CFR) has been a mastermind behind projecting the paradigm in the framework of undertaking The Inquiry, The War and Peace Studies, The WOMP, The 1980s, etc. Carrying out these projects coincided with waging World War I, World War II, and the Cold War. A key role in implementing the paradigm belongs to the Bilderberg Group, the Trilateral Commission, the World State Forum, and many other influential elitist organizations which altogether represent global networking of elites and intellectuals focused on the promotion of the "liberal" world order.

Finally, the paradigm has been empowering fundamental historical process, which might be figuratively compared to global *geopolitical Gulf Stream,* which had originated yet in the ancient past. Since then it has been reflecting the "big picture", that is, transforming the international system towards what might be identified today as being the system of global governance (potentially, the world government). The "big picture" constitutes a chain of interconnected events incorporating, among other, the following milestones: The Four crusades against the Byzantine Empire, the Revolution in France (1789), Napoleon's military campaign into Russia, the Revolution in Russia (1917), World War I, World War II, the Cold War as being the American crusade against communism, the War on Terror, and the ongoing Cyber War. Therefore, implementing the new world order paradigm has been a constant warfare.

The U.S. "grand strategy" is a *tool of establishing the new world order.* The strategy has been driven with a certain mechanism which led the United States through the stages of its evolution to gain a superpower position, namely, isolationism, globalism, and the stage of American hegemony which, at present, came to its end. During the stage of isolationism, the United States accumulated considerable power to entering the world arena in the aftermath of World War I. The stage of globalism started in the wake of World War II and lasted through the period of the Cold War. Because of subverting the Soviet Union, the stage of U.S. global hegemony began.

After the Cold War, important milestones of successive process of establishing the new world order have been the Clinton Doctrine ("democracy enlargement" concept), the Bush Doctrine ("preemptive warfare" concept) and, eventually, the Obama Doctrine ("just warfare" concept). The Clinton administration (1993-2000) policy focused on active engagement into Eurasia and former spheres of influence of the Soviet Union starting with NATO's bombing of Yugoslavia in 1999. The Bush administration (2000-2008) launched the War on Terror in the Middle East in 2001. The Obama administration signalized the beginning of the Cyber War. The latter was proclaimed as if to countering "cyber threats". However, as Edward Snowden's revelations demonstrated, the key objective of the Cyber War has been gaining control over the informational flows within the cyber space. This fact corresponds to the well-known saying: anyone who has the information owns the world. Thus, the process of implementing the paradigm has been *constant warfare.*

The *mechanism of realization* of the U.S. "grand strategy" consists of three components, namely, informational, economic, and military and political. The key role in mechanism's functioning belongs to the factor of threat. Indeed, the "image of enemy" has been constantly used to justifying American global expansion. Referring to the struggle between "good" and "evil" creates uniting tension to shifting power resources for interventions abroad. Under the pretext of confronting threats to U.S. national interests the new world order paradigm has been projected around the globe.

"Threats" to the new world order were presented by the Soviet communism (the "Soviet threat"), then by the international terror (the "Islamic threat") and, finally, by non-state actors ("empowered individuals", the Islamic State movement, etc.). Thus, proclamation of the "iron curtain" and "evil empire" in the face of the Soviet Union directed the process of creation of Pax Americana into the course of the Cold War. Declaring "rogue states", "axis of evil" and, finally, the "terror threat" established a strategic framework for carrying out the War on Terror. At present, the U.S. leaders has been invoking moralism and liberal ideology for public support of the "grand strategy", in much the same way as they did after the end of World War II. So far, identifying threats to the new world order has been a strategic requirement in terms of realizing the U.S. foreign policy.

The U.S. "grand strategy" shapes *dimensions of the new world order*, namely, informational, economic, military and political. After World War II these dimensions were established by means of the Truman Doctrine, the Marshall Plan, and NATO. In the aftermath of the Cold War the U.S. "global control" has been extended worldwide.

The *informational dimension* has been consolidated in the framework of carrying out the Information and Psychological Warfare (the IPW concept[21], "mind control" concept, etc.). This dimension has been widening by means of "global social engineering", the promotion of "mass culture", etc. (e.g. Hollywood's "liberal" propaganda, the activities of Tavistock Institute of Human Relations, certain Internet technologies, the U.S. global electronic control networks). These phenomena bring

---

21 The IPW concept was first adopted within U.S. military doctrines during the Cold War.

about secular world order. It has been underpinned by means of carrying out various social movements that expand "global values" (e.g. "peace education" movement, human rights movements, the LGBT movement, etc.). Certain ideas of these movements disseminate the "seeds of destruction" which penetrate traditional cultures and, thus, erode the concept of national sovereignty, especially, within multiethnic and multinational states.

Thus, the new world order paradigm has been replacing ideals belonging to traditional cultures and civilizations. Its informational dimension might be identified although somewhat pejoratively as being the Third Opium War, in which information plays crucial role. From a theological perspective, the promotion of secular world order foreshadows the appearance of antichrist and the Armageddon, that is, the last battle between good and evil predicted in the Bible.

The *economic dimension* has been established by means of carrying out the "open door" policy. It was underpinned by free market principles and the dominant role of U.S. dollar. The economic dimension emerged, so far, as a result of creating the "open-door" world of free trade and global market economy. It comprised the Bretton Woods institutions, transnational corporations (TNCs), global economic forums (The World Economic Forum, G8/7, G20), etc. These institutions direct economic processes to a subnational level and consolidate global (secular) market economy.

The *military and political dimension* has been shaped in terms of persistent geopolitical expansion of the United States and its determination to "lead" the world. Washington has been deploying American military forces for "constabulary duties" around the globe. During the Cold War, from 1946 until the end of 1980-s, the U.S. military has been used in approximately 300 overseas operations [294; 99; 121].

Besides, indirect foreign engagement included providing weaponry to Afghan mujahidin, such as Taliban movement, and other jihadist movements of radicalized Islam, supporting coup d'états in Latin America as well as in the former Soviet geopolitical space. After the end of the Cold War stage the military dimension of the new world order has been extended because of eastwards NATO enlargement, creating Anti-Missile infrastructure in Eurasia, deploying U.S. military bases in key geopolitical and strategic regions in the world.

At present, there are around 1,000 different overseas bases used by the U.S. military [123].

In the 20th century, the process of implementing the new world order paradigm has been visible in terms of carrying out three attempts aimed at gaining world`s domination. The *first attempt* followed in the aftermath of World War I. Its means was the *world revolution movement*. In Russia, this movement was led by Bolshevik`s current, namely, Trotskyites`. American financiers provided financial support to Trotsky and his adherents who organized the policy of "red terror" [251]. Such policy was focused on undermining Russian power potential, though, under the slogan of arranging the world revolution. The movement was thwarted by Stalin who eliminated the Trotskyites` bloc using their own methods of political repressions. Indeed, the "red terror" in Russia had emerged long before Stalin came to power.

From its side, the United States proclaimed the Wilson Doctrine and incepted the League of Nations as being a prototype for the system of global governance. The ideology of Bolshevism conceptualized in the form of Trozkism on the one hand and Western liberalism, on the other hand, might be considered as being two sides of the same coin. Both ideologies sought world`s domination. The difference between them was the means towards that end. Notably, Trozkism was the source of inspiration for Leo Strauss, the founding father of the American neo-conservative thought.

The *second attempt* at gaining world`s domination was undertaken in the wake of World War II in terms of the activities of the *world government movement*. At this stage, the United States already possessed preeminent economic and military might which was applied to establishing foundations of the new world order. In 1944, economic foundations were settled in Bretton Woods making the U.S. dollar a world reserve currency. In 1945, political foundations were created in the face of the United Nations. In 1949, military foundations of Pax Americana were laid out following the creation of NATO. However, the world government movement was, again, opposed by Stalin`s Soviet Union. Hence, the Cold War emerged as being the requirement of creating Pax Americana to a larger extent, than clashing between the two ideological and geopolitical camps represented by the Soviet Union and the United States.

The *third attempt* at gaining world's hegemony followed during the Cold War. The first post-World War II decade was a climactic period which highlighted the direction of America's foreign policy for the second half of the 20th century. During this period Washington projected the U.S. power capabilities, accumulated during World War II, into the world arena. It replaced isolationism with the new globalism. This marked the historical transformation of U.S. foreign policy, and established the "grand strategy". The strategy focused on subverting the Soviet Union which used to be the only geopolitical impediment to Pax Americana. Therefore, the Cold War played crucial role in approaching the new world order.

After the collapse of the Soviet Union, Washington confirmed its intention to further "lead" the world. As William Cohen stated, for instance, in the flush of victory in the Cold War, America must *again* shoulder responsibility and benefits of the sole superpower - the United States must be actively engaged in the world, and seek to shape world events in favourable direction [56, p. 2]. Thus, a clear strategic parallel exists between the first post-war decade and post-Cold War period. The power vacuum, which was caused by the collapse of the Soviet Union created wide strategic opportunities for Washington to further expansion and transforming the international system according to American interests.

Important enough, the U.S. Cold War "strategy of containment" and the current process of "deterring" China's influence have been based on the same *geopolitical imperatives*. The key imperative has been preventing the emergence of an independent power center or their combination (s) in Eurasia which might challenge the new world order paradigm and stimulate others to overcome American hegemony. Although the U.S. "grand strategy" has been focused, firstly, on undermining Russia's power potential as well as its spiritual might in the face of the Russian Orthodox creed, it suggests subverting any power center that impedes the promotion of the new world order paradigm.

At the modern stage, the paradigm implies carrying out the so-called *managed chaos doctrine*. It aims at bringing about "order out of chaos" (Order ab Chao – lat.). Realization of such scenario requires further splitting the Eurasian geopolitical space, its "balkanization" and, thus, spreading the global chaos. In doing so, the U.S.-led NATO military interventions were carried out in former Yugoslavia, Iraq, Afghanistan, and Libya. The United States also inspired "colour revolutions" on the post-Soviet space, particularly, in Georgia, Kyrgyzstan, Ukraine as well as supported realization of "regime change" scenarios in the Middle East during the Arab Spring. Besides, the U.S. has been triggering protest movements in Latin America, China (Hong Kong), and other countries. This demonstrates strategic continuum of the U.S. "grand strategy" to imposing the new world order paradigm. Obviously, such policy has been provoking escalation of inter-ethnic and inter-religious controversies, rising of separatists` and nationalists` movements, so far, bringing about the global (world) revolution phenomena.

In terms of realizing the managed chaos doctrine, the U.S.-led War on Terror has been radicalizing Islam worldwide. Following American military engagement into the Middle East, which had been provoked by the events of 9/11, the "three evil forces" of separatism, extremism and terrorism have been generating uncontrolled centrifugal forces within the international system. These forces might cause unpredictable consequences for the whole mankind as it had already happened three times in the 20th Century - during World War I, World War II, and the Cold War. Indeed, Syria and Libya have been economically developed countries yet in the not too distant past. Iraq and Afghanistan were not plunged into chaos until the U.S. intervened to "promoting democracy" into the Middle East.

The Islamic State movement emerged as a result of "unintended consequences" [212] of the American invasion in Iraq in 2003. The movement has been creating preconditions for launching "global jihad". Potentially, it might be directed against geopolitical power centers in Eurasia, including Russia and China. Yet its long-term objective seems to have been clashing Islam with Christianity. This imminent global security threat conceals the roots of the "clash of civilizations".

The end of Pax Americana requires implementing a new matrix to ensure creating just and equitable world order. Establishing the new system of international order means generating synergy between world`s power centers, integrational units and states that are willing to remain independent subjects in history rather than manipulated objects by the new world order in terms of its grand geopolitical "chess play". Therefore, new inter-civilizational model of world order, exclusively, might balance the international system and help eliminate the fatal line of Apocalypse. This is a prerequisite for world`s peaceful development and the requirement of our time.

Economic basis of the new system of international order can be established by means of expanding Chinese experience of building up a socially oriented market economy. This would ensure complementarity (synergy), first, of the BRICS countries` economies as well as of their allies and prospective members. In that regard, carrying out mutual payments in national currencies with a perspective of introducing a new world`s reserve currency (e.g. Chinese RMB) is essential.

Military basis of the balanced and harmonious world order implies enhancing broader security of the Eurasian integration process, including the creation of the New Silk Road economic belt by means of using the mechanisms established within the SCO, the CSTO, etc. Yet, coping with common security threats might require creating a joint Eurasian military force. In this context Egypt`s initiative to create a joint Arab military force might be considered.

Conceptual basis of the new system of international order appears as being the system of principles constituting the Doctrine of Greater (United) Eurasia. It was incepted by the Russian geopolitical school yet at the end of 19th century. Also, the mentioned Chinese idea of "Great Unity under Heaven" as well as the concept of creating the "community of common destiny" might strengthen the Eurasian doctrine. Besides, the concept of achieving unity through diversity and the principle of peaceful co-existence among nations are important along with fundamental principles of the international law.

Geopolitical basis of the new system of international order has been established in terms of carrying out the Eurasian integration process. In the framework of this process, establishing new geopolitical pivots, including the New Silk Road, is a necessary precondition to connecting key continental power centers, including Russia, Germany, China, India, Iran, Turkey, and Pakistan. Thus, the Eurasian Alliance can emerge provided the named countries would elaborate appropriate mechanisms to coordinating their state interests while facing similar global threats. Many of these threats have been generated in terms of implementing the new world order paradigm. Finally, the Eurasian Alliance would apply the "integration of integrations" principle to strengthen geopolitical gravity of Eurasia, balance the continent and, thus, establish a *Union by the unions.*

Therefore, strategic networking between the Eurasian Union, the BRICS, ASEAN, ALBA, etc. is necessary. This implies realizing *Joint Eurasian and Intercontinental Strategy* (JES) consisting of informational, economic (e.g. BRICS` Strategy for Economic Cooperation) and military components. To elaborating such strategy new type of think tanks must be established at the intergovernmental level, for example, *Center for United Eurasia* (CUE). This idea corresponds to the Chinese initiative concerning strengthening the construction of new types of think tanks. So far, arranging geostrategic networking between the new type of think tanks and respective Governments will project the new matrix of world`s harmonious development into the world arena. This would ensure mutual understanding and cooperation between world`s civilizations, consolidate the new system of international order, and direct the might of all international players without an exception into a constructive course.

Bibliography

1. A conversation with U.S. Secretary of State Hillary Rodham Clinton [Electronic resource]: Washington, Sept. 8, 2010 // Council on Foreign Relations. – Mode of access: http://www.cfr.org/diplomacy-and-statecraft/conversation-us-secretary-state-hillary-rodham-clinton/p22896. – Date of access: 01.06.2015.
2. Adams, J. T. The epic of America / J. T. Adams. – Boston: Little, Brown a. Co, 1931. – 405 p.
3. Address by Ms. Irina Bokova on her installation as Director-General of the United Nations Educational, Scientific and Cultural Organization (UNESCO) [Electronic resource]: plenary meet. 18th, Paris, 23 Oct. 2009 // UNESDOC Database. – Mode of access: http://unesdoc.unesco.org/images/0018/001855/185556e.pdf. – Date of access: 01.06.2015.
4. Address by Jacques Delors, President of the European Commission, to the Royal Institute of International Affairs [Electronic resource]: Sept. 7, 1992 // European Commission. – Mode of access: http://europa.eu/rapid/press-release_SPEECH-92-81_en.htm?locale=en. – Date of access: 02.05.2015.
5. Address by Rene Maheu, Director-General of UNESCO [Electronic resource]: Sept. 25, 1974, DG/74/12 // UNESDOC Database. – Mode of access: http://unesdoc.unesco.org/images/0001/000116/011681eb.pdf. – Date of access: 01.06.2015.
6. Anniversary remembrance [Electronic resource] // Time. – 1951. – 2 July. – Mode of access: http://www.time.com/time/magazine/article/0,9171,815031,00.html?promoid=googlep. – Date of access: 17.10.2014.
7. Арапова, Е. США и Транс-Тихоокеанское партнерство: социальные интересы против экономических и политических [Электронный ресурс] / Е. Арапова // МГИМО Университет. – Режим доступа: http://www.mgimo.ru/news/experts/document247280.phtml. – Дата доступа: 01.06.2015.
8. Astore, W. J. Operation enduring war [Electronic resource] / W. J. Astore // Asia Times Online. – Mode of access: http://www.

atimes.com/atimes/Middle_East/LG10Ak01.html. – Date of access: 01.06.2015.

9. Балиев, А. Последний проект Сталина [Электронный ресурс] / А. Балиев // Столетие. – Режим доступа: http://www.stoletie.ru/territoriya_istorii/poslednij_projekt_stalina_685.htm. – Дата доступа: 01.06.2015.

10. Barash, D. P. Introduction to peace studies / D. P. Barash. – Belmont: Wadsworth Publ., 1991. – XVI, 613 p.

11. Baratta, J. P. The politics of world federation: in 2 vol. / J. P. Baratta. – Westport: Praeger, 2004. – Vol. 1: United Nations, U.N. reform, atomic control. – 299 p.; Vol. 2: From world federalism to global governance. – P. 300–696.

12. Бартольд, В. В. Ислам / В. В. Бартольд. – М.: Кн. клуб Книговек, 2012. – 346 с.

13. Behravesh, M. The thrust of Wendtian constructivism [Electronic resource] / M. Behravesh // E-International relations. – Mode of access: http://www.e-ir.info/2011/03/09/the-thrust-of-wendtian-constructivism. – Date of access: 01.06.2015.

14. Beitz, C. International liberalism and distributive justice: a survey of recent thought / C. Beitz // World Politics. – 1999. – Vol. 51, iss. 2. – P. 269–296.

15. Belton, C. Putin: Why not price oil in euros? [Electronic resource] / C. Belton // The Moscow Times. – 2003. – 10 Oct. – Mode of access: http://www.themoscowtimes.com/business/article/putin-why-not-price-oil-in-euros/235338.html. – Date of access: 02.06.2015.

16. Benford, R. L. Lies, liberty and the pursuit of happiness / R. Benford. – [S. l.]: Russell Lawrence Benford, 2013. – 562 p.

17. Бешлосс, М. На самом высоком уровне: закулисная история окончания «холодной войны» / М. Бешлосс; пер. с англ. Н. Изосимова [и др.]. – М.: Все для Вас, 1994. – 398 с.

18. Бескровный, Л. Г. Армия и флот России в начале XX в.: очерки воен.-экон. потенциала / Л. Г. Бескровный; отв. ред. А. Л. Нарочницкий. – М.: Наука, 1986. – 237 с.

19. Beveridge, A. J. March of the flag [Electronic resource]: address to an Indiana Republican Meeting, Indianapolis, Indiana, 16 Sept. 1898 / A. J. Beveridge // National Humanities Center. – Mode

of access: http://nationalhumanitiescenter.org/pds/gilded/empire/text5/beveridge.pdf. – Date of access: 02.06.2015.

20. Black, C. E. A new world order? / C. E. Black. – Princeton: Center of Intern. Studies: Woodrow Wilson School of Public A. Intern. Studies: Princeton Univ., 1975. – 87 p.

21. Black, H. The new world / H. Black. – New York: F. H. Revell, 1915. – 240 p.

22. Blair, A. C. Address to British Ambassadors in London [Electronic resource] // The Guardian. – 2003. – 7 Jan. – Mode of access: http://www.theguardian.com/politics/2003/jan/07/foreignpolicy.speeches. – Date of access: 02.06.2015.

23. Bolton, K. R. Origins of the cold war: how Stalin foiled a 'New world order'. Relevance for the present [Electronic resource] / K. R. Bolton // Foreign Policy J. – 2010. – 31 May. – Mode of access: http://www.foreignpolicyjournal.com/2010/05/31/origins-of-the-cold-war-how-stalin-foild-a-new-world-order. – Date of access: 09.05.2012.

24. Бомбежки Ливии – наказание Каддафи за попытку введения золотого динара? [Электронный ресурс] // Anvictory.org. – Режим доступа: http://anvictory.org/blog/2011/03/22/bombezhki-livii-%e2%80%93-nakazanie-kaddafi-za-popytku-vvedeniya-zolotogo-dinara. – Дата доступа: 02.06.2015.

25. Boren, D. The world needs an army on call [Electronic resource] / D. Boren // New York Times. – 1992. – 26 Aug. – Mode of access: http://www.nytimes.com/1992/08/26/opinion/the-world-needs-an-army-on-call.html. – Date of access: 09.05.2012.

26. Boyle, F. A. Foundations of world order: the legalist approach to international relations, 1898–1921 / F. A. Boyle. – Durham: Duke Univ. Press, 1999. – IX, 220 p.

27. Bridge, R. Clinton's 'Sovietization' comment attracts Kremlin's ire [Electronic resource] / R. Bridge // RT. – 2012. – 19 Dec. – Mode of access: http://rt.com/politics/clinton-russia-cis-peskov-371. – Date of access: 02.05.2015.

28. Brinkley, A. American history, a survey: in 2 vol. / A. Brinkley. – 9th ed. – New York: McGraw-Hill, 1995. – Vol. 1: To 1877. – XIV, 446 p.

29. Brinkley, D. Democratic enlargement: the Clinton Doctrine [Electronic resource] / D. Brinkley // Wilson Quarterly Archives. – Mode of access: http://archive.wilsonquarterly.com/in-essence/clinton-doctrine. – Date of access: 02.05.2015.

30. Brown, G. Globalisation [Electronic resource] : speech given by the Chancellor, Gordon Brown at the Press Club Washington, 17 Dec. 2001 / G. Brown // WiredGov. – Mode of access: http://www.wired-gov.net/wg/wg-news-1.nsf/54e6de9e0c383719802572b9005141ed/a102d5a1087f897b802572ab004b4f0c?OpenDocument. – Date of access: 02.05.2015.

31. Brumley, B. Gorbachev asks in Nobel lecture for Western aid [Electronic resource] / B. Brumley // The Times-News. – 1991. – 6 June. – Mode of access: http://news.google.com/newspapers?nid=1665&dat=19910606&id=eO0eAAAAIBAJ&sjid=byQEAAAAIBAJ&pg=6675,1453559. – Date of access: 02.05.2015.

32. Brzezinski, Z. A time of unprecedented instability? [Electronic resource] / Z. Brzezinski // Foreign Policy. – 2014. – July. – Mode of access: http://foreignpolicy.com/2014/07/21/a-time-of-unprecedented-instability. – Date of access: 02.05.2015.

33. Brzezinski, Z. America in the technetronic age. New questions of our time [Electronic resource] / Z. Brzezinski // Encounter. – 1968. – January. – Mode of access: http://www.unz.org/Sun/Encounter-1968jan-00016. – Date of access: 08.01.2015.

34. Brzezinski, Z. Between two ages: America's role in the technetronic era / Z. Brzezinski. – New York : Viking Press, 1970. – XVII, 334 p.

35. Brzezinski, Z. Strategic vision: America and the crisis of global power / Z. Brzezinski. – New York : Basic Books, 2013. – 240 p.

36. Brzezinski, Z. The grand chessboard: American primacy and its geostrategic imperatives / Z. Brzezinski. – New York : Basic Books, 1998. – XIV, 223 p.

37. Bush`s letter to students [Electronic resource] // The Tech. – 1991. – Vol. 110, iss. 59. – Mode of access: http://tech.mit.edu/V110/PDF/V110-N59.pdf. – Date of access: 02.05.2015.

38. Bush, G. Address before a joint session of the Congress on the Persian Gulf crisis and the federal budget deficit [Electronic resource] : Sept. 11, 1990 / G. Bush // The American Presidency Project. – Mode of access: http://www.presidency.ucsb.edu/ws/

index.php?pid=18820&st=&st1=#ixzz2jkpm7nFI. – Date of access: 02.05.2015.

39. Bush, G. W. A charge to keep / G. W Bush. – New York : Morrow, 1999. – XVI, 253 p.

40. Butler, H. A new world takes shape [Electronic resource] / H. Butler // Foreign Affairs. – 1948. – July. – Mode of access: http://www. foreignaffairs.com/articles/70676/sir-harold-butler/a-new-world-takes-shape. – Date of access: 02.05.2015.

41. Butten, S. The new world order / S. Butten. – Philadelphia : Amer. Baptist Publ. Soc., 1919. – 175 p.

42. Cai Mingzhao. The Chinese dream and its appeal [Electronic resource] : keynote speech at the Intern. Dialogue on the Chinese dream, Dec. 7, 2013 / Cai Mingzhao // China.org.cn. – Mode of access: http://china.org.cn/china/Chinese_dream_dialogue/2013-12/07/content_30827106.htm. – Date of access: 02.05.2015.

43. Campaign for World Government [Electronic resource] : rec. of the New York office, 1917–1972, MssCol 461 // The New York Public Library. Manuscripts and Archives Division. – Mode of access: http:// www.nypl.org/sites/default/files/archivalcollections/pdf/ cwg.pdf. – Date of access: 02.05.2015.

44. CCP General Office and State Council General Office opinions concerning strengthening the construction of new types of think tanks with Chinese characteristics [Electronic resource] // China Copyright and Media. – Mode of access: https://chinacopyrightandmedia.wordpress.com/2015/01/20/ccp-general-office-and-state-council-general-office-opinions-concerning-strengthening-the-construction-of-new-types-of-think-tanks-with-chinese-characteristics/?utm_source=The+Sinocism+China+Newsletter&utm_campaign=a617de8ac0-Sinocism01_21_15&utm_medium=email&utm_term=0_171f237867-a617de8ac0-29631745&mc_cid=a617de8ac0&mc_eid=f671861b8a. – Date of access: 20.01.2015.

45. Chavez, U. Speech at 60th UN General Assembly [Electronic resource] / U. Chavez // Embassy of Venezuela to the U.S. – Mode of access: http://www.embavenez-us.org/news.php?nid=1745. – Date of access: 18.06.2013.

46. Чертович, В. Война по законам подлости [Электронный ресурс] / В. Чертович // Profilib : электрон. б-ка. – Режим доступа: http://profilib.com/chtenie/129716/vladimir-chertovich-voyna-po-zakonam-podlosti-118.php. – Дата доступа: 02.05.2015.

47. Chinese president proposes Asia-Pacific dream [Electronic resource] // Xinhua. – 2014. – 9 Nov. – Mode of access: http://news.xinhuanet.com/english/china/2014-11/09/c_133775812.htm. – Date of access: 02.05.2015.

48. Churchill, W. S. The Congress of Europe, May 7, 1948 / W. S. Churchill // Europe unite: speeches 1947 and 1948 / W. S. Churchill ; ed. R. S. Churchill. – London [etc.], 1950.

49. Churchill, W. S. Zionism versus Bolshevism: a struggle for the soul of the Jewish people [Electronic resource] / W. S. Churchill // Focal point publications : David Irving's website. – Mode of access: http://www.fpp.co.uk/bookchapters/WSC/WSCwrote1920.html. – Date of access: 02.05.2015.

50. Clark, G. A New world order – the American lawyer's role [Electronic resource] / G. Clark // Indiana Law J. – 1944. – Vol. 19, iss. 4. – Mode of access: http://www.repository.law.indiana.edu/ilj/vol19/iss4/2. – Date of access: 02.05.2015.

51. Grenville Clark [Electronic resource] // NNDB. Tracking the entire world. – Mode of access: http://www.nndb.com/people/218/000169708. – Date of access: 02.05.2015.

52. Clinton addresses Gay-Rights group but Ducks 'Ellen' [Electronic resource] // Los Angeles Times. – 1997. – 9 Nov. – Mode of access: http://articles.latimes.com/1997/nov/09/news/mn-51995. – Date of access: 02.05.2015.

53. Bill Clinton new world order speech [Electronic resource] : [Washington, DC, Kennedy Center] // YouTube. – Mode of access: https://www.youtube.com/watch?v=-j1b5RlXQkk&feature=youtu.be. – Date of access: 02.05.2015.

54. Clinton, H. R. American global leadership at the center for American progress [Electronic resource] : remarks, Washington, DC, Oct. 12, 2011 / H. R. Clinton // U.S. Department of State. – Mode of access: http://www.state.gov/secretary/20092013clinton/rm/2011/10/175340.htm. – Date of access: 02.05.2015.

55. Clover, C. Clinton vows to thwart new Soviet Union [Electronic resource] / C. Clover // Financial Times. – 2012. – 6 Dec. – Mode of access: http://www.ft.com/cms/s/0/a5b15b14-3fcf-11e2-9f71-00144feabdc0.html#axzz3N0GXxPnR. – Date of access: 06.12.2012.

56. Cohen, W. «Marshall`s legacy: a guide for tomorrow» [Electronic resource] / W. Cohen // U.S. Department of Defense. – Mode of access: http://www.defense.gov/Speeches/Speech.aspx?-SpeechID=646. – Date of access: 04.06.2015.

57. Communism`s collapse poses a challenge to America`s military // U.S. News a. World Rep. – 1991. – 14 Oct. – P. 28–34.

58. Concept of participation of the Russian Federation in BRICS [Electronic resource] // Президент России. – Mode of access: http://eng.kremlin.ru/media/events/eng/files/41d452b13d9c2624d228.pdf. – Date of access: 03.06.2015.

59. Congressional Record 87:1828–31, U.S. Congress, House, 77th Cong., 1st sess., 5 March 1941

60. Continuing the inquiry. The second transformation [Electronic resource] // Council on Foreign Relations. – Mode of access: http://www.cfr.org/about/history/cfr/second_transformation.html. – Date of access: 03.06.2015.

61. Culbertson, E., The preliminary draft of a world constitution, by the Committee to frame a world constitution [Electronic resource] / E. Culbertson // Indiana Law J. – 1949. – Vol. 24, iss. 3. – Mode of access: http://www.repository.law.indiana.edu/ilj/vol24/iss3/20. – Date of access: 03.06.2015.

62. Cuomo, J. Ronald Reagan and the prophecy of Armageddon [Audiobook] / J. Cuomo. – [Sydney] : Austral. Broadcasting Corp., 1984. – 1 sound cassette.

63. Curtis, L. Civitas Dei: the commonwealth of God / L. Curtis. – London : MacMillan, 1938. – LXIV, 985 p.

64. Curtis, L. World Order. (Civitas Dei) / L. Curtis. – New York : Toronto : Oxford Univ. Press, 1939. – 985 p.

65. Curtis, L. World revolution in the cause of peace / L. Curtis. – New York : MacMillan, 1949. – XVI, 135 p.

66. Danzig, J. Winston Churchill: a founder of the European Union [Electronic resource] : 10 Nov. 2013 / J. Danzig // EU ROPE :

a blog by Jon Danzig. –Mode of access: http://eu-rope.ideasoneurope.eu/2013/11/10/winston-churchill-a-founder-of-the-european-union. – Mode of access: 03.06.2015.

67. Дао Сюй: Китаю и России следует создать Евразийский альянс [Электронный ресурс] // Жэньминь Жибао он-лайн. – 2012. – 30 янв. – Режим доступа: http://russian.people.com.cn/95181/7714612.html. – Дата доступа: 03.06.2015.

68. Denyer, S. China promotes 'Asia-Pacific Dream' to counter U.S. 'pivot' [Electronic resource] / S. Denyer // The Washington Post. – 2014. – 11 Nov. – Mode of access: http://www.washingtonpost.com/world/chinas-promotes-asia-pacific-dream-to-counter-us-pivot/2014/11/11/1d9e05a4-1e8e-4026-ad5a-5919f8c0de8a_story.html. – Дата доступа: 03.06.2015.

69. Dittman, R. Sustainable development, the New International Scientific Order and UN reform [Electronic resource] / R. Dittman // SlideServe. – Mode of access: http://www.slideserve.com/chin/sustainable-development-the-new-international-scientific-order-and-un-reform. – Date of access: 03.06.2015.

70. Documents on the history of European integration : in 4 vol. / ed.: W. Lipgens, W. Loth. – Berlin ; New York : de Gruyter, 1985–1991.– Vol. 3 : The struggle for the European Union by political parties and pressure groups in Western European countries, 1945–1950. – 1988. – XXII, 849 p.

71. Doenecke, J. D. Storm on the horizon: the challenge to American intervention, 1939–1941 / J. D. Doenecke. – Lanham ; Oxford : Rowman & Littlefield, 2003. – 552 p.

72. «Don't say population control» – Dr. Guillebaud promotes depopulation at Cambridge [Electronic resource] // Internet Archive. – Mode of access: https://archive.org/details/dontSayPopulationControl-Dr.GuillebaudPromotesDepopulationAt. – Date of access: 03.06.2015.

73. 1992 draft defense planning guidance [Electronic resource] : [last updated Mar. 12, 2008] // Right Web. – Mode of access: http://rightweb.irc-online.org/profile/1992_Draft_Defense_Planning_Guidance. – Date of access: 03.06.2015.

74. Drezner, D. W. The new New world order [Electronic resource] / D W. Drezner // Foreign Affairs. – 2007. – Vol. 86, № 2. – Mode

of access: https://www.foreignaffairs.com/articles/2007-03-01/new-new-world-order. – Date of access: 03.06.2015.

75. Dugan, A. In search of a new world order: WPI history. Part I [Electronic resource] : Febr. 28, 2012 / A. Dugan // The World Policy Institute. – Mode of access: http://www.worldpolicy.org/blog/2012/02/28/search-new-world-order-wpi-history-part-i. – Date of access: 03.06.2015

76. Dugan, A. The world order models project: WPI history. Part III [Electronic resource] : Mar. 7, 2012 / A. Dugan // The World Policy Institute. – Mode of access: http://www.worldpolicy.org/blog/2012/03/07/world-order-models-project. – Date of access: 03.06.2015.

77. Dugan, A. Toward a new global platform: WPI history. Part IV [Electronic resource] : Mar. 10, 2012 / A. Dugan // The World Policy Institute. – Mode of access: http://www.worldpolicy.org/blog/2012/03/10/toward-new-global-platform. – Date of access: 03.06.2015.

78. Dugan, A. World peace through world law: WPI history. Part II [Electronic resource] : Mar. 1, 2012 / A. Dugan // The World Policy Institute. – Mode of access: http://www.worldpolicy.org/blog/2012/03/10/world-peace-through-world-law-wpi-history-part-ii. – Date of access: 03.06.2015.

79. Einstein, A. Towards a world government (1946) / A. Einstein // Out of my later years: the scientist, philosopher and man portrayed through his own words / A. Einstein. – New York, 1956.

80. Electromagnetic spectrum strategy, 2013. A call to action [Electronic resource] / U.S. Department of Defense. – Washington, 2013. – Mode of access: http://www.defense.gov/news/dodspectrumstrategy.pdf. – Date of access: 03.06.2015.

81. Estulin, D. Bilderberg report 2012 [Electronic resource] / D. Estulin // Official Web site of Daniel Estulin. – Mode of access: http://www.danielestulin.com/bilderberg-reportinforme-2012. – Date of access: 03.06.2015.

82. Exceptionalism – Manifest Destiny [Electronic resource] // Encyclopedia of the New American Nation. – Mode of access: http://www.americanforeignrelations.com/E-N/Exceptionalism-Manifest-destiny.html. – Date of access: 03.06.2015.

83. Faisal, I. Iraq nets handsome profit by dumping dollar for euro [Electronic resource] / I. Faisal // The Guardian. – 2003. – 16 Febr. – Mode of access: http://www.theguardian.com/business/2003/feb/16/iraq.theeuro. – Date of access: 03.06.2015.

84. Falk, R. A. Re-imagining human global governance / R. A. Falk. – London : Routledge, 2013. – 208 p.

85. Falk, R. A. The Constitutional foundations of world peace / R. A. Falk, R. C. Johansen, S. S. Kim. – Albany : State Univ. of New York Press, 1993. – XIV, 388 p.

86. Ferrell, R. Harry S. Truman and the modern American presidency / R. Ferrell. – Boston : Little, Brown, 1983. – 220 p.

87. Finley, G. Puritan belief and «Manifest Destiny» [Electronic resource] / G. Finley // End Time Pilgrim. – Mode of access: http://www.endtimepilgrim.org/puritans03.htm. – Date of access: 03.06.2015.

88. Фроянов, И. Я. Архитекторы, прорабы и вольные каменщики перестройки / И. Я. Фроянов // Совет. Россия. – 2002. – 20 июля. – С. 3–4.

89. Gardner R. N. The hard road to World Order [Electronic resource] / R. N. Gardner // Foreign Affairs. – 1974. – Vol. 52, iss. 3. – Mode of access: http://archive.org/stream/TheHardRoadToWorldOrder/HardRoadtoWorldOrder_djvu.txt. – Date of access: 03.06.2015.

90. Face the nation transcripts May 11, 2014: Rogers, Gates, Warren [Electronic resource] // CBS news. – Mode of access: http://www.cbsnews.com/news/face-the-nation-transcripts-may-11-2014-rogers-gates-warren. – Date of access: 11.05.2014.

91. G. H. Walker & Co [Electronic resource] // Wikipedia : the free encycl. – Mode of access: http://en.wikipedia.org/wiki/G._H._Walker_%26_Co. – Date of access: 03.06.2015.

92. Global trends 2030: alternative worlds [Electronic resource] : rep., 10 Dec. 2012 / Nat. Intelligence Council // Public Intelligence. – Mode of access: https://publicintelligence.net/global-trends-2030. – Date of access: 03.06.2015.

93. Gorbachev foreign policy tour, May 6, 1992 [Electronic resource] // C-SPAN. – Mode of access: http://www.c-span.org/video/?25965-1/gorbachev-foreign-policy-tour. – Date of access: 03.06.2015.

94. Gorbachev, M. Acceptance speech [Electronic resource] : 10 Dec. 1990 / M. Gorbachev // Nobelprize.org : the offic. web site of the

Nobel Prize. – Mode of access: http://www.nobelprize.org/nobel_ prizes/peace/laureates/1990/gorbachev-acceptance.html. – Date of access: 03.06.2015.

95. Gorbachev, M. Nobel lecture [Electronic resource] : 5 June 1991 / M. Gorbachev // Nobelprize.org : the offic. web site of the Nobel Prize. – Mode of access: http://www.nobelprize.org/nobel_prizes/ peace/laureates/1990/gorbachev-lecture.html. – Date of access: 03.06.2015.

96. Gorbachev, M. The road we traveled, the challenges we face : speeches, art., interviews / M. Gorbachev. – Moscow : Ves Mir, 2006. – 149 p.

97. Gorbachev proposes new global forum to augment 'Lame UN' [Electronic resource] : Nov. 21, 2014 // RT. – Mode of access: http://rt.com/news/207787-gorbachev-program-stabilize-world. – Date of access: 21.11.2014.

98. Grosse, P. Continuing the inquiry. The Council on Foreign Relations from 1921 to 1996 [Electronic resource] / P. Grosse // Council on Foreign Relations. – Mode of access: http://www.cfr.org/histo-ry-and-theory-of-international-relations/continuing-inquiry/p108. – Date of access: 03.06.2015.

99. Grossman, Z. From Wounded Knee to Syria: a century of U.S. mil-itary interventions [Electronic resource] / Z. Grossman // Academic Computing @ Evergreen. – Mode of access: http://academic. evergreen.edu/g/grossmaz/interventions.html. – Date of access: 03.06.2015.

100. Guide to the Committee to Frame a World Constitution records 1945–1951 [Electronic resource] // University of Chicago Library. – Mode of access: http://www.lib.uchicago.edu/e/scrc/findingaids/ view.php?eadid=ICU.SPCL.CFWC. – Date of access: 03.06.2015.

101. Guide to the World Movement for World Federal Government. Records 1947–1951 [Electronic resource] // The University of Chicago Library. – Mode of access: http://www.lib.uchi-cago.edu/e/scrc/findingaids/view.php?eadid=ICU.SPCL. WMWFG&q=World%20Association%20of%20World%20 Federalists. – Date of access: 04.06.2015.

102. Hague Conventions, 1899 & 1907 [Electronic resource] // Council on Foreign Relations. – Mode of access: http://www.cfr.org/

international-law/hague-conventions-1899-1907/p9597. – Date of access: 04.06.2015.

103. Harley, J. A. Role of information warfare: truth and myths / J. A. Harley. – Newport : Joint Military Operations Dept. : Naval War College, 1996. – II, 23 p.

104. Held, D. Democracy and the global order: from the modern state to cosmopolitan governance / D. Held. – Stanford : Stanford Univ. Press, 1995. – XII, 324 p.

105. Heritage, T. Ukraine holds key to Putin's dream of a new union [Electronic resource] / T. Heritage // Reuters. – Mode of access: http://www.reuters.com/article/2013/11/29/us-ukraine-eu-putin-idUSBRE9AS0F320131129. – Date of access: 29.11.2013.

106. Hicks, F. C. The new world order, international organization, international law, international cooperation / F. C. Hicks. – New York : Doubleday, Page & Co, 1920. – VIII, 496 p.

107. History. The Institute for World Order and the World Order Models Project [Electronic resource] // World Policy Institute. – Mode of access: http://www.worldpolicy.org/history. – Date of access: 04.06.2015.

108. The Politics of World Federation: Vol. 1, United Nations, U.N. reform, atomic control, Vol. 2, From world federalism to global governance (Praeger, 2004) [Electronic resource] // History of World Federation. – Mode of access: http://josephpbaratta.com. – Date of access: 04.06.2015.

109. Home Rule Globally [Electronic resource]. – Mode of access: http://www.homeruleglobally.org. – Date of access: 04.06.2015.

110. Hooper, J. Pope Calls for a new world order [Electronic resource] / J. Hooper // The Guardian. – 2004. – 2 Jan. – Mode of access: http://www.theguardian.com/world/2004/jan/02/catholicism.religion. – Date of access: 04.06.2015.

111. Howard, G. K. America and a new world order / G. K. Howard. – New York : C. Scribner's Sons, 1940. – 121 p.

112. Hulsman, J. C. Paradigm for the new world order: a schools-of-thought analysis of American foreign policy in the post-cold war era / J. C. Hulsman. – New York : St. Martin's Press, 1997. – XI, 212 p.

113. Human Development Report 1994 / UN Development Progr. – New York : Oxford Univ. Press for the UNDP, 1994. – XI, 226 p.

114. Huntington, S. P. The clash of civilizations and the remaking of world order / S. P. Huntington. – New York : Simon & Schuster, 1996. – 367 p.

115. Huntington, S. P. The erosion of American national interests [Electronic resource] / S. P. Huntington // Mount Holyoke College. – Mode of access: http://www.mtholyoke.edu/acad/intrel/hunting3.htm. – Date of access: 09.07.2014.

116. Hutchins, R. M. The State of the University, 1929–1949 / R. M. Hutchins. – [Chicago : s. n.], 1949. – 44 p.

117. Ильин, И. Что сулит миру расчленение России? [Электронный ресурс] / И. Ильин // Православие. – Режим доступа: http://www.pravoslavie.ru/put/2444.htm. – Дата доступа: 04.06.2015.

118. Rathmell, A. J. Information warfare: implications for arms control / A. J. Rathmell // Bull. of Arms Control. – 1998. – Vol. 29. – P. 8–14.

119. Members of the Union [Electronic resource] // Inter-Parliamentary Union. – Mode of access: http://www.ipu.org/english/membshp.htm. – Date of access: 04.06.2015.

120. International meeting of experts on the new international economic order – philosophical and socio-cultural implications, Vienna, 2–3 April, 1979 [Electronic resource] : communiqué // International Progress Organization. – Mode of access: http://www.i-p-o.org/nieo.htm. – Date of access: 04.06.2015.

121. Ирак и прочие интервенции [Электронный ресурс] // Темная сторона Америки : независимый информ. ресурс. – Режим доступа: http://www.usinfo.ru/intervencyiindex.htm. – Дата доступа: 04.06.2015.

122. Jacobson, M. F. Barbarian virtues: the United States encounters foreign peoples at home and abroad, 1876–1917 / M. F. Jacobson. – New York : Hill a. Wang, 2001. – XII, 324 p.

123. Johnson, C. The arithmetic of America`s military bases abroad: what does it all add up to? [Electronic resource] / C. Johnson // HNN: history news network. – Mode of access: http://historynewsnetwork.org/article/3097. – Date of access: 04.06.2015.

124. Woolbert, R. G. Recent books on international relations. General: economic and social [Electronic resource] / R. G. Woolbert // Foreign Affairs. – 1946. – April. – Mode of access: https://www.

foreignaffairs.com/reviews/capsule-review/1946-04-01/world-order-its-intellectual-and-cultural-foundations. – Date of access: 04.06.2015. – Book rev.: Johnson, F. E. World order: its intellectual and cultural foundations / F. E. Johnson. – New York : Harper & Br., [1945]. – IX, 247 p.

125. Jones, C. Global justice: defending cosmopolitanism / C. Jones. – Oxford ; New York : Oxford Univ. Press, 2001. – XIII, 249 p.

126. Каддафи призвал создать объединенную армию Африки [Электронный ресурс] // Взгляд. – 2010. – 15 дек. – Режим доступа: http://www.vz.ru/news/2010/12/15/454859.html. – Дата доступа: 04.06.2015.

127. Kagan, R. Multilateralism, American style [Electronic resource] / R. Kagan // Carnegie Endowment for International Peace. – Mode of access: http://carnegieendowment.org/2002/09/13/multilateralism-american-style. – Date of access: 04.06.2015.

128. Kahler, E. The case for world government, 6 January 1947 [Doc. 119] / E. Kahler // Common Cause. – 1947. – 1 July. – P. 6–7.

129. Al Kamen. George W. Bush and the G-Word [Electronic resource] / Al Kamen // Washington Post. – 2005. – 14 Oct. – Mode of access: http://www.washingtonpost.com/wp-dyn/content/article/2005/10/13/AR2005101301688.html. – Date of access: 04.06.2015.

130. Kemp, G. Strategic geography and the changing Middle East [Electronic resource] / G. Kemp, R. Harkavy // Foreign Affairs. – 1999. – Vol. 76, № 6. – Mode of access: http://www.foreignaffairs.com/articles/53542/l-carl-brown/strategic-geography-and-the-changing-middle-east. – Date of access: 04.06.2015.

131. Kennan, G. F. Measures short of war: the lectures at the National War College, 1946–1947 / G. F. Kennan ; ed.: G. D. Harlow, G. C. Maerz. – Washington : Nat. Defense Univ. Press, 1991. – XXXIII, 326 p.

132. Kennedy, J. F. Address «The President and the Press» before the American Newspaper Publishers Association, New York City, April 27, 1961 [Electronic resource] / J. F. Kennedy // The American Presidency Project. – Mode of access: http://www.presidency.ucsb.edu/ws/index.php?pid=8093. – Date of access: 04.06.2015.

133. Kerr, F. From Empire to Commonwealth [Electronic resource] / F. Kerr // Foreign Affairs. – 1922. – Vol. 1, iss. 2. – Mode of access: http://www.foreignaffairs.com/articles/68364/philip-kerr/from-empire-to-commonwealth. – Date of access: 04.06.2015.

134. Kessler, B. R. Bush's new world order: the meaning behind the words [Electronic resource] : a research paper presented to the Research Dep. Air Command a. Staff College in Partial Fulfillment of the Graduation Requirements of ACSC / B. R. Kessler // Internet Archive. – Mode of access: https://archive.org/details/BushsNewWorldOrderTheMeaningBehindTheWords. – Date of access: 04.06.2015.

135. King, A. The first global revolution [Electronic resource] : a rep. by the Council of the Club of Rome / A. King, B. Schneider // GeoEngineering Watch. – Mode of access: http://www.geoengineeringwatch.org/documents/TheFirstGlobalRevolution_text.pdf. – Date of access: 25.10.2014.

136. Kissinger, H. Diplomacy / H. Kissinger. – New York: Simon&Schuster, 1994. – 912 p.

137. Kissinger, H. World order / H. Kissinger. – New York : Penguin Press, 2014. – 432 p.

138. Конобеев, В. Битва за Римленд: ресурс стран Восточной Европы в геостратегии США в Евразии [Электронный ресурс] / В. Конобеев // Беларус. думка. – 2009. – № 3. – Режим доступа: http://beldumka.belta.by/isfiles/000167_422107.pdf. – Дата доступа: 05.06.2015.

139. Krever, M. Russia can't be 'firefighter and arsonist' in Ukraine, says U.S. [Electronic resource] / M. Krever // Amanpour. – Mode of access: http://amanpour.blogs.cnn.com/2014/04/21/exclusive-russia-cant-be-firefighter-and-arsonist-in-ukraine-says-u-s. – Date of access: 28.12.2014.

140. Layne, C. The end of Pax Americana: how Western decline became inevitable [Electronic resource] / C. Layne // The Atlantic. – 2012. – 26 Apr. – Mode of access: http://www.theatlantic.com/international/archive/2012/04/the-end-of-pax-americana-how-western-decline-became-inevitable/256388. – Date of access: 05.06.2015.

141. Layne, C. The global power shift from West to East [Electronic resource] / C. Layne // The National Interest. – 2012. – May/June.

– Mode of access: http://nationalinterest.org/issue/may-june-2012. – Date of access: 05.06.2015.

142. Dong Hwi Lee. Global governance as a way of balancing sovereignty with global responsibility [Electronic resource] / Dong Hwi Lee / The Nuclear Security Governance Experts Group (NSGEG). – Mode of access: http://www.nsgeg.org/Global%20Governance%20as%20 a%20Way%20of%20Balancing%20Sovereignty%20with%20 Global%20Responsibility.pdf. – Date of access: 05.06.2015.

143. Lett, D. G. Phoenix rising: the rise and fall of the American republic / D. G. Lett. – [S. l. : s. n.], 2008. – 600 p.

144. Levin, N. G. Woodrow Wilson and world politics. America's response to war and revolution / N. G. Levin. – Oxford : Oxford Univ. Press, 1968. – XII, 340 p.

145. Libertarian speaker to present ACCENT program [Electronic resource] : Oct. 24, 2012 // News University of Florida. – Mode of access: http://news.ufl.edu/archive/2012/10/libertarian-speaker-to-present-accent-program-thursday.html. – Date of access: 05.06.2015.

146. Lieberthal, K. Addressing U.S.-China strategic distrust [Electronic resource] / K. Lieberthal, Wang Jisi // The Brookings Institution. – Mode of access: http://www.brookings.edu/~/media/research/files/papers/2012/3/30%20us%20china%20lieberthal/0330_china_lieberthal.pdf. – Date of access: 05.06.2015.

147. Ash Jain. Like-minded and capable democracies: a new framework for advancing a liberal world order [Electronic resource] : an IIGG working paper / Ash Jain // Council on Foreign Relations. – Mode of access: http//www.cfr.org/international-organizations-and-alliances/like-minded-capable-democracies-new-framework-advancing-liberal-world-order/p29484. – Date of access: 05.06.2015.

148. Lipkin, M. Moscow economic conference of April 1952: an early bid for peaceful coexistence or ideological warfare? [Electronic resource] / M. Lipkin // Cold war interactions reconsidered : 9th annu. Aleksanteri conf., Helsinki, 29–31 Oct. 2009 / Univ. of Helsinki. – Mode of access: http://www.helsinki.fi/aleksanteri/conference2009/abstracts/lipkin.htm. – Date of access: 15.05.2013.

149. Lippman, W. The American destiny / W. Lippman // Life. – 1939. – Vol 6, № 23. – P. 47–74.

150. Li Hui. Chinese dream in accord with Russian dream [Electronic resource] / Li Hui // People`s Daily Online. – 2014. – 22 May. – Mode of access: http://english.peopledaily.com.cn/n/2014/0522/c98649-8731036.html. – Date of access: 22.05.2014.

151. Liu Chang. Commentary: U.S. fiscal failure warrants a de-Americanized world [Electronic resource] / Liu Chang // Xinhua. – 2013. – 13 Oct. – Mode of access: http://news.xinhuanet.com/english/indepth/2013-10/13/c_132794246.htm. – Date of access: 13.10.2013.

152. Loftus, J. The secret war against the Jews: how western espionage betrayed the Jewish people / J. Loftus, M. Aarons. – New York : St. Martin's Press, 1994. – IX, 658 p.

153. Lubragge, M. T. Manifest Destiny – the philosophy that created a nation [Electronic resource] / M. T. Lubragge // American history from Revolution to Reconstruction and beyond / University of Groningen. – Mode of access: http://www.let.rug.nl/usa/essays/1801-1900/manifest-destiny/manifest-destiny---the-philosophy-that-created-a-nation.php. – Date of access: 05.06.2015.

154. Luce, H. R. The American century [Electronic resource] / H. R. Luce // Life. – 1941. – 17 Febr. – Mode of access: http://www.informationclearinghouse.info/article6139.htm.– Date of access: 05.06.2015.

155. Luce, H. R. The American century / H. R. Luce // The New York Times. – 1941. – 4 Mar. – P. 14–15/

156. Luce, H. R. The American century / H. R. Luce // Reader's Digest. – 1941. – April. – P. 45–49.

157. Luce, H. R. The American century / H. R. Luce. – New York : Farrar a. Rinehart, 1941. – 89 p.

158. Лукашенко, А. Г. О судьбах нашей интеграции [Электронный ресурс] / А. Г. Лукашенко // Известия. – 2011. – 17 окт. – Режим доступа: http://izvestia.ru/news/504081. – Дата доступа: 05.06.2015.

159. Lynch, F. H. Challenge: the church and the new world order / F. H. Lynch. – New York : Chicago Fleming H. Revell Co, 1916. – 263 p.

160. Lynch, F. H. The peace problem: the task of the twentieth century / F. H. Lynch. – New York : Fleming H. Revell Co, 1911. – 127 p.

161. Ma Jiali. Chinese dream vs Indian dream: advantages and constraints [Electronic resource] / Ma Jiali // China – US Focus. – Mode of access: http://www.chinausfocus.com/political-social-development/chinese-dream-vs-indian-dream-advantages-and-constraints. – Date of access: 19.12.2013.

162. MacAskill, E. George Bush: «God told me to end the tyranny in Iraq» [Electronic resource] / E. MacAskill // The Guardian. – 2005. – 7 Oct. – Mode of access: http://www.theguardian.com/world/2005/oct/07/iraq.usa. – Date of access: 05.06.2015.

163. Mackinder, H. J. Democratic ideals and reality: a study in the politics of reconstruction / H. J. Mackinder. – Washington : Nat. Defence Univ. Press, 1996. – XXIII, 213 p.

164. Mackinder, H. J. The geographical pivot of history / H. J. Mackinder // Geogr. J. – 1904. – Vol. 23, № 4. – P. 421–437.

165. Maessen, J. Legitimizing global tyranny – moving towards world government [Electronic resource] / J. Maessen // Global Research: Center for Research on Globalization. – Mode of access: http://www.globalresearch.ca/legitimizing-global-tyranny-moving-towards-world-government/30961. – Date of access: 05.06.2015.

166. Malinin, S. Latin American revolutionaries make bizarre attempt to bite USA in the side [Electronic resource] / S. Malinin // Pravda. ru. – 2009. – 20 Apr. – Mode of access: http://english.pravda.ru/world/americas/20-04-2009/107426-sucre-0. – Date of access: 05.06.2015.

167. Mandela's sharp statements rarely cited in mainstream media [Electronic resource] // RT. – 2013. – 6 Dec. – Mode of access: http://rt.com/news/mandela-sharp-quotes-media-860. – Date of access: 08.12.2013.

168. Mandelbaum, M. The ideas that conquered the world: peace, democracy, and free markets in the twenty-first century [Electronic resource] : remarks to the Open Forum, Washington, Sept. 18, 2002 / M. Mandelbaum // U.S. Department of State. Archive. – Mode of access: http://2001-2009.state.gov/s/p/of/proc/tr/15162.htm. – Date of access: 05.06.2015.

169. Mandelbaum, M. The ideas that conquered the world: peace, democracy, and free markets in the twenty-first century / M. Mandelbaum. – New York : Public Affairs, 2002. – X, 496 p.

170. Marshall, A. G. Are we witnessing the start of a global revolution?: North Africa and the global political awakening. Pt. 1 [Electronic resource] / A. G. Marshall // Global Research: Center for Research on Globalization. – Mode of access: http://www.globalresearch.ca/ are-we-witnessing-the-start-of-a-global-revolution/22963. – Date of access: 27.01.2011.

171. The new world order / ed. F. S. Marvin. – London : Oxford Univ. Press, 1932. – 188 p.

172. Maund, C. P. Will the US succeed in breaking Russia to maintain dollar hegemony? [Electronic resource] / C. P. Maund // Clive P. Maund. – Mode of access: http://www.clivemaund.com/arti-cle.php?art_id=3278&PHPSESSID=858d95f877010a9291c0b-959c269ab82. – Date of access: 05.06.2015.

173. McFadden, L. T. [Speech in the House of Representatives, 10 June 1932] [Electronic resource] / L. T. McFadden // Alachua Freenet. – Mode of access: http://www.afn.org/~govern/mcfaddengif.html. – Date of access: 05.06.2015.

174. Mead, W. R. God`s country? [Electronic resource] / W. R. Mead // Foreign Affairs. – 2006. – Vol. 85, № 5. – Mode of access: http://www.foreignaffairs.com/articles/61914/walter-russell-mead/ gods-country. – Date of access: 05.06.2015.

175. Mead, W. R. Recent books on international relations. The United States [Electronic resource] / W. R. Mead // Foreign Affairs. – 2002. – Sept./Oct. – Mode of access: https://www.foreignaffairs.com/ reviews/capsule-review/2002-09-01/ideas-conquered-world-peace-democracy-and-free-markets-twenty. – Date of access: 08.06.2015. – Book rev.: Mandelbaum, M. The ideas that conquered the world: peace, democracy, and free markets in the twenty-first century / M. Mandelbaum. – New York : Publ. Affairs, 2002. – X, 466 p.

176. Milestones: 1899–1913: Secretary of State John Hay and the Open Door in China, 1899–1900 [Electronic resource] // U.S. Department of State, Office of the Historian. – Mode of access: https://history.state.gov/milestones/1899-1913/hay-and-china. – Date of access: 08.06.2015.

177. Milestones: 1914–1920: the League of Nations, 1920 [Electronic resource] // U.S. Department of State, Office of the Historian.

– Mode of access: https://history.state.gov/milestones/1914-1920/league. – Date of access: 08.06.2015.

178. Milestones: 1914–1920: Wilson's fourteen points, 1918 [Electronic resource] // U.S. Department of State, Office of the Historian. – Mode of access: https://history.state.gov/milestones/1914-1920/fourteen-points. – Date of access: 08.06.2015.

179. Mitrovich, G. Undermining the Kremlin: America`s strategy to subvert the Soviet Bloc, 1947–1956 / Mitrovich G. – New York : Cornell Univ. Press, 2000. – X, 235 p.

180. Moynihan, D. P. A dangerous place / D. P. Moynihan, S. Weaver. – Boston : Little, Brown & Co, 1978. – X, 297 p.

181. Нарочницкая, Н. А. Россия и русские в мировой истории / Н. А. Нарочницкая. – М. : Междунар. отношения, 2005. – 533 с.

182. National Security Strategy, February 2015 [Electronic resource] / The White House // National Security Strategy Archive. – Mode of access: http://nssarchive.us/wp-content/uploads/2015/02/2015.pdf. – Date of access: 08.06.2015.

183. Назарбаев, Н. Евразийский Союз: от идеи к истории будущего [Электронный ресурс] / Н. Назарбаев // Известия. – 2011. – 25 окт. – Режим доступа: http://izvestia.ru/news/504908. – Дата доступа: 08.06.2015.

184. Study of communication problems – implementation of resolutions 4/19 and 4/20 adopted by the General conference at its twenty-first session [Electronic resource] : 22 C/96, 7 Oct. 1983 // UNESDOC Database. – Mode of access: http://unesdoc.unesco.org/images/0005/000572/057205eo.pdf. – Date of access: 15.06.2015.

185. A report to the National Security Council – NSC 68 [Electronic resource] : Apr. 12, 1950. President's secretary's file, Truman papers // Harry S. Truman Library and Museum. – Mode of access: https://www.trumanlibrary.org/whistlestop/study_collections/coldwar/documents/pdf/10-1.pdf. – Date of access: 08.06.2015.

186. Oakley, R. Analysis: crisis may lead to new world order [Electronic resource] : 1 Apr. 1, 2009 / R. Oakley / CNN. – Mode of access: http://edition.cnn.com/2009/WORLD/europe/04/01/oakley.summit/index.html. – Date of access: 08.06.2015.

187. Obama, B. H. A just and lasting peace [Electronic resource] : Nobel lecture, Oslo, 10 Dec. 2009 / B. H. Obama // Nobelprize.org : the offic. web site of the Nobel prize. – Mode of access: http://www. nobelprize.org/nobel_prizes/peace/laureates/2009/obama-lecture_ en.html. – Date of access: 08.06.2015.

188. Press conference by the President Barack Obama [Electronic resource] : Aug. 1, 2014 // The White House. – Mode of access: http://www.whitehouse.gov/the-press-office/2014/08/01/ press-conference-president. – Date of access: 08.06.2015.

189. Obama, B. H. Remarks at the United States Military Academy commencement ceremony [Electronic resource] : West Point, New York, May 28, 2014 / B. H. Obama // The White House. – Mode of access: https://www.whitehouse.gov/the-press-office/2014/05/28/ remarks-president-west-point-academy-commencement-ceremony. – Date of access: 08.06.2015.

190. Obama, B. H. Remarks in address to the United Nations General Assembly, [Electronic resource] : UN Gen. Assembly Hall, New York, Sept. 24, 2014 / B. H. Obama // The White House. – Mode of access: http://www.whitehouse.gov/the-press-office/2014/09/24/ remarks-president-obama-address-united-nations-general-assem- bly. – Date of access: 08.06.2015.

191. Obama, B. H. Remarks in State of the Union Address [Electronic resource] : Washington, Jan. 24, 2012 / B. H. Obama // The White House. – Mode of access: https://www.whitehouse.gov/the-press- office/2012/01/24/remarks-president-state-union-address. – Date of access: 08.06.2015.

192. Official American commentary on the Fourteen points [Electronic resource] // The intimate papers of Colonel House [Electronic resource] : in 4 vol. / ed. C. Seymour. – Boston ; New York, 1928. – Vol. 4. – Mode of access: http://archive.org/stream/intimatepa- persof007804mbp/intimatepapersof007804mbp_djvu.txt. – Date of access: 08.06.2015.

193. Onuf, N. G. World of our making: rules and rule in social theory and international relations / N. G. Onuf. – Columbia : Univ. of South California Press, 1989. – XII, 341 p.

194. Our global neighborhood / Commiss. on Global Governance. – Oxford ; New York : Oxford Univ. Press, 1995. – XX, 410 p.

195. Nixon, R. Toasts of the President and President Medici of Brazil [Electronic resource] : Dec. 7, 1971 / R. Nixon, Medici // The American Presidency Project. – Mode of access: http://www.presidency.ucsb.edu/ws/?pid=3247. – Date of access: 08.06.2015.

196. Novak, J. The trilateral connection / J. Novak // Atlantic Month. – 1977. – Vol. 15, July. – P. 50–57.

197. Park Geun-hye. Remarks by President at the 2013 International conference on global cooperation in the era of Eurasia [Electronic resource] : Oct. 18, 2013 / Park Geun-hye // Korea.net. – Mode of access: http://www.korea.net/Government/Briefing-Room/Presidential-Speeches/view?articleId=114334. – Date of access: 18.10.2013.

198. Peck, G. T. Universal pattern of law is sought as basis for global community / G. T. Peck // New York Herald Tribune. – 1946. – 3 Nov. – P. X–32.

199. Ли Хуэй. «Пекинская опера» и китайский звездолет [Электронный ресурс] : [беседа с Послом КНР в РФ Ли Хуэй] / Ли Хуэй ; беседовал А. А. Проханов // Жэньминь Жибао он-лайн. – Режим доступа: http://russian.people.com.cn/n/2014/0826/c31521-8774606.html. – Дата доступа: 08.06.2015.

200. People of the world, unite for the complete, thorough, total and resolute prohibition and destruction of nuclear weapons. – Peking : Foreign Lang. Press, 1963. – 208 p.

201. Plashchinsky, A. New world order: cold war and U.S. «Grand Strategy» connection / A. Plashchinsky. – Saarbrücken : LAP Lambert Acad. Publ., 2015. – 88 p.

202. Pogge, T. World poverty and human rights / T. Rogge. – Cambridge : Polity Press, 2002. – 284 p.

203. Ponomareva, E. G. The Eurasian Union: a threat to the new world order [Electronic resource] / E.G. Ponomareva // Atlantic-Community.org. – Mode of access: http://archive.atlantic-community.org/index/Open_Think_Tank_Article/The_Eurasian_Union:_A_Threat_to_the_New_World_Order. – Date of access: 08.06.2015.

204. Benedict XVI. Caritas in veritate [Electronic resource] : encyclical letter to the bishops, priests and deacons men and women religious,

the lay faithful and all people of good will on integral human development in charity and truth, 29 June 2009 / Pontiff Benedict XVI // The Holy See. – Mode of access: http://www.vatican.va/holy_father/ benedict_xvi/encyclicals/documents/hf_ben-xvi_enc_20090629_ caritas-in-veritate_en.html. – Date of access: 08.06.2015.

205. Towards reforming the international financial and monetary systems in the context of global public authority [Electronic resource] : Oct. 24, 2011 / Pontifical Council for Justice and Peace // The Holy See. – Mode of access: http://www.vatican.va/roman_curia/pontifical_ councils/justpeace/documents/rc_pc_justpeace_doc_20111024_ nota_en.html. – Date of access: 08.06.2015.

206. Francis. Holy Mass [Electronic resource] : celebration presided over by Pope Francis at the Military Memorial in Redipuglia on the occasion of the 100th anniversary of the outbreak of First World War, 13 Sept. 2014 / Pope Francis // The Holy See. – Mode of access: http:// w2.vatican.va/content/francesco/en/homilies/2014/documents/ papa-francesco_20140913_omelia-sacrario-militare-redipuglia. html. – Date of access: 08.06.2015.

207. John Paul II. Message [Electronic resource] : of His Holiness Pope John Paul II for the celebration of the World Day of Peace, 1 Jan. 2004 / Pope John Paul II. // The Holy See. – Mode of access: http:// www.vatican.va/holy_father/john_paul_ii/messages/peace/documents/hf_jp-ii_mes_20031216_xxxvii-world-day-for-peace_en.html#fn5. – Date of access: 08.06.2015.

208. John Paul II. Homily [Electronic resource] : Solemnity of Mary, Mother of God, XXXVII World Day of Peace, 1 Jan. 2004 / Pope John Paul II. – Mode of access: http://www.vatican.va/ holy_father/john_paul_ii/homilies/2004/documents/hf_jp-ii_ hom_20040101_en.html. – Date of access: 08.06.2015.

209. Paul VI. Populorum progressio [Electronic resource] : encyclical of the Pope Paul VI on the Development of Peoples, Mar. 26, 1967 / Pope Paul VI. – Mode of access: http://www.vatican.va/holy_father/ paul_vi/encyclicals/documents/hf_p-vi_enc_26031967_populorum_en.html. – Date of access: 08.06.2015.

210. Porter, A. G20 Summit: Gordon Brown announces «new world order» [Electronic resource] / A. Porter, R. Winnet, T. Harden // The Telegraph. – 2009. – 3 Apr. – Mode of access: http://www.

telegraph.co.uk/finance/g20-summit/5097195/G20-summit-Gordon-Brown-announces-new-world-order.html. – Date of access: 08.06.2015.

211. Preliminary draft of a world constitution (1947–1948) [Electronic resource] / Comm. to Frame a World Constitution. – Chicago : Univ. of Chicago Press, 1948. – Mode of access: http://www.world-beyondborders.org/chicagodraft.htm. – Date of access: 09.06.2015.

212. President Obama claims rise of Isis is «unintended consequence» of George W. Bush's invasion in Iraq [Electronic resource] // The Independent. – 2015. – 18 Mar. – Mode of access|: http://www.independent.co.uk/news/world/middle-east/president-obama-claims-rise-of-isis-is-unintended-consequence-of-george-w-bushs-invasion-in-iraq-10115243.html. – Date of access: 09.06.2015.

213. Wilson, W. President Wilson's fourteen points: the basis of the new world order / W. Wilson. – Boston : League for Permanent Peace, 1918. – 4 p. – (World peace plans ; collected pamphlets ; № 28).

214. Wilson, W. President Woodrow Wilson's 14 Points (1918) [Electronic resource] / W. Wilson // Our Documents. – Mode of access: http://www.ourdocuments.gov/doc.php?flash=true&doc=62. – Date of access: 09.06.2015.

215. Nixon, R. M. Public papers of the Presidents of the United States: Richard Nixon, 1971 : containing the public messages, speeches, a. statements of the President / R. M. Nixon. – Washington : U.S. G.P.O., 1972. – XLIX, 1362 p.

216. Putin, V. Article by Prime Minister Vladimir Putin «A new integration project for Eurasia: the future in the making» [Electronic resource] / V. Putin // Izvestia. – 2011. – 3 Oct. – Mode of access: http://www.russianmission.eu/en/news/article-prime-minister-vladimir-putin-new-integration-project-eurasia-future-making-izvestia-3-#st-hash.lAbTGX7v.dpuf. – Date of access: 10.06.2015.

217. Putin, V. V. [Speech] [Electronic resource] : meeting of the Valdai Intern. Discussion Club, Sept. 19, 2013 / V. V. Putin // President of Russia. – Mode of access: http://en.kremlin.ru/events/president/news/19243. – Date of access: 10.06.2015.

218. Putin, V. V. [Speech] [Electronic resource] : meet. of the Valdai Intern. Discussion Club, Oct. 24, 2014 / V. V. Putin // President of

Russia. – Mode of access: http://eng.news.kremlin.ru/news/23137. – Date of access: 10.06.2015.

219. Путин, В. В. Новый интеграционный проект для Евразии – будущее, которое рождается сегодня [Электронный ресурс] / В. В. Путин // Известия. – 2011. – 3 окт. – Режим доступа: http://izvestia.ru/news/502761. – Дата доступа: 10.06.2015.

220. Putin, V. V. [Speech] [Electronic resource] : the Congr. of Federation of Independent Trade Unions of Russia, Febr. 7, 2015 / V. V. Putin // President of Russia. – Mode of access: http://eng.kremlin.ru/transcripts/23570. – Date of access: 10.06.2015.

221. Putin, V. V. Speech [Electronic resource] : Munich Conf. on Security Policy, Febr. 10, 2007 / V. V. Putin // President of Russia. – Mode of access: http://archive.kremlin.ru/eng/speeches/2007/02/10/0138_type82912type82914type82917type84779_118123.shtml. – Date of access: 10.06.2015.

222. Quigley, C. The Anglo-American establishment: from Rhodes to Cliveden / C. Quigley. – New York : Books in Focus, 1981. – 285 p.

223. Quigley, C. Tragedy and hope: a history of the world in our time / C. Quigley. – New York : Macmillan, 1966. – XI, 1348 p.

224. Rachman, G. And now for a world government [Electronic resource] / G. Rachman // Financial Times. – 2008. – 9 Dec. – Mode of access: http://blogs.ft.com/the-world/2008/12/and-now-for-a-world-government. – Date of access: 10.06.2015.

225. Rebuilding America`s defences: strategy, forces and resources for a new century : a rep. of the Project for the New Amer. Century [Electronic resource] / T. Donnelly [et al.] ; project co-chairmen: D. Kagan, G. Schmitt. – Washington, 2000. – Mode of access: http://www.informationclearinghouse.info/pdf/RebuildingAmericasDefenses.pdf. – Date of access: 11.06.2015.

226. Recknagel, C. Iraq: Baghdad moves to euro [Electronic resource] : Nov. 1, 2000 / C. Recknagel // Radio Free Europe. – Mode of access: http://www.rferl.org/content/article/1095057.html. – Date of access: 11.06.2015.

227. Declaration on the establishment of a new international economic order [Electronic resource] : resolution adopted by the Gen. Assembly, 6 spec. sess., 1974, 1 May, A/RES/S-6/3201 // UN

Documents. – Mode of access: http://www.un-documents.net/ s6r3201.htm. – Date of access: 11.06.2015.

228. Revision of the United Nations Charter: hearings before a subcommittee of the Committee on Foreign Relations, United States Senate, Eighty-first Congress, second session, on resolutions relative to revision of the United Nations Charter, Atlantic Union, World Federation, etc. February 2, 3, 6, 8, 9, 13, 15, 17, and 20, 1950 / U. S. Congress, Senate, Comm. on Foreign Relations, Subcomm. on Revision of the UN Charter. – Washington : U.S. Gov. Print. Off., 1950. – V, 808 p.

229. Rice, C. Campaign 2000: promoting the national interest / C. Rice // Foreign Affairs. – 2000. – Vol. 79, № 1. – P. 45–51.

230. Rice, C. Rethinking the national interest: American realism for a new world [Electronic resource] / C. Rice // Foreign Affairs. – 2008. – Vol. 87, № 4. – Mode of access: https://www.foreignaffairs.com/ articles/2008-06-01/rethinking-national-interest. – Date of access: 11.06.2015.

231. Robbins, A. Secrets of the tomb: Skull and Bones, the Ivy League, and the hidden paths of power / A. Robbins. – Boston : Little, Brown, 2002. – VII, 230 p.

232. Rockefeller Brothers Fund archives [Electronic resource] // Rockefeller Archive Center. – Mode of access: http://www.rockarch. org/collections/rbf. – Date of access: 11.06.2015.

233. Rockefeller Brothers Fund. Special Studies Project. The Mid-Century Challenge to U.S. Foreign Policy [Electronic resource] // Hathi Trust : Digital Libr. – Mode of access: http://babel.hathitrust.org/ cgi/pt/search?q1=the+nation-state+as+it+was+conceived&id=m-dp.39076005459545&view=image&seq=62&num=48. – Date of access: 18.10.2014.

234. Online books by Rockefeller Brothers Fund [Electronic resource] // The Online Books Library. – Mode of access: http://onlinebooks. library.upenn.edu/webbin/book/lookupname?key=Rockefeller%20 Brothers%20Fund. – Date of access: 11.06.2015.

235. Rockefeller, D. Memoirs / D. Rockefeller. – New York : Random House Trade Paperbacks, 2003. – 560 p.

236. Roosevelt, F. D. Address on Armistice Day, Arlington National Cemetery [Electronic resource] : Nov. 11, 1940 / F. D. Roosevelt

// The American Presidency Project. – Mode of access: http://www.presidency.ucsb.edu/ws/?pid=15898. – Date of access: 11.06.2015.

237. Rostow, W. The United States in the world arena: an essay in recent history / W. Rostow. – New York : Harper, 1960. – XXII, 568 p.

238. Rotherham, L. Controversies: from Brussels and closer to home [Electronic resource] / L. Rotherham. – Mode of access: https://d3n8a8pro7vhmx.cloudfront.net/taxpayersalliance/pages/5197/attachments/original/1422261997/controversies.pdf?1422261997. – Date of access: 11.06.2015.

239. McKinley, W. Interview with President William McKinley [Electronic resource] : 1903, 22 Jan. / W. McKinley ; conversed J. Rusling // Kansas Assessment Program. – Mode of access: http://www.ksassessments.org/sites/default/files/HGSS_Preview_Texts/Grade_11/Interview%20with%20President%20William%20McKinley.pdf. – Date of access: 11.06.2015.

240. Russell, B. The atomic bomb and the prevention of war / B. Russell // Bull. of the Atomic Scientists. – 1946. – Vol. 2, № 7/8. – P. 19–21.

241. Russett, B. The U.N. in a new world order [Electronic resource] / B. Russett, J. S. Sutterlin // Foreign Affairs – 1991. – Vol. 70. – Mode of access: www.foreignaffairs.com/articles/46583/bruce-russett-and-james-s-sutterlin/the-un-in-a-new-world-order. – Date of access: 11.06.2015.

242. Russia`s wrong direction: what the United States can and should do : rep. of an independent task force / ed.: J. Edwards, J. Kemp, S. Sestanovich. – New York: Council on Foreign Relations, 2006. – XIV, 82 p. – (Task Force Report ; № 57).

243. Сакович, В. А. Введение в глобалистику : учеб.-метод. пособие / В. А. Сакович. – Минск : Междунар. ун-т «МИТСО», 2014. – 298 с.

244. Satz, D. Equality of what among whom?: thoughts on cosmopolitanism, statism, and nationalism / D. Satz // Global Justice / ed.: I. Shapiro, L. Brilmayer. – New York, 1999. – P. 67–85.

245. Savka, O. Secret documents reveal Stalin was poisoned [Electronic resource] / O. Savka // Pravda.ru. – 2005. – 29 Dec. – Mode of access: http://english.pravda.ru/history/29-12-2005/9457-stalin-0. – Date of access: 11.06.2015.

246. Scheuerman, W. E. The realist case for global reform / W. E. Scheuerman. – Cambridge : Polity Press, 2011. – 219 p.

247. Schulzinger, R. D. The wise men of foreign affairs: the history of the Council on Foreign Relations / R. D. Schulzinger. – New York : Columbia Univ. Press, 1984. – XIII, 342 p.

248. Sempa, F. P. Spykman`s world [Electronic resource] / F. P. Sempa // American Diplomacy. – Mode of access: http://www.unc.edu/ depts/diplomat/item/2006/0406/semp/sempa_spykman.html. – Date of access: 11.06.2015.

249. The intimate papers of Colonel House [Electronic resource] : in 4 vol. / ed. C. Seymour. – Boston ; New York, 1928. – Vol. 3 : Into the world war, April 1917 – June 1918. – Mode of access: http:// archive.org/stream/intimatepapersof007804mbp/intimatepapersof007804mbp_djvu.txt. – Date of access: 11.06.2015.

250. The intimate papers of Colonel House [Electronic resource] : in 4 vol. / ed. C. Seymour. – Boston ; New York, 1928. – Vol. 4 : The ending of the war, June 1918 – August 1919 // Slideshare. – Mode of access: http://www.slideshare.net/RareBooksnRecords/the-intimate-papersofcolonelhousevol41918to1919600pgspol. – Date of access: 11.06.2015.

251. Шамбаров, В. Опасная история. Кто «заказал» Россию революционерам [Электронный ресурс] / В. Шамбаров // Файл-РФ. – 2012. – 16 нояб. – Режим доступа: http://file-rf. ru/analitics/750. – Дата доступа: 11.06.2015.

252. Шебаршин, Л. Хроники Безвременья. Заметки бывшего начальника разведки [Электронный ресурс] / Л. Шебаршин // Леонид Шебаршин. – Режим доступа: http:// shebarshin.ru/timeless.html. – Дата доступа: 11.06.2015.

253. Шебаршин, Л. Рука Москвы: записки начальника советской разведки [Электронный ресурс] / Л. Шебаршин // Леонид Шебаршин. – Режим доступа:http://shebarshin.ru/ intell.html. – Дата доступа: 11.06.2015.

254. Широнин, В. С. Под колпаком контрразведки: тайная подоплека перестройки / В. С. Широнин. – Набережные Челны : Кам. изд. дом, 1998. – 336 с.

255. Shved, V. The Harvard project [Electronic resource] / V. Shved // Oriental Review. – Mode of access: http://orientalreview. org/2010/05/27/the-harvard-project. – Date of access: 11.06.2015.

256. Slaughter, A. The real new world order [Electronic resource] / A. Slaughter // Foreign Affairs. – 1997. – Vol. 76, № 5. – Mode of access: https://www.foreignaffairs.com/issues/1997/76/5. – Date of access: 11.06.2015.

257. Смело выйдем за флажки [Электронный ресурс] : письмо молодых коммунистов съезду партии / А. Веселов [и др.] // Совет. Россия. – 2003. – 25 дек. – Режим доступа: http:// www.sovross.ru/old/2003/144/144_4_7.htm. – Дата доступа: 11.06.2015.

258. Spykman, N. J. America's strategy in world politics: the United States and the balance of power / N. J. Spykman. – New York : Harcourt, Brace a. Co, 1942. – 500 p.

259. Spykman, N. J. Geography and foreign policy I / N. J. Spykman // The Amer. Polit. Science Rev. – 1938. – Vol. 32, № 1. – P. 28–50.

260. Spykman, N. J. The geography of the peace / N. J. Spykman. – New York : Harcourt, Brace a. Co, 1944. – XII, 66 p.

261. Spykman, N. J. Geographic objectives in foreign policy I / N. J. Spykman, A. A. Rollins // The Amer. Polit. Science Rev. – 1939. – Vol. 33, № 3. – P. 391–410.

262. Стариков, Н. Геополитика. Как это делается / Н. Стариков. – СПб. [и др.] : Питер : Питер Пресс, 2014. – 363 с.

263. Starikov, N. Top Russia public intellectual: Western financial system is driving it to war [Electronic resource] / N. Starikov // Russia Insider. – 2015. – 12 Mar. – Mode of access: http:/russia-insider. com/en/politics/2015/02/19/3646. – Date of access: 11.06.2015.

264. Steinberg, J. Cheney's 'Spoon-Benders' pushing nuclear Armageddon [Electronic resource] / J. Steinberg // Executive Intelligence Rev. – 2005. – 26 Aug. – Mode of access: http://www.larouchepub.com/ other/2005/3233spoonbenders.html. – Date of access: 25.12.2014.

265. Sterligov, G. Interview to Russian channel «Rain» («Dojd») [Electronic resource] : broadcast / G. Sterligov // Лучший. ЖЖ.РФ. Мастерская Позитивных Изменений. – Mode of access: http://kir-t34.livejournal.com/14869.html. – Date of access: 25.12.2014

266. Still, W. T. New world order: the ancient plan of secret societies / W. T. Still. – Lafayette : Huntington House Pub., 1990. – 208 p.

267. Stix, G. Effective world government will be needed to stave off climate catastrophe [Electronic resource] / G. Stix // Scientific Amer. – 2012. – 17 Mar. – Mode of access: http://blogs.scientificamerican.com/observations/2012/03/17/effective-world-government-will-still-be-needed-to-stave-off-climate-catastrophe. – Date of access: 11.06.2015.

268. Study group on new world order [Electronic resource] : July 1, 2000 – June 30, 2004 // Council on Foreign Relations. – Mode of access: http://www.cfr.org/projects/world/study-group-on-new-world-order/pr286. – Date of access: 11.06.2015.

269. Sutton, A. Western technology and Soviet economic development : in 3 vol. / A. Sutton. – Stanford : Hoover Inst. on War, Revolution a. Peace : Stanford Univ., 1968–1973. – 3 vol.

270. Talbott, S. The birth of the global nation [Electronic resource] / S. Talbott // Time mag. – U.S. ed. – 1992. – Vol. 140, № 3. – Mode of access: http://content.time.com/time/magazine/article/0,9171,976015,00.html. – Date of access: 11.06.2015.

271. Talbott, S. The great experiment: the story of ancient empires, modern states, and the quest for a global nation / S. Talbott. – New York : Simon & Schuster, 2008. – X, 478 p.

272. Tan, K. C. Toleration, diversity, and global justice / K. C. Tan. – Univ. Park Penn : The Pennsylvania State Univ. Press, 2000. – XII, 233 p.

273. The Archives Hub [Electronic resource]. – Mode of access: http://archiveshub.ac.uk/features/05120803.html. – Date of access: 11.06.2015. http://socialarchive.iath.virginia.edu/ark:/99166/w6q10dvv

274. Blair, T. The Blair doctrine [Electronic resource] : 1999, 22 Apr. / T. Blair // PBS News hour. – Mode of access: http://www.pbs.org/newshour/bb/international/jan-june99/blair_doctrine4-23.html. – Date of access: 11.06.2015.

275. The Club of Rome [Electronic resource] : overview // The Club of Rome. – Mode of access: http://www.clubofrome.org/?p=199. – Date of access: 11.06.2015.

276. Teaching Eleanor Roosevelt glossary. World War II (1939–1945) [Electronic resource] // The George Washington University. – Mode of access: http://www.gwu.edu/~erpapers/teachinger/glossary/world-war-2.cfm. – Date of access: 11.06.2015.

277. The evolution of world peace : essays / ed. F. S. Marvin. – Oxford : Oxford Univ. Press, 1921. – 191 p.

278. The first global revolution [Electronic resource] : a rep. by the Council of the Club of Rome, 1991 // Internet Archive. – The Club of Rome, September 3, 1991. 184 p. / https://archive.org/details/TheFirstGlobalRevolution

279. Woolbert, R. G. Recent books on international relations. General: political, military and legal [Electronic resource] / R. G. Woolbert // Foreign Affairs. – 1941. – July. – Mode of access: http://www.foreignaffairs.com/articles/103069/walter-h-c-laves/the-foundations-of-a-more-stable-world-order. – Date of access: 11.06.2015. – Book rev.: Laves, W. H. C. The foundations of a more stable world order / W. H. C. Laves. – Chicago : Univ. of Chicago Press [1941]. – XIII, 192 p.

280. The free and balanced flow of information in a new communication order [Electronic resource] : rep. of the Meet. of consultants, Paris, 18–21 Dec. 1978 // UNESDOC Database. – Mode of access: http://unesdoc.unesco.org/images/0003/000371/037151eb.pdf. – Date of access: 11.06.2015.

281. The Gorbachev Foundation. About us: the Foundation projects and structural subdivisions [Electronic resource] // The International Foundation for Socio-Economic and Political Studies (The Gorbachev Foundation). – Mode of access: http://www.gorby.ru/en/gorbi_fund/about. – Date of access: 11.06.2015.

282. The Great Seal of the United States [Electronic resource] / U.S. Dep. of State, Bureau of Public Affairs // U.S. Department of State. – Mode of access: http://www.state.gov/documents/organization/27807.pdf. – Date of access: 11.06.2015.

283. U.S. Government. The Great Seal [Electronic resource] // U.S. Diplomatic Mission to Germany. – Mode of access: http://usa.usembassy.de/government-seal.htm. – Date of access: 11.06.2015.

284. The Harvard project on the Soviet social system online [Electronic resource] // Harvard College Library. – Mode of access: http://

hcl.harvard.edu/collections/hpsss/about.html. – Date of access: 12.06.2015.

285. The International Institutions and Global Governance Program. World order in the 21st century [Electronic resource] : concept doc. // Council on Foreign Relations. – Mode of access: http://www.cfr. org/thinktank/iigg/mission.html. – Date of access: 12.06.2015.

286. The new world order. Select list of references on regional and world federation; together with some special plans for world order after the war / comp. H. L. Scanlon ; under the direction of M. A. Matthews. – Washington : Carnegie Endowment for Intern. Peace, 1940. – 17 p. – (Select bibliographies ; № 10).

287. François, L. The right to education: from proclamation to achievement, 1948–1968 / L. François. – Paris : UNESCO, 1968. – 101 p.

288. The State of the World Forum. Our mission [Electronic resource] // State of the World Forum. – Mode of access: http://worldforum. percepticon.com/mission/index.html. – Date of access: 12.06.2015.

289. The United Nations and the future of global governance [Electronic resource] : expert roundup / P. M. Defarges [et al.] // Council on Foreign Relations. – Mode of access: http://www.cfr.org/international-organizations-and-alliances/united-nations-future-global-governance/p29122. – Date of access: 12.06.2015.

290. The war and peace studies of the Council on foreign relations, 1939–1945 / Council on Foreign Relations. – New York : The Harold Pratt House, 1946. – 48 p.

291. The World Revolution [Electronic resource]. – Mode of access: http://www.worldrevolution.org. – Date of access: 12.06.2015.

292. Thompson, K. W. Winston Churchill`s world view: statesmanship and power / K. W. Thompson. – Baton Rouge : Louisiana State Univ. Press, 1983. – 364 p.

293. Thyssen, F. I paid Hitler / F. Thyssen. – New York ; Toronto : Farrar & Rinehart, 1941. – XXIX, 281 p.

294. Torreon, B. S. Instances of use of United States armed forces abroad, 1798–2015 [Electronic resource] : 15 Jan. 2015 / B. S. Torreon // Federation of American Scientists. – Mode of access: https://fas.org/sgp/crs/natsec/R42738.pdf. – Date of access: 12.06.2015.

295. Toynbee, A. J. The trend of international affairs since the war / A. J. Toynbee // Intern. Affairs. – 1931. – Vol. 10, № 6. – P. 803–826.

296. Treaty of Versailles, 28 June 1919 [Electronic resource] // First World War. – Mode of access: http://www.firstworldwar.com/source/versailles31-117.htm. – Date of access: 12.06.2015.

297. Turner, F. G. The significance of the frontier in American history [Electronic resource] / F. G. Turner // The Annenberg Foundation. – Mode of access: http://www.learner.org/workshops/primarysources/corporations/docs/turner.html. – Date of access: 12.06.2015.

298. Ullman, H. War on terror is not the only threat [Electronic resource] / H. Ullman // Atlantic Council. – Mode of access: http://www.atlanticcouncil.org/blogs/new-atlanticist/war-on-terror-is-not-the-only-threat. – Date of access: 12.06.2015.

299. Decisions adopted by the Executive Board at its 181st Session [Electronic resource] : Paris, 30 May 2009 // UNESDOC Database. – Mode of access: http://unesdoc.unesco.org/images/0018/001826/182664E.pdf. – Date of access: 12.06.2015.

300. Introducing UNESCO [Electronic resource] // United Nations Educational, Scientific and Cultural Organization. – Mode of access: http://en.unesco.org/about-us/introducing-unesco. – Date of access: 12.06.2015.

301. Huxley, J. UNESCO: its purpose and its philosophy [Electronic resource] / J. Huxley ; Commiss. of the UNESCO // UNESDOC Database. – Mode of access: http://unesdoc.unesco.org/images/0006/000681/068197eo.pdf. – Date of access: 12.06.2015.

302. UNESCO 1991 prize for peace education [Electronic resource]. – Paris : UNESCO, 1992. – Mode of access: http://unesdoc.unesco.org/images/0012/001227/122733Eo.pdf. – Date of access: 12.06.2015.

303. The free and balanced flow of information in a new communication order [Electronic resource]: - Paris : UNESCO, 1979. Mode of access: http://unesdoc.unesco.org/images/0003/000371/037151eb.pdf – Date of access: 12.06.2015.

304. The Unity of Western civilization : essays / ed. F. S. Marvin. – London ; New York : H. Milford, 1915. – 315 p.

305. Urbin, B. The 147 companies that control everything [Electronic resource] / B. Urbin // Forbes. – 2011. – 22 Oct. – Mode of access: http://www.forbes.com/sites/bruceupbin/2011/10/22/the-147-companies-that-control-everything. – Date of access: 11.06.2015.

306. US hoped to cause mass protests in Russia by sanctions – senior security official [Electronic resource] // TASS : Russ. news agency. – 2015. – 4 Mar. – Mode of access: http://tass.ru/en/russia/781118. – Date of access: 11.06.2015.

307. USUN progress report: a new era of engagement: advancing America's interests in the world [Electronic resource] : press statement, New York, Apr. 29, 2009 // U.S. Department of State. – Mode of access: http://www.state.gov/p/io/rm/2009/122451.htm. – Date of access: 11.06.2015.

308. Vallely, P. From PSYOP to Mind War: the psychology of victory [Electronic resource] / P. Vallely, M. A. Aquino // Internet Archive. – Mode of access: https://archive.org/details/pdfy-Mv-q4qGq8_TBPcwL. – Date of access: 20.09.2014.

309. Venier, P. The geographical pivot of history and early 20th century geopolitical culture / P. Venier // Geogr. J. – 2004. – Vol. 170, № 4. – P. 330–336.

310. Walzer, M. Arguing about war / M. Walzer. – New Haven : Yale Univ. Press, 2004. – 224 p.

311. Assange, J. Wanted by the CIA: the man who keeps no secrets [Electronic resource] : Julian Assange tells Matthew Bell why governments fear Wikileaks / J. Assange // The Independent. – 2010. – 18 July. – Mode of access: http://www.independent.co.uk/news/media/online/wanted-by-the-cia-the-man-who-keeps-no-secrets-2029083.html. – Date of access: 11.06.2015.

312. Warburg, J. P. The West in crisis / J. P. Warburg. – New York : Doubleday, 1959. – 192 p.

313. Weinberg, A. K. Manifest destiny: a study of nationalist expansion in American history / A. K. Weinberg. – Baltimore : The Johns Hopkins Press, 1935. – 559 p.

314. Wells, H. G. Anticipations of the reaction of mechanical and scientific progress upon human life and thought / H. G. Wells. – New York ; London : Harper a. br., 1902. – 342 p.

315. Wells, H. G. Open conspiracy: blue prints for a world revolution / H. G. Wells. – Garden City : Doubleday, Doran a. Co, 1928. – XII, 200 p.

316. Wells, H. G. The new world order: whether it is attainable, how it can be attained, and what sort of world a world at peace will have to be / H. G. Wells. – New York : Alfred A. Knopf, 1940. – 145 p.

317. Wendt, A. Why a world state is inevitable / A. Wendt // Europ. J. of Intern. Relations. – 2003. – Vol. 9, № 4. – P. 491–542.

318. Whitney, M. Only Moscow can stop it. Washington's war on Russia [Electronic resource] / M. Whitney // CounterPunch. – 2015. – 18 Mar. – Mode of access: http://www.counterpunch.org/2015/03/18/washingtons-war-on-russia. – Date of access: 11.06.2015.

319. Wilson, W. Address to a joint session of Congress requesting a Declaration of war against Germany, April 2, 1917 [Electronic resource] / W. Wilson // The American Presidency Project. – Mode of access: http://www.presidency.ucsb.edu/ws/?pid=65366. – Date of access: 11.06.2015.

320. Wilson, W. The new freedom: a call for the emancipation of the generous energies of a people / W. Wilson. – New York : Doubleday, Page & Co, 1913. – 313 p.

321. Wines, M. New study supports idea Stalin was poisoned [Electronic resource] / M. Wines // The New York Times. – 2003. – 5 Mar. – Mode of access: http://www.nytimes.com/2003/03/05/world/new-study-supports-idea-stalin-was-poisoned.html. – Date of access: 11.06.2015.

322. Wisnewski, G. The Bilderbergers – puppet-masters of power?: an investigation into claims of conspiracy at the heart of politics, business and the media / G. Wisnewski. – [S. l.] : Clairview Books, 2014. – 288 p.

323. Woods, T. E. Idolatry of the Market? [Electronic resource] / T. E. Woods // LewRockwell.com. – Mode of access: http://archive.lewrockwell.com/woods/woods181.html. – Date of access: 11.06.2015.

324. Woods, T. E. Must reads on the new Vatican document [Electronic resource] / T. E. Woods // TomWoods. – Mode of access: http://tomwoods.com/blog/must-reads-on-the-new-vatican-document-2. – Date of access: 11.06.2015.

325. Foundations for world order / E. L. Woodward [et al.]. – [Denver] : Univ. of Denver Press, 1949. – 174 p.

326. Woodward, E. L. The historical and political foundations for world order / E. L. Woodward // Foundations for world order / E. L. Woodward [et al.]. – [Denver], 1949. – P. 1–29.

327. Woolbert, R. G. Recent books on international relations. General: political, military and legal [Electronic resource] / R. G. Woolbert // Foreign Affairs. – 1938. – April. – Mode of access: http://www. foreignaffairs.com/articles/96283/lionel-curtis/civitas-dei. – Date of access: 08.06.2015. – Book rev.: Curtis, L. Civitas Dei : in 3 vol. / L. Curtis. – London : Macmillan, 1934–1937. – 3 vol.

328. Woolbert, R. G. Recent books on international relations. General: political, military and legal [Electronic resource] / R. G. Woolbert // Foreign Affairs. – 1949. – July. – Mode of access: https://www. foreignaffairs.com/reviews/capsule-review/1949-07-01/founda-tions-world-order. – Date of access: 05.06.2015. – Book rev.: Foundations for world order / E. L. Woodward [et al.]. – [Denver] : Univ. of Denver Press, 1949. – 174 p.

329. World federalist movement – Institute for global policy: about [Electronic resource] // WFM–IGP. – Mode of access: http://www. wfm-igp.org/about/overview. – Date of access: 11.06.2015.

330. World government [Electronic resource] // Stanford Encyclopedia of Philosophy. – Mode of access: http://plato.stanford.edu/entries/ world-government. – Date of access: 11.06.2015.

331. World Parliament Association Archive [Electronic resource] // University of Sussex. – Mode of access: http://www.sussex.ac.uk/ library/speccoll/collection_catalogues/wpa.html. – Date of access: 11.06.2015.

332. World policy institute. History [Electronic resource] // World Policy Institute. – Mode of access: http://www.worldpolicy.org/history. – Date of access: 11.06.2015.

333. Wreszin, M. Villard Oswald Garrison: pacifist at war / M. Wreszin. – Bloomington : Indiana Univ. Press, 1965. – 264 p.

334. Xi Jinping. Promoting friendship between our people and working together to build a brighter future [Electronic resource] : speech at Nazarbayev Univ., Astana, Sept. 7, 2013 / Xi Jinping // China News a. Rep. – 2013. – № 20. – Mode of access: http://english.cri.cn/ mmsource/images/2013/10/15/eng131015.pdf. – Date of access: 11.06.2015.

335. Xi Jinping. [Speech] [Electronic resource] : meet. marking the 60th anniversary of the initiation of the five principles of peaceful coexis-tence, June 28, 2014 / Xi Jinping // President of China. – Mode of

access: http://china.org.cn/world/2014-07/07/content_32876905. htm. – Date of access: 17.06.2015.

336. Xi Jinping. Towards a community of common destiny and a new future for Asia [Electronic resource] : keynote speech at the Boao Forum for Asia, annu. conf., 2015, Mar. 28 / Xi Jinping // Xinhua. – Mode of access: http://news.xinhuanet.com/ english/2015-03/29/c_134106145.htm?utm_source=The+Sino-cism+China+Newsletter&utm_campaign=67173362fc-Sino-cism03_30_15&utm_medium=email&utm_ter-m=0_171f237867-67173362fc-29637885&mc_cid=67173362f-c&mc_eid=8c3579d6e3. – Date of access: 11.06.2015.

337. Zahn, D. Kissinger: Obama primed to create «New world order» [Electronic resource] / D. Zahn // WND : America's independent news network. – Mode of access: http://www.wnd. com/2009/01/85442. – Date of access: 11.06.2015.

338. Obama, B. Obama on Russian relations [Electronic resource] : [interview President Obama, 31 Jan. 2015] / B. Obama ; conversed F. Zakaria // CNN. – Mode of access: http://edition.cnn.com/vid-eos/tv/2015/01/31/exp-gps-obama-sot-putin.cnn. – Date of access: 31.01.2015.

339. Zoakos, C. A conspiracy of morons: the CFR Project 1980s [Electronic resource] / C. Zoakos // Execut. Intelligence Rev. – 1979. – Vol. 6, № 9. – Mode of access: http://www.larouchepub. com/eiw/public/1979/eirv06n19-19790515/index.html. – Date of access: 11.06.2015.

340. 100 academic documents confirming the new world order [Electronic resource] // Docstoc: make your business better. – Mode of access: http://www.docstoc.com/docs/173594628/100-Aca-demic-Documents-Confirming-the-New-World-Order. – Date of access: 11.06.2015.

341. America`s geopolitical dilemmas [Electronic resource] / Canad. Intern. Council // Vimeo, Your Videos Belong Here. – Mode of access: https://vimeo.com/11303942

342. Beveridge, A. J. [Speech] [Electronic resource] : In Support of an American Empire, Jan. 9, 1900 / J. Beveridge // U.S. Senator. – Mode of access: https://www.mtholyoke.edu/acad/intrel/ajb72. htm. – Date of access: 17.06.2015

www.ingramcontent.com/pod-product-compliance
Lightning Source LLC
Chambersburg PA
CBHW020529270326
41927CB00006B/505

* 9 7 8 1 9 4 3 3 5 0 7 1 1 *